20 —

Critical Thinkers for Islamic Reform

A Collection of Articles from Contemporary Thinkers on Islam

Abdullahi An-N—
A'
Ahmed S
Aish.
Aisha
Ali B
Arnold
Ayman A. ——an
Caner Taslaman
Chibuzo Casey Ohanaja
Christopher Moore
Dilara Hafiz
Edip Yuksel
El-Mehdi Haddou
Eman M. Ahmed
Fereydoun Taslimi
Farouk A. Peru
Germaine A. Hoston
Ghayasuddin Siddiqui
Irshad Manji
Kassim Ahmad
Layth Saleh al-Shaiban
Melody Moezzi
Mike Ghouse
Mohammad Mova al Afghani
Mustafa Akyol
Naser Khader
Raymond Catton
Richard S. Voss
Ruby Amatulla
Shabbir Ahmed
T.O. Shanavas
Taj Hargey
Yasar Nuri Ozturk
Yahya Yuksel

BrainbowPress
Iconoclastic Books

1

© 2009 Edip Yuksel

All rights reserved. No part of this book may be used, transmitted, or reproduced in any form or by any means whatsoever without the written permission of the editor except in the case of brief quotations in reviews and critical articles. For permission requests or other information, contact the publisher or Edip Yuksel electronically through:

www.19.org
www.yuksel.org
www.quranix.com
www.islamicreform.org
www.brainbowpress.com

ISBN: 978-0-9796715-7-9

9 780979 671579   5 2 4 9 5

Printed in the United States of America

10 9 8 7 6 5 4 3 2

CONTENTS

3

بسم الله الرحمن الرحيم

•17:36•10:100•39:17-18•41:53•42:21•34:46•6:114-116•10:36•11:17•12:111•4:174•8:42•74:30-37•
•5:111•10:72•98:5•4:125•22:78•2:112,131•4:125•6:71•22:34•40:66•3:83•33:30•35:43•3:86•
•2:111•21:24•74:30•35:28•4:162•9:122•22:54•27:40•29:44,49•29:20•2:48•9:31-34•
•9:34•2:41,79,174•5:44•9:9•6:164•2:256•18:29•10:99•88:21-22•42:38•
•5:12•58:11•2:188•4:58•5:8•4:148•2:215•59:7•5:32•13:11•49:12•
•49:12•2:282•53:38•2:85,188•4:29•24:29•59:6-7•2:275•
•5:90•3:130•6:141•7:156•49:13•3:195•4:124•
•16:97•5:90•2:62•2:135-136,208•4:97-98•
•60:8-9•8:60•42:20•17:33.•4:75•
•16:90•3:110•25:63-76•
•31:12-20•23:1-11•
•6:19, 38, 114•
•3:19, 85•
•39:45•
•1:1•
•

Before putting anything in our mouths we observe the color, smell its odor. If it looks rotten or smells bad we do not touch it. If food passes the eye and nose tests, then our taste buds will be the judge. If a harmful bit fools all those examinations, our stomach come to rescue; it revolts and throws them up. There are many other organs that function as stations for testing, examination, and modification of imported material into our bodies. They ultimately meet our smart and vigilant nano-guards: white cells. Sure, there are many harmful or potentially harmful foods that pass all the way through our digestive system into our blood, such as alcohol and fat. Nevertheless, without using our reasoning faculty much if at all, we have an innate system that protects our body from harmful substances. It would be a mystery then how we can input information and assertions, especially the most bizarre ones, into our brains without subjecting them to the rigorous test of critical thinking. Our brains should never become trashcans of false ideas, holy viruses, unexamined dogmas and superstitions. We should be wise!

How can we protect our minds and brains? Do we have an innate system that protects us from harmful or junky ideas, especially dogmas or jingoisms that could turn us into zombies or self-righteous evil people? Yes we do: our logic is the program that detects and protects us against the most harmful viruses, which usually find their way when we are hypnotized by crowds, salespeople, politicians or clergymen.

5

Indeed, our brain comes with a pre-installed virus-protection program, called reasoning, logic or inference.[1] Unfortunately, this program is constantly attacked by false ideas, prejudices, dogmas, and contradictory stories. We are fed lies all the time, from fairy tales in cradles to silly stories in holy guises in places of worship. Fiction books are the best selling. Actors whose entire profession is based on faking other characters are treated like gods and goddesses. They are meteorites and hence are called 'stars!' Similarly, we reward liars in politics and in our relationship. We prefer to walk around with ketchup on our nose, since we do not expect our friends to be truthful as a mirror.

Centuries after the revelation of the Quran, we Muslims have accumulated more than ketchup on our noses. We have sunk in dirt until our eyebrows since we have traded the sound, liberating, and progressive message of the Quran, with the contradictory, enslaving and regressive dogmas of fabricated sects.

This book is the by-product of "A Celebration of Heresy Conference: Critical Thinking for Islamic Reform", in Atlanta on March 28-30 of 2008. It was a conference that I had prayed for years before it took place. When Fereydoun Taslimi offered his help and then Abdullahi an-Naim joined us, the idea became a reality. I offered Critical Thinking for Islamic Reform as the title, while Abdullahi insisted on using the word Heresy in the title. After a lengthy and hot debate among us, we finally agreed to combine both suggestions.[2] With the support of Fereydoun's family and friends, about hundred Critical Thinkers gathered in Atlanta to discuss the imperative of Islamic Reform.

The contributors of this book do not necessarily agree on every issue. However, we all agree on the imperative of a radical reformation in the Muslim world. A reform under the guidance of the Quran with the light of reason, our Creator's greatest gift to us... *Inshallah*, we are planning to continue organizing these conferences under the title "Critical Thinking for Islamic Reform" and publish the articles of the participants in annual anthologies with the same title.[3]

Edip Yuksel
Arizona, USA
April 2009

---

[1] The complete list of the 19 inferences can be found inside the cover of the most widely used textbook in America on logic, which I have been using for about a decade in my logic courses: Introduction to Logic, Irving M. Copi and Carl Cohen, Prentice Hall, Eleventh Edition, 2001, page 361 and inside cover.

[2] For the record, I have a 16-page discussion on the name of the first conference. The participants of the discussion were: Fereydoun Taslimi, Abdullahi al-Naim, Layth al-Shaiban, Thomas Haidon, Arnold Yasin, Aisha Juman, Aisha Musa, Kassim Ahmad, Ruby Amutulla, Amina Wadud, and Edip.

[3] We did not receive the articles on time from some associates whose names were typed in *italic* in the list in the title page: Germaine A. Hoston, Naser Khader, Raymond Catton, Taj Hargey, and Yaşar Nuri Öztürk. Hopefully, we will have them for the next annual issue.

The Critical Thinkers

Abdullahi an-Naim, PhD.is the Charles Howard Candler Professor of Law at Emory University School of Law. His specialties include human rights in Islam and cross-cultural issues in human rights, and he is the director of the Religion and Human Rights Program at Emory. He also participates in Emory's Center for the Study of Law and Religion. Abdullahi was formerly the Executive Director of the African bureau of Human Rights Watch. He argues for a synergy and interdependence between human rights, religion and secularism instead of a dichotomy and incompatibility between them. Abdullahi is originally from Sudan, where he was greatly influenced by the Islamic reform movement of Mahmoud Mohamed Taha. He is the author of numerous journal articles and books on human rights, international law, democracy, and Islamic reform. His most recent book is Islam and the Secular State: Negotiating the Future of Shari'a Cambridge, MA and London, England: Harvard University Press (2008).
● http://people.law.emory.edu/~aannaim/ ●

Abdur Rab, PhD. graduated with Honors and received a Master's degree from Dhaka University and a PH.D. from Harvard. He has had a long career in economic research and consultation, analyzing various public policy issues ranging from public resource mobilization to industrial development and trade policy reform, while serving the Pakistan Institute of Development Economics, the Industrial Development Bank of Pakistan and the Bangladesh and former undivided Pakistan governments, and various international organizations. He served the Pakistan Tariff Commission as a Member, and the Bangladesh Planning Commission as a Section Chief and a senior Consultant. He worked as an Industrial Development Officer with the United Nations Industrial Development Organization (UNIDO), Vienna. He worked as a financial adviser for the government of Uganda under a World Bank assignment, and as a senior industrial economist for the Qatar government under a UNIDO assignment. Under a UNDP assignment, he contributed to part of a business plan for an industrial development bank of the Economic Co-operation Organization (whose founding members are Iran, Turkey and Pakistan). He also worked on various development projects of Bangladesh supported by donor agencies such as the World Bank, USAID and the Asian Development Bank. He also consulted as an agricultural trade specialist for the US-based International Fertilizer Development Center (IFDC). Abdur Rab grew up in a traditional Bengali Muslim family. Since his school days he has been very devoted to religion. A turning point in his religious approach came when he came in contact with a virtually unknown but versatile Bengali spiritual guide Shah Aksaruddin Ahmad who possessed deep Quranic and spiritual knowledge. Under his guidance, Abdu received some preliminary lessons in spiritual exercises. Inspired by him, Abdu closely studied the Quran and the Hadith and relevant Islamic literature of modern scholars. His website: ● www.exploreQuran.org ●

Ahmed Subhy Mansour, PhD. is Former Assistant Professor at Al Azhar University, Egypt. He is also a political asylee in the U.S as well as a visiting Fellow at the Human Rights Program, Harvard Law School. An Egyptian national now living in the U.S., Ahmed is a distinguished scholar of Islam with expertise in Islamic history, culture, theology and politics. He was an advocate for democracy and human rights in Egypt for many years, during which time he was isolated and persecuted by religious extremists and by the regime, including having served time in prison for his liberal political, religious and social views. Having graduated with honors from Al Azhar University of Cairo, one of the oldest and most well respected centers of Islamic thought in the world, he later received his PhD with highest honors from Al Azhar as well. In May 1985, Ahmed was discharged from his teaching and research position there due to his liberal views that were not acceptable to the ultra-conservative religious authorities who controlled much of university policies and programs. In 1987 and 1988 he was imprisoned by the Egyptian government for his "progressive" views, including the advocacy of religious harmony and tolerance between Egyptian Muslims, Christian Copts, and Jews. Ahmad has authored 24 books and some 500 articles in Arabic, dealing with many aspects of Islamic history, culture, and religion. His organization's website: • www.ahl-alQuran.com •

Aisha Jumaan, PhD, MPH is the President of the Islamic Society of Atlanta.

Aisha Y. Musa, PhD, is the author of "Hadith as Scripture: Discussions on the Authority of Prophetic Traditions in Islam". Her training at Harvard was focused on early Islamic scriptural history, specifically the relative authority of the Quran and Prophetic Traditions (Hadith). Her book, Hadith as Scripture: Discussions on the Authority of Prophetic Traditions in Islam (Palgrave, 2008)-explores the development of the doctrine of duality of revelation and issues surrounding the relative authority of the Quran and the Prophetic Traditions (Hadith) through an examination of early Islamic texts in a variety of genres from the 8th and 14th centuries CE and compares the early controversies to their current counterparts. The question of the relative authority of the Quran and the Prophetic Traditions is part of usul al-fiqh (roots of jurisprudential methodology). How early Muslims answered that question has helped to shape Islamic theology and jurisprudence throughout the Muslim world for the past 1200 years. As part of the work, she produced the first English translation of al-Shafi'i's Kitab Jimā' al 'ilm, one of the most important early texts dealing with the authority of Prophetic Traditions.. The current resurgence of debates over the authority of Prophetic Traditions relative to the Quran, make it a contemporary question of both academic interest and personal importance to Muslims. Her research and teaching interests extend from the early classical period to the present and include translation of classical Arabic texts, Quranic interpretation, women's issues, and modern day reformist and neo-traditionalist movements. Aisha is an Assistant Professor of Islamic Studies in the Department of Religious Studies at Florida International University. Her website: • www.askmusa.org •

Ali Behzadnia, M.D. is a Medical Doctor who came to the United Stated near forty years ago. Ali is a life time student of Islam and is interested in Quranic research and Interfaith Dialogue. He is socio-politically active and was a member in the first cabinet after the revolution in Iran, as Deputy Minister of Health and welfare, acting Minister of Education and associate professor in Medicine at Teheran University. He opposed the non-democratic religious regime of Iran, and returned to the United States, after nearly two years. Ali is a member of several academic and religious organizations and is in private practice in California.

Arnold Yasin Mol is born and raised in Holland. Coming from a Catholic background, he started to research many faiths and beliefs, and while studying biochemistry at college, he discovered the Quran and found it to have a logical social and scientific message. Arnold embraced Islam at the age of 20. Being first drawn into classical Islamic doctrine, he studied its message and history thoroughly and found it contradicted the Quranic message on many points, and decided to study Theology at college to study how history, religions and cultures influenced another. Now only accepting the Quran as a divine source based on its social and scientific message and make up, he has founded an organization together with several Muslim thinkers to study the Quranic message as the

basis for a secular social global society and works with several modern Islamic thinkers. Currently he has studied Arabic at the University of Rotterdam, the Netherlands and is starting Social Theology at Amsterdam College. Arnold's website:
● www.deenresearchcenter.com ●

Ayman Abdullah M.D. is of Egyptian origins and has a PHD in Mathematics. Many of his articles are published at: ● www.free-minds.org ●

Caner Taslaman, PhD. was born in 1968 in Istanbul, and graduated from the sociology department at Bosporus University, Caner pursued his studies for MA and PhD degrees, in Philosophy-Theology, and Political Science. He is post doctorate scholar at Harvard University. His range of interests, not being limited to philosophy, sociology and political sciences, stretched to such fields of positive sciences as physics and biology, and he produced works on the said disciplines as well. In all these scientific treatises, dealing in widely differing subjects, his focus point has always been religion. Like many modern reformists, Like many modern monotheists, Caner too was influenced by Rashad's *Quran, Hadith and Islam.* Among his works are; *Quran Unchallengeable Miracle; The Big Bang, Philosophy and God; Evolution, Philosophy and God; Modern Science, Philosophy and God; Quantum Theory, Philosophy and God.* Some of his websites:
● www.canertaslaman.com/english/ ● www.quranic.org ● www.quranmiracles.com ●

Chibuzo Casey Ohanaja was born and raised in Dallas, Texas. Coming from a Nigerian Christian background he was not introduced to Islam until High School through a close friend from Pakistan. As a Political Science/Arabic and Middle Eastern studies major at the University of Notre Dame he began to deeply research and study various faiths, beliefs and systems of life. Allured by the message of Islam he discovered the Quran and found that it had the most humane, logical and pragmatic system of life. He reverted to Islam at the age of 20. Although through further studies of the Muslim history, hadith, fiqh, the Arabic language and observations through his travels in Africa and the Middle East he found that the traditional Islam prevalent around the world was incompatible with the message of Islam in the Quran. Now realizing that only the Quran can be used to guide and bring peace to mankind he has dedicated himself to informing and lecturing to people about the true message of Islam which is preserved in the Quran. Casey is currently the President of the Muslim Student Organization in Notre Dame, Indiana and is a coordinator for the University of Notre Dame Interfaith Fellowship. After graduation from the University Notre Dame he hopes to continue his studies in law, Arabic and Islamic studies.

Christopher Moore was born in Nicosia, Cyprus, which was under British rule at the time, soon after gaining independence. Due to his father's devotion to Military Service his education was conducted by the Military. Now married for years to his wife Linda and the grandparent of two young granddaughters. Like Cyprus, he gained independence from British rule at the age of 49 to retire to Turkey. Since retiring he has been able to feed his growing passion for Quranic Islamic studies.

Dilara Hafiz is a retired investment banker, Sunday school teacher, interfaith activist and co-author of *The American Muslim Teenager's Handbook* along with her daughter, Yasmine, and son, Imran. This abridged article originally appeared in Altmuslim.com and is distributed with permission by the Common Ground News Service (CGNews). Her work can be found at: ● www.theamth.com ● www.altmuslim.com ●

9

Irshad Manji is a Canadian feminist, author, journalist, activist and professor of leadership. Manji is Director of the Moral Courage Project at New York University. The Moral Courage Project aims to teach young leaders to speak truth to power in their own communities. She is author of *The Trouble with Islam Today: A Muslim's Call for Reform in Her Faith*, now published in more than 30 countries. She is also creator of the Emmy-nominated documentary, *Faith Without Fear*, which launched the American Islamic Congress 2008 "Think Different" Film Festival. Her websites:● www.irshadmanji.com ●

Edip Yuksel, J.D., was born in Turkey in 1957 as the son of Sadreddin Yuksel, a prominent Sunni scholar. During his youth he was an outspoken Islamist, and spent years in prison for his political views. While a popular Islamist author and youth leader, he adopted the Quran Alone philosophy after corresponding with Rashad Khalifa and reading his landmark book, *Quran, Hadith and Islam*. This led him to brake with the Sunni sect in 1st of July, 1986. In 1989, he was sponsored for immigration to the US by Rashad Khalifa. Worked with Rashad for one year in Masjid Tucson, and became a prominent member of the United Submitters International. After the assassination of Rashad he broke away from the United Submitters International as he objected to the new cult-like ideas arising among its members. Edip is the author of over twenty books on religion, politics, philosophy and law in Turkish, and numerous articles and several books in English. His current work is as the co-author of: *Quran: a Reformist Translation* and the author of the *Manifesto for Islamic Reform* which are available at brainbowpress.com. Edip is the founder of Islamic Reform organization and his online books, interviews, and articles are published at: ● www.19.org ● www.islamicreform.org ● www.yuksel.org ● www.quran.org ● www.quranix.com ● www.mpjp.org ● www.opednews.com ● *Edip's books can be ordered at* ● www.brainbowpress.com ● www.ozanyayincilik.com ● *and his English email list* ● http://groups.google.com/group/19org ●

El Mehdi Haddou, MD. is a 37 year-old Canadian veterinary Doctor originating from Morocco. At the age of 24, he started to question his faith, Islam, the purpose of this life and the existence of God. In November 2006, after reading Rashad Khalifa's book: *'Quran, Hadith and Islam'* posted at www.submission.org, he began to verify Rashad Khalifa's ideas of code 19 and confirmed the findings. Recognizing that God has answered his questions and had given the proof that I was always looking for. Since that day, he witnessed a big change in his spirituality. "Now", he says, "Without hesitation I have attained certainty. I am following only the Quran, the whole Quran and nothing but the Quran."

Eman M. Ahmed Originally from Pakistan, Eman came to Canada in 2000. She is currently the Projects Coordinator at CCMW. In Pakistan she worked in areas related to social development and human and women's rights. She was also the managing editor for the Heinrich Boll Foundation book series on Women and Religion. Her publications include "A Dangerous mix: Religion & Development Aid", (WHRNet), "Violence Against Women: The Legal System and Institutional Responses" in *Violence, Law and Women's Rights in South Asia*, (Sage Publications); and "Promoting Inclusivity: Protecting (whose) Choice?" (AWID). Eman has MAs in Publishing (SFU), Social Anthropology (Oxford) and English (Pb)

F.K. is a Kurdish-American monotheist with dozens of patents in computer hardware technology. He has a PhD in mathematics. He is originally from Kurdistan of Iraq.

Farouk A. Peru is a human being in the world. This is where his discourse begins and ends. As a human being, he addresses the problem of the human condition by being a

student of Quran, which he considers to God's descriptions of and prescriptions for humankind. Farouk is also a novice academic whose interests include: The Study of Quran according to its Author. The resurrection of the Author's voice towards discovering His authentic philosophy from the text Quranic streams of thoughts and tendencies in Islam. How Muslims are reproaching Quran in a variety of manners in an effort to understand and reform their faith. The true nature of Islamic fundamentalism as an exclusivist philosophy. How Islamic fundamentalism roots itself in Islamic thought and manifests itself in Islamic institutions and discovering the alternative to this world-view. Philosophy, especially the study of being. To build upon Heidegger's concept of being by expounding how being in the world is the basis of all philosophical thought. His website:
• www.farouk.name •

Fereydoun Taslimi is an entrepreneur philanthropist who came to Islam after rejecting it. "I was not a Muslim until I rejected all that I thought was Islam, heresy is my path to salvation." He is the co-founder of Noor Foundation and founder of several High-tech companies. Prior to joining PerformanceIT, Mr. Taslimi was co-founder and CTO at infoGO, Inc. Before that, he was Vice President of ESI, Inc. from 1986 to 1996, co-founding the company along with Mr. Mittel. During his tenure, Mr. Taslimi was instrumental in the design and development of several successful product lines in the area of voice processing and Internet Telephony servers. Prior to ESI, Mr. Taslimi started Adax, Inc. in 1984, a company that developed a programmable PC-based phone system. While finishing graduate school, Mr. Taslimi founded Informatics Sciences a company that developed multi-lingual computers and applications systems that was subsequently sold in 1984. Mr. Taslimi graduated with honors from University of London in 1975 and received a Masters degree in computer science from Georgia Tech. His websites:
• www.noor.org • www.muslimheretics.com •

Ghayasuddin Siddiqui, PhD., is one of the leading spokespeople of the Muslim community in Britain. He is regarded as an expert on Islamic fundamentalism and Muslim political thought. He is one of the first Muslim leaders who has championed women's causes, against forced marriage, domestic violence and murder in the name of honour. Last year, together with some senior clerics, he launched Muslim Marriage Contract to protect rights of women. He is now leading a campaign against child abuse within faith-based environment. He has consistently opposed the invasion of Afghanistan and subsequently that of Iraq, joining the Anti-war Coalition at its inception, becoming a member of its central executive. As a patron of Guantanamo Human Rights Commission and active member of 'Campaign Against Criminalizing Communities' (CAMPACC), Ghayasuddin has campaigned against detention without trial of people held in Guantanamo Bay and Belmarsh. As director of one of the oldest Muslim think tanks, the Muslim Institute, he has promoted dialogue across all barriers: social, cultural and political. His website: • www.muslimparliament.org.uk •

Kassim Ahmad is Malaysia's foremost thinker and philosopher. Kassim was born on 9 September, 1933 in Kedah, Malaysia. He received his Bachelor of Art's degree in Malay language and literature, but also read widely in political science and Islamic philosophy. He grabbed national headlines in the 1950s with his dissertation on the characters of Hang Tuah (Perwatakan Hang Tuah), the Malay literary classic. He taught Malay language and literature for a time in the London's School of Oriental and African Studies and then in a secondary school in Penang where he has been staying with his family since 1966. Kassim was jailed for nearly five years under the ISA for daring to express openly his political views, an experience which he recounted in his book, Universiti Kedua

(Second University). Like many modern reformists, after reading Rashad Khalifa's book, *Quran, Hadith, and Islam*, Kassim experienced a paradigm change. He shook the Malay world with his *Hadith: A Re-Examination* in which he challenges the infallibility of the purported words of Prophet Muhammad. He is awarded an honorary doctorate in Letters by the National University of Malaysia. He has written several books on Malay literature as well as on Islamic subjects. His English and Malay articles are published at:
● www.kassimahmad.blogspot.com ●

Layth Saleh al-Shaiban is one of the leading muslim intellectuals for Islamic Reform. Like many modern reformists, he re-discovered the Quran after reading Rashad Khalifa's book, *Quran, Hadith, and Islam*. Layth is the founder of Progressive Muslims and Free-Minds organizations. He is the co-author of the Quran: a Reformist Translation, and the author of The Natural Republic. Layth lives in Saudi Arabia and works as a financial adviser. Layth's websites: ● www.free-minds.org ● www.progressivemuslims.org ●

Melody Moezzi, J.D. is a writer, activist, author and attorney. Her first book, War on Error: Real Stories of American Muslims, was published in the fall of 2007 by the University of Arkansas Press. Ms. Moezzi has a regular column in Muslim Girl Magazine and has written essays and articles for several other print and online publications, including Parabola, Dissident Voice, American *Chronicle, Urban Mozaik*, and the *Yale Journal for Humanities in Medicine*. She has also appeared as a commentator on NPR's All Things Considered. Born in Chicago in 1979, Melody grew up mostly in Dayton, Ohio amid a strong and vibrant Iranian-American diaspora. Today, she lives in Atlanta, with her husband, Matthew, and their cats, Olyan and Talula. She is a graduate of Wesleyan University and Emory University School of Law, as well as the Emory University School of Public Health. Melody's website: ● www.melodymoezzi.com ●

Mike Mohamed Ghouse is a Speaker, Thinker and a Writer. He co-chairs the center for interfaith inquiry of the Memnosyne Foundation, president of the Foundation for Pluralism and is a frequent guest on talk radio and local television network discussing interfaith, political and civic issues. Ghouse is originally from Yelahanka-Bangalore, and Dallas, Texas has been his home town for nearly three decades. Mike is the founding president of World Muslim Congress with a simple theme: Good for Muslims and good for the world. His comments, news analysis and columns can be found on the Websites and Blogs listed at his personal website: ● www.MikeGhouse.net ●

Mohammad Mova Al Afghani works at a Jakarta-based Lawfirm and lectured at Universitas Ibn Khaldun Bogor. He founded the Center for Law Information (CeLI), a law information NGO in 1999. He is a frequent contributor at Daily Jakarta Post and has had several international publications. Mr. Al Afghani is also a member of the Center for Responsible Nanotechnology (CRN) Task Force on Implication and Policies. He graduated from the law faculty of Universitas Indonesia and -- with the scholarship from Deutsches Akademisches Austausch Dienst (DAAD) -- obtained a master in European Law from University of Bremen (with distinction).

Mustafa Akyol is son of a well known journalist, Taha Akyol. He has criticized both Islamic extremism and Turkish secularism, which he likens to Jacobinism and fundamentalism. He is an outspoken promoter of intelligent design. Mustafa was born in 1972 and received his early education in Ankara. He graduated International Relations Department of Bosphorus University. He earned his masters in the History Department of the same university. He is currently a columnist for the Turkish Daily News and Director of International Relations at the Intercultural Dialogue Platform, a subsidiary of the

Journalists and Writers Foundation. He has given seminars in several universities in the U.S. and the U.K. on issues of faith, science, religious tolerance or inter-faith dialogue. Mustafa's articles on Islamic issues, in which he mostly argues against Islamic extremism and terrorism from a Muslim point of view and defends the Islamic faith, have appeared in publications like The Weekly Standard, The Washington Times, The American Enterprise, National Review, FrontPage Magazine, Newsweek, and Islam Online. His book on Kurdish issue questioned the official taboos and offered practical solutions. Mustafa is a co-host in a Turkish TV program and his Turkish articles are published at:
• www.mustafaakyol.org •

Richard S. Voss, Ph.D. teaches business management courses at Troy University, where he is pursuing several research tracks, among which his favorite involves an ongoing project to integrate established theories of national cultural, universal human values, and civilizations into a unified civilizational theory. Richard embraced Islâm in Morocco in 1983 and adopted his Islâmic Reformist orientation upon discovering Dr. Rashâd Khalifa's book, Quran, Hadith, and Islam, in the bookstore of the University of California at Riverside, his undergraduate alma mater where he had studied foreign language, shortly after his return to the United States. Several of his articles are posted at:
• www.19.org •

Ruby Amatulla is an American Muslim business woman who is an activist to promote understanding and constructive engagements between the West and the Muslim world. She is a writer and a speaker for the cause. She is the president of a recently formed non-profit organization, Muslims for Peace, Justice and Progress (MPJP). • www.amipi.org • www.mpjp.org •

Shabbir Ahmed MD. is a writer of books in both Urdu and English on history and Islam. He was born in Pakistan in 1947 and currently resides in Florida, United States. A medical doctor by profession, he started his military career in the Pakistan Army under Emergency Commission as a young Captain in 1971. Then he served in Royal Saudi Army (Medical Corps) and became a Brigadier General at an age of just 31. He has since made a new career as an Islamic scholar, and been published in various magazines and newspapers. Being a young member of the royal medical staff of Kingdom of Saudi Arabia, Shabbir learned the Arabic language and was trained in Islamic Theology and Quranic exegesis in the 1970s under the auspices of Malik Faisal bin Abdul Aziz and Malik Khalid bin Abdul Aziz of Saudi Arabia and has widely traveled the Muslim world and has been a visitor to many Islamic centers of knowledge. Shabbir's website:
• www.ourbeacon.com •

T.O. Shanavas, M.D. is a physician based in Michigan. He is the author of the book *Creation and/or Evolution* wherein he discusses the Quranic view on evolution and its roots in Islamic history.

Yahya Yuksel is a freshman at the University of Arizona, studying Journalism and Political science. He has been in leadership position since elementary school; at age 11 he was interviewed by the local CBS affiliate TV station for the evening news for his survey and its analysis at his elementary school. In 2008, he received the Senior Student of the Year award from City of Tucson for his various leadership activities including for founding Teen Court at Mountain View High School and receiving grant for its initial costs. He is on the board of several educational and social committees and organizations and became the youngest member of the Human Relations Committee of the City of Tucson. In 2008, he received Certificate of Congressional Recognition from US congresswoman Gabrielle Gifford for his civic contribution. As the co-founder of TeenDemocrats or Democrateens organization, in 2004 Yahya campaigned for John Kerry, and then in 2008 for Barack Obama. Besides, English, Yahya knows Persian and little Turkish.

Being a Teen Named Yahya in America

Yahya Yuksel

At the age of seventeen, I had the privilege of attending the 2008 Celebration of Heresy Conference and the great honor of hosting the first night where I met many distinguished professors, authors, and critical thinkers. And I've decided to briefly describe my life so far as a Muslim.

Since my birth I have lived with a very unique name. The story is long and prophetic, and my name is its fruit. So there I was, with no power of negotiations, brought into the world named Yahya Yuksel, a name that would bring me much hardship and generate nuisance and embarrassment at times but would strengthen my character. It's not like I was paralyzed or had speech impediments, but a weird name like 'Yahya' is a little harder to live with than a "John" or "Aaron." My name, uncommon and difficult to pronounce, hints at and whispers of my religious or ethnic background to everyone I meet, including police officers, security guards, cashiers and of course, potential friends and employers.

In elementary school I remember not having issues with being perceived as a Muslim. The kids didn't really understand or care much for religion. However, my name brought a few unfavourable nicknames and bullying. "Yo-yo" was the most common, and really wasn't all that bad except when the girl I had a crush on in 5th grade says "Hey Yo-yo can you pass the glue stick?" Naively thinking she liked me deep down, I told myself she was just trying to socialize.

High school was the beach of Normandy in my life. The moment I delicately stepped off the boat, I was shot at with brutal and painful nicknames, from every direction, even by friendly fire. It was very difficult to heal and mend my persona, but I eventually did. Every time I talked to a friend, a stranger, and sometimes a teacher I had to listen to their version of my name, and 'cute' terrorist jokes. I became desensitized to people making fun of my name and assumed religion. Of course I wouldn't give in completely; I put up fights when I believed it was necessary. People are interesting; they make fun of you but claim to be your friend. They say "I'm just joking Yak. Don't get so mad,"even though it was the thousandth time I heard the dumb joke! By senior year I realized that I had overcome the adversity. With every new encounter with my peers I emitted a more confident vibe when introducing myself. I was poised and direct; I looked everyone in the eye, not once giving them a chance to attack my name. I gained as much respect back as an outsider could. I was elected president of my class Junior and Senior year, was president of two other clubs on campus, and nominated for prom royalty; and yet, because of my non-American name, people still called me terrorist…

So I pondered. Coming up with a brilliant idea. It was gutsy and would most likely be embarrassing. I grew my beard for two months, nurturing it with much love and conditioner. Finally it was time! The day had come where my two months of alienation by the ladies at school, the long explanations of why I'm growing beard out, and the constant unrecognizable look I gave myself in the mirror, all were about to come to an end. I wore a legit Arab outfit to school that Friday, including the limited edition fitted turban.

Where could I find an authentic Arabian garb? My mom offered help. "Let me see if we have one." All of a sudden, returning from the garage, she whipped out this blanket looking dress and red bundle of cloth. It was the outfit. My parents don't wear Arab dresses or turbans. I never saw it before in my life and wondered why we even had it.

So here I was walking to school from the back parking lot, palms sweating, eyes wide open, and with a sudden and constant tingling down my spine. I entered the school's plaza, the students' congregation hot spot before school. It was dead quiet. Every little pupil was focused on my delicate and vulnerable brown skin. I thought to myself, "It was nice knowing you. Good luck to you."

That day went well. I received an unusual amount of praise for showing courage and having "huevos", as my Latino homies declared to me later. Even though I was sent to the assistant principal's office, I wasn't in any trouble and showed to my peers that just because I was wearing a turban it did not imply "KABOOM!" What it did was prove I could crack a happy smile and could be a gentle human.

Being called a sand-nigger got me thinking about racism and xenophobia in my country. Ironically, I was neither an Arab nor yet consciously chosen a religion. My parents were Kurdish and Persian and I have yet to decide about my religion. My father, who suffered from religious oppression by his family and countrymen, had already warned me not be a Muslim just because of my parents are Muslim. I consider that warning and I am still holding my judgment on this important issue. I do believe in one God, the First Cause, and an Intelligent Designer.

Yet, I did match their color and did have a cool name. This labeling was occurring while the Neocon government we voted for had invaded and terrorized a country based on a series of lies and deceptions, and directly or indirectly caused the death of more than a million "sand-niggers," displaced and injured millions more, and subjected thousands of innocent people with weird names to humiliation and appalling tortures!

At graduation I gave a speech and received the loudest applause when handed my diploma, I'm not sure how I'll be treated in college when I attend the University of Arizona in the fall. But I know I made the best of my blessed situation and gained the respect I deserved as an individual.

My father reminded me a verse from the Quran God that instructs people not to not make fun of people's names. I understand why… it's something you had no control over and was given to you with love and thought. You live with it wherever you go and it is who you are, mine has made me unique and strengthened my self-esteem.

Racism is a virus that turns its victims into potential criminals. The wars, massacres, and genocides of the past that we all condemn were committed by self-righteous people who had opened their minds and hearts to the most deadly virus in human history. Though I am not sure about its divine origin, I would like to quote a verse from the Quran that emphasizes equality of humanity regardless their gender and color:

> 49:13　O people, We created you from a male and female, and We made you into nations and tribes, that you may know one another. Surely, the most honorable among you in the sight of God is the most righteous. God is Knowledgeable, Ever-aware.

A Journey

Christopher Moore

A long journey, they say, starts with the first step. For submitters, that long journey started before we arrived on this earth albeit not known to us at the time. In a physical sense my journey started before I could take my first step.

This short story is not one of my life but one of reflection of how God came into my life continually knocking at my door until I opened it and let Him in.

Born into a "Christian" family it was and is still customary to have the child baptized with a suitable name into the Church of Christ. At my baptism my chosen name was changed at the last minute to Christopher, why, neither I nor my parents know. This, with hindsight was the very first step on the journey to submission. I was given this name after the Patron Saint of travel, Saint Christopher who also is depicted as being the carrier of the boy Jesus. These two elements became significant in my early and later life that directly put me on a path that became the right path to submission.

I have always had a sense of spirituality about my person. From a very young age, I have found comfort in being alone with my thoughts, a sort of child-like meditation. I certainly showed signs of a travel lust and whenever, which was frequent, I was not at home for the evening dinner a search party was sent out. The search never lasted for long as I was generally to be found in the local church. What I was doing there my memory fails me but now, looking back it is clear to see that I was starting to resemble my name. Clearly one well "chosen".

If my early years showed small signs of my life ahead my teen years showed intention. It is unusual for any teenager to devote so much time to a topic – religion – when so many outdoor activities were available. I, for whatever reason, shunned most team sports in favour of a spiritual adventure. The time spent in church, in study and debate, grew and I am told it was expected that one day I would take up the cloth. It was an enlightening period of my life that showed me the power of belief and a strong sense of community solidarity however misguided.

It did have its drawbacks however; the school bully took great pleasure in throwing a few well aimed punches at me. They called it character building in those days. I called it painful.

My studies continued but were enlarged to include other branches of Christianity. Many hours were spent in discussion with Jehovah Witnesses, Christadelphians and Roman Catholics to name but a few. Some of the most interesting nights were spent eating the obligatory popcorn whilst debating The Book of Mormon.

My period as being "a student of religion" as I was once called began to take a backward step as I started to question deeply the spirituality of these ritualistic religions. Each claimed to be right and yet they all differed, in many cases significantly. That, unfortunately has not changed but at the time doubts and cracks started to appear, not in my faith but in my belief. The belief I held had been built on a soft foundation of blind adherence to tenants of religion that found no basis in its origins as my study of history had shown. What had been the backbone of society was nothing more than the creation of "movers and shakers" of the post Jesus era and haughty emperors seeking a late salvation.

I had reached a crossroads in my life that knowledge, not spirituality had led me to, and it angered me. A lesson I learnt from this though was a good one; while knowledge is power wisdom is freedom.

In my late teens I had reached a conclusion that no matter how well meaning, the church, its leaders and its practices had little to do with God but more to do with status. This conclusion could be well challenged and debated as it most surely was, especially by me, and it was to surface again and again in the future.

This "student of religion", this great debater, this defender of religious practices had been defeated and the taste of defeat sat heavy with me to the point where the only path that lay open to me was the one that led out.

Falling off the rails is a very interesting phrase. While it denotes the current situation of a person it also shows how narrow is the path that an upstanding citizen has to take. I had been on those rails, walking that narrow path for a good number of years and now, short of my 20th birthday it was time to get a taste of the fruits that life had to offer.

The actions of a person trying to rid themselves of "baggage" cannot be classed as calculated, irrational is the best word to use, and that is what I became. I started missing tutorials and followed that with the decision that higher education was not for me. I got a job and for the first time had money in my pocket. I purchased a car and took advantage of this freedom by taking myself on undefined trips, sometimes not returning in time for work. I found pubs and clubs had a certain appeal and as I had rarely showed interest in the fairer sex I thought that may be a bit of fun as well. I excelled in the pubs and clubs, drinking obscene amounts of alcohol but I had little success with the females. This period of my life was, on reflection a necessary episode but at the time it was an utter disaster albeit I had no intention of changing it.

Although at the back of my mind, during this period, faith was never too far away and had I wanted or been wise enough I could have, with prayer lifted myself from the pit I had fallen into. I had not counted on the strong hand of God who knocked and guided me once more.

I managed through a certain amount of guile and arrogance to acquire a new job that paid well and provided a company car. Of course this new position demanded a certain amount of dedication and accountability which I had been lacking for some time. However I was persuaded by my Mother to turn over a new leaf and give it my best.

The job was heaven sent as it did pull me out of that dark pit and it also opened a new chapter for me in my journey, my search for something that I did not even know existed.

With a new set of "wheels" and a new purpose in life I set about my new job with gusto and embraced willingly the rituals of a corporate existence. My career, which the job became, enabled me to take the first steps in realizing my growing passion for travel, albeit mainly in the UK. The experience of new places resonated with my longing for knowledge and it was during one of my trips that that thirst was quenched, and the guidance God offers for those who seek it became apparent.

The U.K. is not a country filled with many Christian denominations so I was intrigued to spot a building that did not follow the traditional architecture of a "Church of England". I stopped to enquire and had stumbled across an Orthodox church, a Serbian Orthodox church to be exact. The very word orthodox conjures up a meaning of originality which offered a potential answer to my questioning the tenets of the Christian experiences I had had. After a few weeks discussion with the priest I felt that I had found my answers and Christ was back on my shoulders.

I soon learnt that the rituals of this church were even greater than those of Catholicism. Despite this I had a great feeling of returning home and the comfort I derived from the method of worship was immense. I could not see, nor did I consider that the kissing of statues and icons was the gravest form of idolatry that can be imagined. It bothered me little as it gave me a refuge, a home and a need fulfilled.

The informed reader of this story may justifiably ask how I equate idolatry with God's guidance. If that question had been asked at the time I could not have offered an answer. Now I can. There is no doubt in my mind that for me it was important to experience what religions have to offer and to eliminate them before I could truly say that I have found God. God had found me, not that He had lost me in the first place but He was showing me all that I needed to see before I could take the biggest step in my journey.

Having now become an active member of a new community I was growing in confidence and discussions and debates were now back on the agenda. I had not felt this good for years and my devotion returned and knowledge was growing once again, wisdom however still eluded me.

My schism with this church occurred following a gift of a book from the priest. It was one of the first publications in English of "The life of the Saints". One saint for every day of the year detailing his history, how he died, his significance in orthodoxy and a prayer to help save his soul. One such saint lifted himself from the page as I read the book in earnest. I cannot remember the saint's name or the day his life is celebrated but if there is a league table for saints he, for me would be at the top. This particular saint was executed for heresy, an apostate, propagating the outrageous suggestion that there is only One God and that Jesus is not the son of God. Conflict immediately entered my mind; a man who propagates "lies" about the identity of Jesus is celebrated by those whose forbears executed him. This was a case for debate which I duly took up with the priest only to be told, "That's just the way things are". I don't and didn't accept that principle and that was the day I voted with my feet and left, returning to the world of darkness.

After this episode I decided to change my life completely. I got a new job and relocated to another part of the country and it was here that I met my future wife and so starts a new chapter and one that would finally lead me to the ultimate goal, submission.

If I had known what the episodes of my life meant, and if I had known what was ahead and where my journey was taking me, it would be easy to say that the summit was in sight. None of these were the case, but the events of the next few years brought clarity and definition to my former existence.

I met my wife one evening at the squash club I had joined upon arrival in the area. She was playing that night and I had just visited to see the facilities. As she turned around she afforded me the most welcoming smile, (I later found out that she mistook me for someone else). Inevitably, what other word can you use when God controls everything, inevitably our paths crossed again and a relationship soon developed? We had very little in common. She was a fiery character, a determination that bordered on obsession. I on the other hand was controlled, a deep thinker not prone to impulsive decisions. However, and there always is, we did share one common passion – travel. This part of my journey, and hers too took us to many places before being led to our final earthly destination.

We were, without our knowledge well blessed; we were being groomed for our lives together under the banner of submission.

We eventually got married and started enjoying the fruits of our labour. We worked to travel and experienced some amazing sights and sounds, Egypt for example became our second home. The colours and fragrances of India excited us and the devotion of the monks in Tibet enthralled us. We saw, as God had planned it numerous examples of idol worship and unbeknownst to us these events would make our acceptance and understanding of Quran so much easier.

It would be true to say that Linda was not a religious person and any attempt on my part, and they were few, to discuss the topic fell on stony ground. That is not to say she did not have a belief, she did in her own way and occasionally visited a church for quiet contemplation. I maintained a modest devotion to my faith which was more inward now as a show of faith may have upset the balance we had achieved in our short relationship.

Nineteen-ninety was the year that my inner faith was put to the test once again. We had planned yet another vacation, this time to Thailand. God had other plans. A few weeks before our departure the company we were traveling with went into liquidation and a new destination was hurriedly sought. We chose to travel to Mexico, see the sights of Mexico City and take some well earned rest in a resort in the mountains.

Mexico City is a wonderful place to visit. Its ruins are amazing and its museums full of treasures that rival the greatest museums in any country. Having left one of these museums we stopped outside for coffee and proceeded to discuss what we had seen. I have often asked myself when I recount this episode; how it was that we got on to the subject of religion. Maybe it was the idols and perhaps I related them to those we had previously seen, or maybe it was just God's hand at work once again. For once Linda took an interest and I duly went into a sermon on religion and the fact that despite the depth and length of the Bible I still felt that there was something missing. My exact words "there has to be something else". Topic closed we left and made our way to our next destination in the mountains.

Without going into detail our expectations of the resort were not met so we planned to leave the next day. As we swept the resort one final time we overheard some English speaking voices and so began our introduction to submission.

Ray and Sophie Catton are two of the nicest and devout submitters you could ever wish to meet. When we met we had no idea as to their religious persuasion nor did they offer them. We laugh about it now as we recount the interrogation by Linda over lunch as to why they didn't eat pork and how my body shuddered when I realized they were Muslims, the enemy of the Christian world. Not withstanding this we enjoyed each others company and the thought of leaving left us and so began the first lesson, the first lesson on submission that lasted for the remaining period of our vacation.

I lay in bed during that period digesting what we had been introduced too and what it meant and would eventually mean. I knew then that the questions I had had for so many years were starting to be answered and that frightened me. I was, with Christianity, in my comfort zone, after all. Although not comfortable with the establishment, I had studied for years and felt I could control my version of Christianity. My main stumbling block was the divinity of Jesus. I knew it was wrong and that that martyred saint was right, but without the resurrection and the divinity of Jesus there was no Christianity. To take out a brick that would cause the building to fall is a decision not to be taken in haste. Haste was not a problem for Linda, she had no baggage and guidance was soon upon her and she embraced submission before we left having not once read the words of Quran. For me it took another few weeks and upon reading Yusuf Ali's translation I new that The Quran was and still is the "something else" I had been searching for.

My journey was at an end, at least I thought. Embracing submission is just the start of another journey as all submitters are well aware of. That particular journey continues and the influence submission has had in my life is not the subject of this short story. What is, is the role of God in our lives should we choose to accept Him. Not only as the Almighty or The Creator or The Sustainer, whichever title you give Him. Accepting God is not about attributes however important they may seem. Accepting God is not about believing in God it is about believing Him. There is a difference, when you find Him you will experience and know that difference.

I had thought that over the years of my journey I had acquired a knowledge of God, an understanding of God that would serve me well for the rest of my life. When I embraced submission I came to realize that my understanding was superficial and further clarity was required. There comes a point in all of our lives when that clarity is achieved and with it a greater understanding of our lives.

That point in my life took 33 years to arrive at. I had, during that time given up on God, but He never gave up on me.[1]

---

[1]   BrainbowPress is interested in publishing a book containing stories like this (1000 to 3000 words). Please contact Edip Yuksel for more information.

Was Ayesha a Six-Year-Old Bride? The Ancient Myth Exposed[1]

T.O. Shanavas

A Christian friend asked me once, "Would you marry your seven year-old daughter to a fifty year-old man?" I kept my silence. He continued, "If you would not, how can you approve the marriage of an innocent seven year-old, Ayesha, with your Prophet?" I told him, "I don't have an answer to your question at this time." My friend smiled and left me with a thorn in the heart of my faith. Most Muslims answer that such marriages were accepted in those days. Otherwise, people would have objected to Prophet's marriage with Ayesha.

However, such an explanation would be acceptable only for those who are naive enough to believe it but unfortunately, I was not satisfied with the answer.

The Prophet was an exemplary man. All his actions were most virtuous so that we Muslims can emulate them. However, most people in our Islamic Center of Toledo including myself, would not think of betrothing our seven year-old daughter to a fifty-two year old man. If a parent agrees to such a marriage, most people, if not all, would look down upon the child's father and the old husband.

In 1923, registrars of marriage in Egypt were instructed not to register and issue official certificates of marriage for brides less than sixteen and grooms less than eighteen years of age. Eight years later, the Law of the Organization and Procedure of Sheriah courts of 1931 consolidated the above provision by not hearing the marriage disputes involving brides less than sixteen and grooms less than eighteen years old. (*Women in Muslim Family Law*, John Esposito, 1982). It shows that even in the Muslim-majority country of Egypt the child marriages are unacceptable.

So I believed, without solid evidence other than reverence to my Prophet, that the stories of the marriage of seven-year-old Ayesha to 50-year-old Prophet are only myths. However, my long pursuit in search of the truth on this matter proved my intuition correct. My Prophet was a gentleman. And he did not marry an innocent seven or nine year old girl. The age of Ayesha has been erroneously reported in the hadith literature. Furthermore, I think that the narratives reporting this event are highly unreliable. Some of the hadith (traditions of the Prophet) regarding Ayesha's age at the time of her wedding with prophet are problematic.

I present the following evidences against the acceptance of the fictitious story by Hisham ibn 'Urwah and to clear the name of my Prophet as an irresponsible old man preying on an innocent little girl.

---

[1] This article first appeared in The Minaret in March 1999.

EVIDENCE #1: Reliability of Source

Most of the narratives printed in the books of hadith are reported only by Hisham ibn 'Urwah, who was reporting on the authority of his father. First of all, more people than just one, two or three should logically have reported. It is strange that no one from Medina, where Hisham ibn 'Urwah lived the first 71 years of his life narrated the event, despite the fact that his Medinan pupils included the well-respected Malik ibn Anas. The origins of the report of the narratives of this event are people from Iraq where Hisham is reported to have shifted after living in Medina for most of his life.

Tehzibu'l-Tehzib, one of the most well known books on the life and reliability of the narrators of the traditions of the Prophet, reports that according to Yaqub ibn Shaibah: "He [Hisham] is highly reliable, his narratives are acceptable, except what he narrated after moving over to Iraq" (*Tehzi'bu'l-tehzi'b*, Ibn Hajar Al-'asqala'ni, Dar Ihya al-turath al-Islami, 15th century. Vol 11, p. 50).

It further states that Malik ibn Anas objected on those narratives of Hisham which were reported through people in Iraq: "I have been told that Malik objected to those narratives of Hisham which were reported through people of Iraq" (*Tehzi'b u'l-tehzi'b*, Ibn Hajar Al-'asqala'ni, Dar Ihya al-turath al-Islami, Vol.11, p. 50).

Mizanu'l-ai'tidal, another book on the life sketches of the narrators of the traditions of the Prophet reports: "When he was old, Hisham's memory suffered quite badly" (*Mizanu'l-ai'tidal*, Al-Zahbi, Al-Maktabatu'l-athriyyah, Sheikhupura, Pakistan, Vol. 4, p. 301).

CONCLUSION: Based on these references, Hisham's memory was failing and his narratives while in Iraq were unreliable. So, his narrative of Ayesha's marriage and age are unreliable.

CHRONOLOGY: We must also consider some dates in the history of Islam:

> Pre-610 CE: Jahiliya (pre-Islamic age) before revelation
> 610 CE: First revelation
> 610 CE: AbuBakr accepts Islam
> 613 CE: Prophet Muhammad begins preaching publicly.
> 615 CE: Emigration to Abyssinia
> 616 CE: Umar bin al Khattab accepts Islam
> 620 CE: Generally accepted betrothal of Ayesha to the Prophet
> 622 CE: Hijrah (emigation to Yathrib, later renamed Medina)
> 623/624 CE: Generally accepted year of Ayesha living with the Prophet

EVIDENCE #2: The Betrothal

According to Tabari (also according to Hisham ibn 'Urwah, Ibn Hambal and Ibn Sa'd), Ayesha was betrothed at seven years of age and began to cohabit with the Prophet at the age of nine years.

However, in another work, Al-Tabari says: "All four of his [Abu Bakr's] children were born of his two wives during the pre-Islamic period" (*Tarikhu'l-umam wa'l-mamlu'k*, Al-Tabari (died 922), Vol. 4, p. 50, Arabic, Dara'l-fikr, Beirut, 1979).

If Ayesha was betrothed in 620 CE (at the age of seven) and started to live with the Prophet in 624 CE (at the age of nine), that would indicate that she was born in 613 CE and was nine when she began living with the Prophet. Therefore, based on one account of Al-Tabari, the numbers show that Ayesha must have born in 613 CE, three years after the beginning of revelation (610 CE). Tabari also states that Ayesha was born in the pre-Islamic era (in Jahiliya). If she was born before 610 CE, she would have been at least 14 years old when she began living with the Prophet. Essentially, Tabari contradicts himself.

CONCLUSION: Al-Tabari is unreliable in determining Ayesha's age.

EVIDENCE # 3: The Age of Ayesha in Relation to the Age of Fatima

According to Ibn Hajar, "Fatima was born at the time the Ka'bah was rebuilt, when the Prophet was 35 years old... she was five years older than Ayesha" (*Al-isabah fi tamyizi'l-sahabah*, Ibn Hajar al-Asqalani, Vol. 4, p. 377, Maktabatu'l-Riyadh al-haditha, al-Riyadh, 1978).

If Ibn Hajar's statement is factual, Ayesha was born when the Prophet was 40 years old. If Ayesha was married to the Prophet when he was 52 years old, Ayesha's age at marriage would be 12 years.

CONCLUSION: Ibn Hajar, Tabari an Ibn Hisham and Ibn Hambal contradict each other. So, the marriage of Ayesha at seven years of age is a myth.

EVIDENCE #4: Ayesha's Age in relation to Asma's Age

According to Abda'l-Rahman ibn abi zanna'd: "Asma was 10 years older than Ayesha (*Siyar A'la'ma'l-nubala'*, Al-Zahabi, Vol. 2, p. 289, Arabic, Mu'assasatu'l-risalah, Beirut, 1992).

According to Ibn Kathir: "She [Asma] was elder to her sister [Ayesha] by 10 years" (*Al-Bidayah wa'l-nihayah*, Ibn Kathir, Vol. 8, p. 371, Dar al-fikr al-'arabi, Al-jizah, 1933).

According to Ibn Kathir: "She [Asma] saw the killing of her son during that year [73 AH], as we have already mentioned, and five days later she herself died. According to other narratives, she died not after five days but 10 or 20, or a few days over 20, or 100 days later. The most well known narrative is that of 100 days later. At the time of her death, she was 100 years old." (*Al-Bidayah wa'l-nihayah*, Ibn Kathir, Vol. 8, p. 372, Dar al-fikr al-'arabi, Al-jizah, 1933)

According to Ibn Hajar Al-Asqalani: "She [Asma] lived a hundred years and died in 73 or 74 AH." (*Taqribu'l-tehzib*, Ibn Hajar Al-Asqalani, p. 654, Arabic, Bab fi'l-nisa', al-harfu'l-alif, Lucknow).

According to almost all the historians, Asma, the elder sister of Ayesha was 10 years older than Ayesha. If Asma was 100 years old in 73 AH, she should have been 27 or 28 years-old at the time of the hijrah.

If Asma was 27 or 28 years old at the time of hijrah, Ayesha should have been 17 or 18 years-old. Thus, Ayesha, being 17 or 18 years of at the time of Hijra, she started to cohabit with the Prophet between at either 19 to 20 years of age.

Based on Hajar, Ibn Kathir, and Abda'l-Rahman ibn Abi Zanna'd, Ayesha's age at the time she began living with the Prophet would be 19 or 20. In Evidence # 3, Ibn Hajar suggests that Ayesha was 12 years-old and in Evidence #4 he contradicts himself with a 17 or 18-year-old Ayesha. What is the correct age, twelve or eighteen?

CONCLUSION: Ibn Hajar is an unreliable source for Ayesha's age.

EVIDENCE #5: The Battles of Badr and Uhud

A narrative regarding Ayesha's participation in Badr is given in the hadith of Muslim, (Kitabu'l-jihad wa'l-siyar, Bab karahiyati'l-isti'anah fi'l-ghazwi bikafir). Ayesha, while narrating on the journey to Badr and one of the important events that took place in that journey, says: "when we reached Shajarah". Obviously, Ayesha was with the group travelling towards Badr. A narrative regarding Ayesha's participation in the Battle of Uhud is given in Bukhari (Kitabu'l-jihad wa'l-siyar, Bab Ghazwi'l-nisa' wa qitalihinna ma'a'lrijal): "Anas reports that on the day of Uhud, people could not stand their ground around the Prophet. [On that day,] I saw Ayesha and Umm-i-Sulaim, they had pulled their dress up from their feet [to avoid any hindrance in their movement]." Again, this indicates that Ayesha was present in the Battles of Uhud and Badr.

It is narrated in Bukhari (Kitabu'l-maghazi, Bab Ghazwati'l-khandaq wa hiya'l-ahza'b): "Ibn 'Umar states that the Prophet did not permit me to participate in Uhud, as at that time, I was 14 years old. But on the day of Khandaq, when I was 15 years old, the Prophet permitted my participation."

Based on the above narratives, (a) the children below 15 years were sent back and were not allowed to participate in the Battle of Uhud, and (b) Ayesha participated in the Battles of Badr and Uhud

CONCLUSION: Ayesha's participation in the Battles of Badr and Uhud clearly indicates that she was not nine years old but at least 15 years old. After all, women used to accompany men to the battlefields to help them, not to be a burden on them. This account is another contradiction regarding Ayesha's age.

EVIDENCE #6: Surat al-Qamar (The Moon)

According to the generally accepted tradition, Ayesha was born about eight years before hijrah. But according to another narrative in Bukhari, Ayesha is reported to have said: "I was a young girl (*jariyah* in Arabic)" when Surah Al-Qamar was revealed (Sahih Bukhari, kitabu'l-tafsir, Bab Qaulihi Bal al-sa'atu Maw'iduhum wa'l-sa'atu adha' wa amarr).

Chapter 54 of the Quran was revealed eight years before hijrah (*The Bounteous Koran*, M.M. Khatib, 1985), indicating that it was revealed in 614 CE. If Ayesha started living with the Prophet at the age of nine in 623 CE or 624 CE, she was a newborn infant (*sibyah* in Arabic) at the time that Surah Al-Qamar (The Moon) was revealed. According to the above tradition, Ayesha was actually a young girl, not an infant in the year of revelation of Al-Qamar. *Jariyah* means young playful girl (Lane's *Arabic English Lexicon*). So, Ayesha, being a *jariyah* not a *sibyah* (infant), must be somewhere between 6-13 years old at the time of revelation of Al-Qamar, and therefore must have been 14-21 years at the time she married the Prophet.

CONCLUSION: This tradition also contradicts the marriage of Ayesha at the age of nine.

EVIDENCE #7: Arabic Terminology

According to a narrative reported by Ahmad ibn Hanbal, after the death of the Prophet's first wife Khadijah, when Khaulah came to the Prophet advising him to marry again, the Prophet asked her regarding the choices she had in mind. Khaulah said: "You can marry a virgin (*bikr*) or a woman who has already been married (*thayyib*)". When the Prophet asked the identity of the *bikr* (virgin), Khaulah mentioned Ayesha's name.

All those who know the Arabic language are aware that the word *bikr* in the Arabic language is not used for an immature nine-year-old girl. The correct word for a young playful girl, as stated earlier, is *jariyah*. *Bikr* on the other hand, is used for an unmarried lady without conjugal experience prior to marriage, as we understand the word "virgin" in English. Therefore, obviously a nine-year-old girl is not a "lady" (*bikr*) (Musnad Ahmad ibn Hanbal, Vol. 6, p. .210, Arabic, Dar Ihya al-turath al-'arabi, Beirut).

CONCLUSION: The literal meaning of the word, *bikr* (virgin), in the above hadith is "adult woman with no sexual experience prior to marriage." Therefore, Ayesha was an adult woman at the time of her marriage.

EVIDENCE #8. The Quranic Text

All Muslims agree that the Quran is the book of guidance. So, we need to seek the guidance from the Quran to clear the smoke and confusion created by the eminent men of the classical period of Islam in the matter of Ayesha's age at her marriage. Does the Quran allow or disallow marriage of an immature child of seven years of age?

There are no verses that explicitly allow such marriage. There is a verse, however, that guides Muslims in their duty to raise an orphaned child. The

Quran's guidance on the topic of raising orphans is also valid in the case of our own children. The verse states:

> 4:5-6   "And make not over your property (property of the orphan), which Allah had made a (means of) support for you, to the weak of understanding, and maintain them out of it, clothe them and give them good education. And test them until they reach the age of marriage. Then if you find them maturity of intellect, make over them their property..."

In the matter of children who have lost a parent, a Muslim is ordered to (a) feed them, (b) clothe them, (c) educate them, and (d) test them for maturity "until the age of marriage" before entrusting them with management of finances.

Here the Quranic verse demands meticulous proof of their intellectual and physical maturity by objective test results before the age of marriage in order to entrust their property to them.

In light of the above verses, no responsible Muslim would hand over financial management to a seven- or nine-year-old immature girl. If we cannot trust a seven-year-old to manage financial matters, she cannot be intellectually or physically fit for marriage. Ibn Hambal (Musnad Ahmad ibn Hambal, vol.6, p. 33 and 99) claims that nine-year-old Ayesha was rather more interested in playing with toy-horses than taking up the responsible task of a wife. It is difficult to believe, therefore, that Abu Bakr, a great believer among Muslims, would betroth his immature seven-year-old daughter to the 50-year-old Prophet. Equally difficult to imagine is that the Prophet would marry an immature seven-year-old girl.

Another important duty demanded from the guardian of a child is to educate them. Let us ask the question, "How many of us believe that we can educate our children satisfactorily before they reach the age of seven or nine years?" The answer is none. Logically, it is an impossible task to educate a child satisfactorily before the child attains the age of seven. Then, how can we believe that Ayesha was educated satisfactorily at the claimed age of seven at the time of her marriage?

Abu Bakr was a more judicious man than all of us. So, he definitely would have judged that Ayesha was a child at heart and was not satisfactorily educated as demanded by the Quran. He would not have married her to anyone. If a proposal of marrying the immature and yet to be educated seven-year-old Ayesha came to the Prophet, he would have rejected it outright because neither the Prophet nor Abu Bakr would violate any clause in the Quran.

CONCLUSION: The marriage of Ayesha at the age of seven years would violate the maturity clause or requirement of the Quran. Therefore, the story of the marriage of the seven-year-old immature Ayesha is a myth.

EVIDENCE #9: Consent in Marriage

A women must be consulted and must agree in order to make a marriage valid (*Mishakat al Masabiah*, translation by James Robson, Vol. I, p. 665). Islamically, credible permission from women is a prerequisite for a marriage to be valid.

By any stretch of the imagination, the permission given by an immature seven-year-old girl cannot be valid authorization for marriage.

It is inconceivable that AbuBakr, an intelligent man, would take seriously the permission of a seven-year-old girl to marry a 50-year-old man.

Similarly, the Prophet would not have accepted the permission given by a girl who, according to the hadith of Muslim, took her toys with her when she went live with Prophet.

CONCLUSION: The Prophet did not marry a seven-year-old Ayesha because it would have violated the requirement of the valid permission clause of the Islamic Marriage Decree. Therefore, the Prophet married an intellectually and physically mature lady Ayesha.

SUMMARY:

It was neither an Arab tradition to give away girls in marriage at an age as young as seven or nine years, nor did the Prophet marry Ayesha at such a young age. The people of Arabia did not object to this marriage because it never happened in the manner it has been narrated.

Obviously, the narrative of the marriage of nine-year-old Ayesha by Hisham ibn 'Urwah cannot be held true when it is contradicted by many other reported narratives. Moreover, there is absolutely no reason to accept the narrative of Hisham ibn 'Urwah as true when other scholars, including Malik ibn Anas, view his narrative while in Iraq, as unreliable. The quotations from Tabari, Bukhari and Muslim show they contradict each other regarding Ayesha's age. Furthermore, many of these scholars contradict themselves in their own records. Thus, the narrative of Ayesha's age at the time of the marriage is not reliable due to the clear contradictions seen in the works of classical scholars of Islam.

Therefore, there is absolutely no reason to believe that the information on Ayesha's age is accepted as true when there are adequate grounds to reject it as myth. Moreover, the Quran rejects the marriage of immature girls and boys as well as entrusting them with responsibilities.

1Man = 2 Women?

Layth Saleh al-Shaiban

According to today's Muslim scholars and leaders, women are not fit to rule or hold any office of significance because God has indicated that they are deficient when compared to men. The Muslim scholars will tell you that in the Quran God has made the testimony of ONE man equal to that of TWO women because women are forgetful and emotionally driven.

Any sane and rational person who has worked or studied with women will know that they can be just as smart, if not smarter, than most of their male counterparts. At the same time, I have yet to find this fictional woman who forgets or whose memory is weaker than a man's (although we all wish this was the case sometimes). Let us examine the verse where all these unequal and sexist conclusions have been drawn:

> 2:282   Oh you who believe, if you borrow until a delayed period then you will write it amongst you, and let he who is an official record keeper write between you, and let him not refuse to write as God has commanded it. And when he writes, let he who has borrowed give the details of the transaction and he shall fear his Lord God and not omit anything. If the one who has borrowed is not fit, or if he is weak, or if he can't complete the information; then let he who is responsible for him fill-in on his behalf. And you shall have TWO witnesses from your men, and if they are not two men then let them be ONE man and TWO women from those whose testimony you accept, so if one of them is mis-guided <Tudhil>, then one will remind the other.....

The word used in 2:282 which has caused the misunderstanding of the witnessing requirement is '*Tudhil*'.

-Khalifa has translated this as: 'biased'.

-Yusif Ali used: 'errs'.

There are also a few translations which used: 'forgets'. The word for 'forgets' in Arabic is '*Tansa/Nasi*'...Thus we can rule out this possibility from the start. '*Dhalall*' is used in opposition to '*Huda*' (guidance)...Thus its prime translation could be '*Misguided*'.

"You guide (*Tahdi*) whom you will, and you misguide (*Tidhil*) whom you will'.

Its derivative *Al-Dhalleen* (those who are misguided) is also used in Sura 1, Al-Fatiha. Thus, looking at 2:282 we can say:

> 2:282   If you cannot find, then one man and two women FROM WHO'S TESTIMONY IS ACCEPTABLE TO YOU. If one of them is 'Tudhil', then one will remind the other...

Please note that the issue of 'honesty/biasness' is not at question since the choice of witnesses has to be of people who are already acceptable or honest.

We also said that 'Forgetfullnes' is not a possible translation.

Tudhil = *Becomes Misguided; Lost*

A clearer undertsanding of 2:282 takes place when we analyze the steps involved:

1. If there is a financial transaction involving debt between two or more parties and whose repayment will be at a later stage, then it must be documented.

2. The documentation of such a transaction is to be done through an official record keeper or institution.

3. The one who has incurred the debt will be the one giving the record keeper the details of the transaction as he/she will put his signature or print on the document.

4. If the one who borrowed is incapacitated for any reason from giving information, then his/her guardian shall take such responsibility.

5. Two witnesses are required to seal the transaction.

6. It is preferable that the two witnesses be males, but if that is not possible then one man and two women will suffice.

7. At the time of testimony ONLY TWO witnesses are required, if one of the women is incapacitated then the other must take her place.

The question we should all ask ourselves is "What would cause one of the women to be 'misguided' in her testimony?"

The answer is obvious: the key difference between men and women is their physiology. Women give birth and men don't, women must rest for a lengthy period after child birth while men don't, women as mothers must suckle their children while men don't, women have menstrual cycles while men don't. These differences exist as a matter of physical fact and have nothing to do with intellegence or will.

It is obvious from the Quran that God calls on TWO witnesses to be present (this is clear from the sequence of words in the verse). God being the knower and creator of all things knows that having one man and one women as a witness is not practical since on the day they are called the women may be incapacitated while the man may not, and since God calls on TWO witnesses, then the chances of having both present becomes much higher when TWO women and ONE man are selected so at the time of calling there are three people to choose from (please note that had God meant that the testimony of ONE man equals TWO women then He would have continued the verse and said: If TWO women and One man are not available then you shall select FOUR women).

This precious Quran speaks of nothing but fairness and equality for both men and women, yet it is the evil wishes of those who have corrupted the religion to turn it into a book that serves their own purposes and desires.

Please note: Other than 'future financial transactions' listed in 2:282, the testimony of 1 woman = 1 man as can be seen:

> 4:15   If any of your women are guilty of lewdness, Take the evidence of four (Reliable) witnesses from amongst you against them; and if they testify, confine them to houses until death do claim them, or Allah ordain for them some (other) way.

> 24:4   And those who launch a charge against chaste women, and produce not four witnesses (to support their allegations),- flog them with eighty stripes; and reject their evidence ever after: for such men are wicked transgressors;-

In fact, there is even one instance where the testimony of a woman OVERRIDES that of a man!:

> 24:6-9   And for those who launch a charge against their spouses, and have (in support) no evidence but their own,- their solitary evidence (can be received) if they bear witness four times (with an oath) by Allah that they are solemnly telling the truth; And the fifth (oath) (should be) that they solemnly invoke the curse of Allah on themselves if they tell a lie. But it would avert the punishment from the wife, if she bears witness four times (with an oath) By Allah, that (her husband) is telling a lie; And the fifth (oath) should be that she solemnly invokes the wrath of Allah on herself if (her accuser) is telling the truth.

May God increase our knowledge and grant us wisdom.

Are Women to be Beaten?

Layth Saleh al-Shaiban

In some parts of the Middle East and other areas of the Muslim world, a woman may be beaten severely by her husband or male relatives for something as ridiculous as not having dinner prepared on time. It is a common theme amongst some male Muslims to beat their women whenever they think it is deserved and they can rest assured that the entire Islamic Scholars will be right behind them for support.

Although this may sound bizarre, the Muslim Scholars have told people that God has ordained in His holy book that women may be beaten if their male counter-part is not pleased with them. The verse that Muslims claim gives a green light to commit violence against their women-folk is the following:

> 4:34   [Yusufali Translation]: Men are the protectors and maintainers of women, because Allah has given the one more (strength) than the other, and because they support them from their means. Therefore the righteous women are devoutly obedient, and guard in (the husband's) absence what Allah would have them guard. As to those women on whose part ye fear "Nushooz" disloyalty and ill-conduct , admonish them (first), (Next), refuse to share their beds, (And last) "Idribuhun" beat them (lightly); but if they return to obedience, seek not against them Means (of annoyance): For Allah is Most High, great (above you all)."

If indeed God had commanded men to beat their 'disloyal' women, then we have no course of action but to 'hear & obey'...However, there is more than meets the eye in accepting the common interpretation of verse 4:34 which is the subject of this article.

The Quran is best studied by placing all similar subject words/verses together (this approach is called 'Tarteel' and has been advised by the Almighty in 73:4).

There are two key words that are central to deriving the correct meaning for this topic:

> *Nushuz* (translated above 'disloyalty & ill-conduct)
>
> *Idribuhun* (translated above as 'beat them').

The first word 'Nushooz' will give us an understanding of what the subject is all about...Is this about a woman who is disloyal and in ill-conduct (an adulteress or temptress perhaps?) Or, has this word been mistranslated based on a backdrop of social ignorance and male domination?

Nushooz means: '*to rise / go above*'.

This can be seen clearly in 58:11 where people are told to 'Nushooz' from the place of gathering/sitting.

> 58:11   [Yusufali Translation]: O ye who believe! When ye are told to make room in the assemblies, (spread out and) make room: (ample) room will Allah provide for you. And when ye are told "Inshuzoo" * to rise up, rise up Allah will rise up, to (suitable) ranks (and degrees), those of you who believe and who have been granted (mystic) Knowledge. And Allah is well-acquainted with all ye do."
>
> * Notice how our translator [Yusufali] has given the correct translation in the verse, whereas in 4:34 it was all about 'disloyalty & ill-conduct'.

Therefore, the issue we are dealing with here is not adultery or some other act of immorality, but rather it is the subject of a woman 'rebelling / going against' her husband (going above them, not acknowledging the other, not listening, deserting them, etc.).

Let us read what the Quran tells us to do when it is the man that is doing the 'Nushooz' and not the woman:

> 4:128   [Yusufali Translation]: If a wife fears cruelty or "Nushooz" ** desertion on her husband's part, there is no blame on them if they arrange an amicable settlement between themselves; and such settlement is best; even though men's souls are swayed by greed. But if ye do good and practise self-restraint, Allah is well-acquainted with all that ye do."
>
> ** Again, we see our translator [yusufali] magically giving the correct meaning by translating 'Nushooz' as 'desertion' when it just happened that the male was the subject matter!

The Quran tells us that if the man is the one who is doing the 'Nushooz' then the couple need to reconcile or part since he obviously has rebelled against his wife (can't stand to be with her, finds himself wanting to leave from her presence, etc..)... The verse does not say that the woman should 'beat' the man into submission or bring her men-folk to do so in order to knock some sense into him...It says they should talk, and reconcile, since obviously this is an issue which needs people to come-back into respecting and loving one another, or part ways.

Now to move back to the verse where the woman is the one doing the 'Nushooz' using the correct translation:

> 4:34 "The men are to support the women by what God has gifted them over one another and for what they spend of their money. The upright women who are attentive, and keep private the personal matters for what God keeps watch over. As for those women from whom you fear a "Nushooz" desertion, then you shall advise them, and abandon them in the bedchamber, and "Idribuhun" Beat them?; if they obey you, then do not seek a way over them; God is High, Great.'

If we look at the subject matter, it is of a woman who cannot stand her man and therefore has rebelled from him...As with the example of the man being the one rebelling, there are steps to 'calm things down' and to bring harmony into the marriage...Beating a woman if she can't stand her man and has rebelled against him will only make her hate him more (not exactly a logical or practical solution to the problem).

Obviously now that the subject has been better understood, it is the second word "Idribuhun" which needs examination in light of the Quran.

> 14:24 [The Message] "Have you not seen how God puts forth (Daraba) the example of a good word is like a good tree, whose root is firm and its branches in the sky."

> 2:273 [The Message] "For the poor who face hardship in the cause of God, they cannot go forth (Darban) in the land; the ignorant ones think they are rich from their modesty; you know them by their features, they do not ask the people repeatedly. And what you spend out of goodness, God is fully aware of it."

Daraba (in its natural state) means: '*to put forth*'

The only reason this word can sometimes mean hit/strike is because a person is 'putting forth' his hand when striking someone (see 8:12, 8:50, 47:27).

> 8:50 "And if you could only see as the Angels take those who have rejected, they "Yadriboon" strike their faces and their backs: 'Taste the punishment of the blazing Fire!'"

Looking back at 4:34, we see that the context of the verse (solving the wife's rejection of her husband) leads us to choose the natural meaning of "Darab" which is: 'to put forth' and not the alternative meaning of 'strike'.

> 4:34 "The men are to support the women by what God has gifted them over one another and for what they spend of their money. The upright women who are attentive, and keep private the personal matters for what God keeps watch over. As for those women from whom you fear a desertion, then you shall 1)

36

advise them, and 2) abandon them in the bedchamber, and 3) "Idribuhun" let them go forth; if they obey you, then do not seek a way over them; God is High, Great."

The approach of choosing the 'best' understanding and/or meaning is both logical and, more importantly, in-line with the guidance for study we are given by God:

> 39:18 "The ones who listen to what is being said, and then follow the BEST of it. These are the ones whom God has guided, and these are the ones who possess intelligence."

What we have now is a comprehensive list of steps in order for a man to deal with his wife who wants to desert her husband and can no longer stand to be with him...

Talk about it. This is obviously the simplest and healthiest method since it opens the communication channel between both parties.

Abstain from sharing the same bed. This is the 2nd approach the man is advised to use if they are unable to reconcile their problem as the lack of sexual contact may lead to the wife to cool down as intimate contact may simply inflame the situation if she is unable to stand her husband.

Separate from each other. The 3rd and final line of advice is designed as a 'cooling-off' period and is mainly designed to help the wife re-think and examine the situation closely without the physical presence of her husband.

The logic and clarity of the above steps are a far cry from the wife beating and bashing claims which this article started off examining....

As for those who have been promoting the evil inherited from their forefathers while claiming falsely it was from God...

> 7:28-30 "And if they commit evil acts, they Say: 'We found our fathers doing such, and God ordered us to it.' Say: 'God does not order evil! Do you say about God what you do not know?' Say: 'My Lord orders justice, and that you be devoted at every temple, and that you call on Him, while being faithful to Him in the system; as He initiated you, so you will return.' A group He has guided and a group have deserved misguidance; that is because they have taken the devils as allies besides God; and they think they are guided!"

Questions / Issues

Below are some arguments/questions which have been presented in support of the understanding to 'beat women' as claimed is the true meaning in 4:34.

In Arabic, the word for 'separate from them' is 'IdribuANhun' and not 'Idribuhun' as used in 4:34. Therefore 'beat' is the correct meaning.

The people who raise such linguistic obstacles fail to notice that God uses the very same word 'Darab' such as in 14:24 without any prefix.

> 14:24   [The Message] "Have you not seen how God puts forth (Daraba) the example of a good word is like a good tree, whose root is firm and its branches in the sky."

Would they claim by the very same linguistic argument that God is 'beating' an example? Or, will they accept that without any prefix the word can mean to 'put forth'?

The word 'Idrib' means 'beat' if applied to a living object/thing and can mean otherwise if applied to a non-living object/thing.

This is mainly an argument put forth by groups who have preconceived notions and wish to keep believing that Islam is a mindless and barbaric system. The argument holds no merit based on linguistics or Arabic grammar. In-fact, the usage of the word 'Idrib' as applied in verse 24:31 puts an end to this argument as the women are obviously not being commanded to 'beat' their bosoms with their shawls, but rather they are commanded to 'put-forth' their shawls:

> 24:31   "And tell the believing women to lower their gaze and keep covered their private parts, and that they should not reveal their beauty except what is apparent, and let them put-forth (YaDribna) their shawls over their cleavage..."

Manifesto For Islamic Reform
(Short Version)[1]

Edip Yuksel

4:174	"O people, a proof has come to you from your Lord, and We have sent down to you a guiding light."
7:85	"…and do not make corruption on the Earth after it has been reformed…"
74:36-37	"It is one of the great ones. A warning to humanity. For any among you who wishes to progress or regress."

The influence of the religion concocted by clerics during the Umayyad and Abbasid dynasties is still dominant in Muslim countries. The idea that the Quran is incomplete, unintelligible, and insufficient for spiritual guidance created a huge demand for religious books, and the scholars and clergymen supplied volumes of them. The masses were told that those books were going to complete, explain, and detail the Quranic revelation. These clerics thus implied that God was not a wise and articulate author; He could not make His message sufficiently clear and He failed to provide guidance on many issues, even issues involving important spiritual principles and practices. Without these supplementary books, the Quran was of limited use to the individual seeking religious guidance. Some even went so far as to declare that reading the Quran alone would mislead the reader. Numerous books of hadith and sectarian jurisprudence (sharia) were labeled "authentic" and for all practical purposes, replaced the Quran. The Quran was not a book to be understood on its own; people needed to read books written by professional narrators, collectors, editors, and scholars of hearsay and speculation. Many people got lost among the volumes of books written to interpret and explain the Quran and did not find sufficient time to study the Quran itself. The privileged few who did find that time had little chance of understanding it, since their minds were tainted with man-made religious instructions, and their logic had been corrupted by contradictory teachings or what we might call "holy viruses."

Although religious scholars, clerics and their blind followers have always demonstrated the utmost formal respect for the Quran as physical media (the

---

[1] This is a shor version of the Manifesto for Islamic Reform. First published in 2007 as the appendix of the Quran: a Reformist Translation, the full text of the Manifesto for Islamic Reform has been published by BrainbowPress as a booklet. It is also available online, with its translations into other languages, at www.IslamicReform.org. To purchase it as a book, visit: www.BrainbowPress.com

leather or paper on which the verses of the Quran were written), they lost faith in, and respect for its message. Verses of the Quran are hung in high places on the walls, touched and treated with utmost reverence, yet the so-called Muslims rarely refer to them for their guidance. They are too confused by the contradictory and tangled maze of thousands of hadith falsely attributed to Muhammad and lost among the trivial details of sectarian books. When they occasionally refer to the Quran, it is most likely to be in an abusive manner, abusing the verses by taking them out of context and using them as slogans to declare holy wars or to justify aggression. The Quran that liberated people from the darkness of ignorance was transformed, soon after Muhammad's departure, to a book whose verses were recited for the dead, an amulet carried by the mentally and physically sick, and a paper idol to be revered and feared.

Though the Quran is considered one of the most read books, millions of the followers of Sunni and Shiite sects read the Quran without understanding it. Even if their native language is Arabic, they are taught not to trust their understanding. The Quran might be the most read book, but unfortunately, due to the concerted effort of religious clerics, it has been turned into the least understood, the least followed popular book in history.

When the mass reversion from the progressive and enlightening message of the Quran started, those who rejected the fabricated *hadith* and *sunna*, the Arab version of the Jewish Mishna and Gemara, were labeled "*murtad*" (apostates) and were threatened, tortured and murdered by the followers of *hadith* and *sunna*. For instance, a critical study of the Muslim history will reveal that Abu Hanifa was one of those courageous monotheists (*hanif*) who was persecuted during both the Umayyad and Abbasid dynasties. During his lifetime, he was accused of not accepting *hadith*. However, the murderers took advantage of his growing reputation after his death and led the creation of a Sunni sect falsely attributed to him.

The Origins of Sectarian Teachings

After the death of the prophet Muhammad, a diabolic event happened. In direct contradiction to the teachings of the Quran, male clerics dedicated the religion not to God alone, but to a "holy" corporation consisting of:

- God +
- Muhammad +
- Muhammad's companions +
- The companions of Muhammad's companions +
- Early sect leaders +
- Late sect leaders +
- Early scholars of a particular sect +
- Late scholars of a particular sect, and so on.

The product of this corporation was the hadith (teachings attributed to Muhammad), the sunna (actions attributed to Muhammad), the ijma (consensus of a select group of early scholars), and the sharia (religious decrees by early scholars). The result was numerous hostile factions that afflicted a great amount of division and atrocities in the land about thirty years after the departure of Muhammad (6:159; 23:52-56). This concoction of medieval Arab/Christian/Jewish cultures was introduced to the masses as God's infallible religion, as delivered by the last prophet. The only thing actually delivered by God to Muhammad, however, was the text of the Holy Quran, which is set out as the final and authoritative divine message to humankind:

> **75:18-19** Once We recite it, you shall follow such a recitation. Then, it is We who will explain it.

Unfortunately, ignorance, intolerance, misogynist teachings, superstitions, and outdated practices have accumulated over the centuries in interpreting and translating the holy book of Islam. It is time to re-introduce the actual message of the Quran. It is time to remove the accumulated layers of man-made dogmas and traditions that have attached themselves to the text (6:21; 7:29; 9:31; 16:52; 39:2,11,14; 40:14,65; 42:21; 45.17; 74:1-56; 98:5).

Under a very cruel theocratic state terror, many men mobilized to participate in the creation that we rightly call Hislam. They did not have much chance to add or subtract to what was considered The Quran, but there was a lot of room for innovations, superstitions, additions and distortions through fabricating hadith. When a man from Bukhara started collecting hearsay more than two hundred years after the departure of the prophet Muhammad, the landscape and social demographics were fertile for all kinds of theological concoctions and mutations. Those people and their parents had participated in numerous sectarian wars and atrocities. Many educated Gentiles, Christians and Jews were converted to Islam for dubious reasons. Most of these converts had never experienced a paradigm change; they just found it convenient to integrate their culture and most of their previous religious ideas with the new one. To justify and promote their version of religion, the elite started packaging and introducing their religious, cultural, and political ideas and practices under the brand names of hadith, sunna, commentaries, and fatwas. Additionally, they fabricated numerous stories called "asbab ul-nuzul" (the reasons for revelation) about why each verse was revealed, thereby distorting the meaning or limiting the scope of many Quranic verses. There was a great effort and competition to distort the meaning of words, taking them out of context to promote the agenda of a certain religion, culture, tribe, sect, cult, or king. Male chauvinists, hermits, misogynists too took advantage of this deformation movement. Hearsay statements attributing words and deeds to Muhammad and his idolized comrades became the most powerful tool or Trojan horse, for the promotion of diverse political propaganda, cultural assimilation, and even commercial advertisement. As a result, the Quran was deserted and its message was heavily distorted.

41

Soon after Muhammad's death, thousands of hadiths (words attributed to Muhammad) were fabricated and two centuries later collected, and centuries later compiled and written in the so-called "authentic" hadith books:

- to support the teaching of a particular sect against another (such as, what nullifies ablution; which sea food is prohibited);
- to flatter or justify the authority and practice of a particular king against dissidents (such as, Mahdy and Dajjal);
- to promote the interest of a particular tribe or family (such as, favoring the Quraysh tribe or Muhammad's family);
- to justify sexual abuse and misogyny (such as, Aisha's age; barring women from leading Sala prayers);
- to justify violence, oppression and tyranny (such as, torturing members of Urayna and Uqayla tribes; massacring the Jewish population in Medina; assassinating a female poet for her critical poems);
- to exhort more rituals and righteousness (such as, nawafil prayers);
- to validate superstitions (such as, magic; worshiping the black stone near the Kaba);
- to prohibit certain things and actions (such as, prohibiting drawing animal and human figures; playing musical instruments; chess);
- to import Jewish and Christian beliefs and practices (such as, death by stoning; circumcision; head scarf; hermitism; rosary);
- to resurrect pre-Islamic beliefs and practices common among Meccans (such as, intercession; slavery; tribalism; misogyny);
- to please crowds with stories (such as the story of Miraj (ascension to heaven) and bargaining for prayers);
- to idolize Muhammad and claim his superiority to other messengers (such as, numerous miracles, including splitting the moon);
- to defend hadith fabrications against monotheists (such as, condemning those who find the Quran alone sufficient); and even
- to advertise products of a particular farm (such as, the benefits of dates grown in a town called Ajwa).

In addition to the above mentioned reasons, many hadith were fabricated to explain the meaning of the "difficult" Quranic words or phrases, or to distort the meaning of verses that contradicted the fabricated hadith, or to provide trivial information not mentioned in the Quran.

Islam versus Sunni and Shiite Religions

Let's first check the Quran and enumerate some of the characteristics of Islam, the system of peace, submission and surrender to God alone. Islam:

- is not a proper name, but a descriptive noun coming from the Arabic root of surrendering/submission/peace, used by God to describe the

42

system delivered by all His messengers and prophets (5:111; 10:72; 98:5, 4:125; 22:78).

- is peacefully surrendering to God alone (2:112,131; 4:125; 6:71; 22:34; 40:66).
- is a system with universal principles, which are in harmony with nature (3:83; 33:30; 35:43).
- requires objective evidence besides personal experience (3:86; 2:111; 21:24; 74:30).
- demands conviction not based on wishful thinking or feelings, but based on reason and evidence (17:36; 4:174; 8:42; 10:100; 11:17; 74:30-31).
- esteems knowledge, education, and learning (35:28; 4:162; 9:122; 22:54; 27:40; 29:44,49).
- promotes scientific inquiry regarding the evolution of humankind on earth (29:20).
- rejects clergymen and intermediaries between God and people (2:48; 9:31-34).
- condemns profiteering from religion (9:34; 2:41,79,174; 5:44)
- stands for liberty and accountability (6:164).
- stands for freedom of expression (2:256; 18:29; 10:99; 88:21).
- requires consultation and representation in public affairs (42:38; 5:12).
- promotes a democratic system where participation of all citizens is encouraged and facilitated (58:11).
- prohibits bribery, and requires strict rules against the influence of interest groups in government (2:188).
- requires election of officials based on qualifications and principles of justice (4:58).
- promises justice for everyone (5:8).
- supports the rights of individual to publicly petition against injustices committed by individuals or government (4:148).
- encourages the distribution of wealth, economic freedom and social welfare (2:215, 59:7).
- promotes utmost respect to individuals (5:32).
- relates the quality of a society to the quality of individuals comprising it (13:11).
- recognizes and protects individual right's to privacy (49:12).
- recognizes the right to the presumption of innocence and right to confront the accuser (49:12).
- provides protection for witnesses (2:282).
- does not punish the innocent for the crimes of others (53:38).
- protects the right to personal property (2:85,188; 4:29; except. 24:29; 59:6-7).
- discourages a non-productive economy (2:275; 5:90; 3:130).

- encourages charity and caring for the poor (6:141; 7:156).
- promotes gender and race equality. (49:13).
- values women (3:195; 4:124; 16:97).
- values intellect (5:90).
- offers peace among nations (2:62; 2:135-136, 208).
- considers the entire world as belonging to all humanity and supports immigration (4:97-98).
- promotes peace and deters aggression (60:8,9; 8:60; 3:110).
- pursues the golden-plated brazen rule of equivalence, that is, retaliation with occasional forgiveness (42:20; 17:33).
- stands for human rights and the oppressed (4:75).
- encourages competition in righteousness (16:90).
- expects high moral standards (25:63-76; 31:12-20; 23:1-11).
- protects the environment (30:41).
- is the only system/law approved by god (3:19,85).

Through hadith, sunna and sectarian jurisprudence, scholars produced various sects, orders, or religions which were later attributed to their names (Shafii, Hanbali, Maliki, Hanafi, Jafari, Vahhabi, etc) to replace God's system of Islam or surrender and peace. The breadth and depth of distortion is astonishing. Here is a sample list of distortions made by the leaders of Sunni and Shiite sects, despite the Quranic teachings to the contrary. The list below is a selection of anti-Quranic teachings, which are found in the most respected Sunni or Shiite sources.

- Man-made sectarian teachings are needed to supplement the Quran.
- Muhammad was an illiterate man and remained illiterate until his death.
- Muhammad tortured people by gauging their eyes with hot nails.
- Married adulterers should be stoned to death.
- There was a verse instructing stoning to death for married adulterers, but it was eaten by a hungry holy goat after Muhammad's death. Though those verses were abrogated through the goat, they are still legally binding and their meaning is valid.
- Omar, the second Caliph, wanted to re-insert the verses eaten by the goat, but could not do it because of he feared from people.
- Some verses of the Quran abrogate other verses of the Quran.
- Even some hadith abrogate verses of the Quran.
- Dividing to sects is a good thing, as long as they are authorized by kings and their paid scholars.
- God initially required us to pray 50 times (not units; times) a day when Muhammad met God in the seventh heaven during his Miraj (ascension). But, thank to Moses, who was residing in the sixth heaven, gave repeated advice to Muhammad for reduction. After

oscillating between God and Moses repeatedly Muhammad haggled for further discount in the numbers of prayers. Thank to Moses and Muhammad we are saved from praying 50 times a day, or for every 28 minutes including day and night!

- Muhammad has the power of intercession and will save us during the Day of Judgment.
- Uttering the name of Muhammad alone without other words of praise, is disrespect to Muhammad and deprives a person from his intercession.
- People cannot make it to heaven without accepting Muhammad's messengership.
- Muhammad is the highest of all prophets and messengers.
- God created the universe for the sake of Muhammad.
- Muhammad is the last messenger.
- The black stone by the Kaba in Mecca is from heaven and should be respected.
- Visiting Muhammad's tomb in Medina is a religious duty.
- Testifying for oneness of God is not enough without adding Muhammad's name.
- Muhammad's name and the names of his closest companions should be displayed next to God's name in mosques.
- We should pray to God alone while we are standing in our daily Salat prayers, but when we sit we should call Muhammad as he is alive, omnipresent and omniscient by addressing him "essalamu alayKA ayyuhann nabiyyu" (o prophet, peace be upon YOU).
- Muhammad showed many miracles, including splitting the moon. According to some narrations, half of the moon fell in Ali's backyard.
- Muhammad was not a human being like us; he was a superman. He had sexual intercourse with nine women in a single night.
- Muhammad had the sexual power of 30 males.
- When Muhammad was 53 years-old, he married Aisha who was only 9 years-old.
- Muhammad was bewitched by a Jew and he wandered in the streets of Medina in utter confusion for weeks.
- Muhammad died poor, so poor that he pawned his personal belonging to Jew for little barley
- The consensus of religious scholars should be considered God's religion.
- Men are superior to women.
- Men may beat their wives if they disobey them.
- The menstruating women should not touch the Quran, should not pray and should not enter the mosques.
- Prayer is nullified if a donkey, a dog, or a woman passes in front of the praying person.

- Women cannot lead congregational prayers.
- Women are mentally and spiritually inferior to men.
- The hell will be filled with mostly women.
- Women should be covered from head to toe under veil.
- Women should be segregated in public places.
- Gold and silk is prohibited for men.
- Drawing pictures of animated creatures is great sin.
- Playing musical instruments other than those used by medieval Arabs is sin.
- Wearing turban and growing beards in a particular fashion is a religious practice of emulating Muhammad.
- Circumcision is needed to correct the male genitals.
- Following the hadith books that were written two centuries after Muhammad is equal to following messenger.
- Women cannot divorce her husband on her own.
- A man can divorce his wife by uttering some words three times.
- Paying the Zakat charity is required only once a year.
- The Hajj pilgrim should be done in several days.
- If one breaks his fast during Ramadan before the sunset, he or she should fast 30 more days for that day as a punishment.
- Dogs especially black dogs are from devil. If a dog touches you, you must wash in a special way.
- Eating the meat of many animals is prohibited and the contradictory list of prohibitions in authorized sects is good. The taste of the Quraysh tribe is the ultimate authority regarding which food is prohibited or not.
- Khalifa, that is succession in leadership, is the right of the Quraysh tribe.
- Arabic is the language of heaven.
- We are ordered to kill people until they declare "la ilaha illallah"
- The Quran is not clear; it is ambiguous.
- The Quran is not detailed; it is general.
- The Quran is not complete; it needs to be completed.
- The Quran alone does not guide; it needs many other books and teachings.
- Those who do not observe daily prayers should be beaten.
- Those who leave the religion of Islam (read Sunni or Shiite) should be killed.
- For the Quranic references and discussions on the above, see:

For the detailed arguments and **full text** of the Manifesto for Islamic Reform, please visit:

www.brainbowpress.com
www.islamicreform.org

Why is an Islamic State Untenable? Why the State should be Secular?

Abdullahi An-Naim

The idea of an Islamic State derives from the unique role that the Prophet Muhammad held in Medina, where the Prophet concurrently asserted political, military and religious leadership. But conflating religion and the state is untenable because only the Prophet was capable of holding all of that authority at once, and Muslims do not accept the possibility of another Prophet.

Furthermore, the idea of an Islamic state is not borne from Islamic culture. The idea stems from a European view where law is positive and the state is totalitarian entity that seeks to form society in the state's image. Historically, Islamic societies have differentiated between state and religious institutions, and permitting a state to force its view upon unwilling citizens violates the principles of Islam that teach individuals to live through personal choice and accept differences and disagreements with others.

Islamic societies have traditionally differentiated between state and religious institutions because religious and political authorities are fundamentally different. Religious authority comes from personal, subjective judgments about a scholar's religious piety and knowledge. Political authority is determined on an objective basis as people assess a leader's ability to exercise coercive power and administrate effectively. Additionally, religious authority invokes divine power, which transcends human challenge, whereas political authority is supposed to represent the views of the population and is thus based upon human judgment which can be challenged by other human beings.

Also, the flexibility of Shari'a conflicts with the state's need for practicability and stability. As demonstrated below, Shari'a is subject to changing human interpretations, and if Shari'a is the entire basis for a state's law, then that law could be undermined by the potential for wholesale change. Further, Shari'a does not provide effective guidance for the state on practical issues like daily administration and international trade.

Practices of the Prophet Muhammad support the idea that a state needs skills that stand apart from religious authority. The Prophet repeatedly appointed a man as commander of the Muslim armies even though the Prophet was dissatisfied with the commander's religious piety.

Just like there is an inherent connectedness between religion and politics, there is interplay between religious and political authority. For example, a political leader may have a degree of religious authority. But the fundamental differences between religious and political authority mandate separating the two precepts.

Why the State should be Secular

The base of this discussion is Professor An-Na'im's belief that the state should be secular (i.e. neutral about religion) and not an enforcer of Shari'a.

First, the state should not commandeer Shari'a because Islam decrees that Muslims practice their religion through personal, voluntary conviction without the influence of state coercion. Additionally, the idea of a secular state is more consistent with Islamic history than the notion of an Islamic state that conflates religious and state institutions.

Second, state enforcement of Shari'a undermines the religious authority of Shari'a and leads to possibilities of hypocrisy (nifaq). For example, consider how some Islamic scholars assert that apostasy (heresy) is punishable by death although the Qur'an does not provide any legal punishment for apostasy. Thus, if a state enforced the views of those scholars, then some Muslims may be forced to contradict their own beliefs, violating their personal freedom of religion, and undermining the credibility and coherence of Islam itself.

Islam: Religion of Peace

Ahmed Subhy Mansour

Two different visions of Islam:

There are two different visions of Islam. The first is seeing Islam through its divine source, namely the Quran. The method of this vision is to understand Islam through its own terminology and language. The Arabic language, as any other language, is a living being whose terminology and words' meaning change depending on the time and place, and also on the sects, the schools of thought and societies in general.

Therefore, he who wants to approach Islam through its divine source (the Quran) needs to understand the Quranic language and then to proceed without any preconceived ideas to trace the subject under research. It is essential to go through all the verses connected to the subject being researched to reach the final conclusion. Quranic verses are of two kinds:

> 1. Mohkamat, the verses that have specific meanings and lay down the general rule

> 2. Motashabehat, the verses that have details of the same subject mentioned in the first. It is easy to collect all the verses of Motashabehat and understand them by its Mohkamat verse of the same subject. After such scrutiny, one reaches the complete and correct view of Islam without any preconceived ideas. This is the Quranic vision of Islam.

The second vision is seeing Islam throughout Muslim tradition. It is a human source as it has many sources, includes the sayings ascribed to the prophet Mohammed some centuries after his death, the tales invented to comment on the Quranic stories according to their point of views, and the saying of the renowned Muslim Scholars or 'the Imams of the Muslim Jurisprudence and the other scholars or Al foqahaa'. By these human resources, they look at the Quranic verses and understand them accordingly.

It's clearly natural to find in these human sources contradicting opinions. Each opinion searches for supporting verses in the Quran often results in the verses being taken out of their context and having their meaning twisted according to the terminology of its tradition

The difference between the two visions:

Since the researcher here is led astray, it's no wonder that his or her understanding of Islam contradicts its' reality and its real vision. It is implicitly out of this second vision of Islam that come the judicial sentences fatwa which puts Islam in a position that allows it to be accused of terrorism, violence, anomalies and fanaticism.

In fact, Muslims during the middle ages like many others living with the mentality of that time, namely with fundamentalism, fanaticism, holy wars and religious trials, and persecutions twisted the meanings of the Quranic verses according to their culture and mentality, along with the invention of the prophetic sayings that served their purpose. Those sayings [Hadeeth] were made holy as if they were really said by the prophet Mohammed. This is the belief of the Sunni Muslims. The Shiite Muslims followed another set of sayings attributed to the prophet Mohammed and his relatives, or [Ahl Al Bait]. The Sufi Muslims also followed the sayings of their holy saints.

Thus from this second human traditional vision of Muslims, we find diversity of sources and sects, and he who chooses this traditional vision of Muslims in order to understand Islam will find nothing but mixture of Middle-ages cultures; some of them full of superstitions [Sufi tradition] or violence[Sunni tradition] and a mixture of the two [The Shiite tradition]. If, however, the researcher goes directly to read the Quran according to its language and understand the Quran using the Quran without any preceding ideas, he/she will be astonished to find that Islam is the religion of peace, forgiveness and all the high values.

I choose to understand Islam through the Quran as it is the only confirmed source of Islam, using a scientific method which adheres to Quranic terminology to understand the Quran by the Quran. By this method, I have previously researched and wrote about Islam and its comparisons to the Muslim Sufi and Sunni traditions, and their history in the middle age, and their contemporary Islamic movement which purported to bring the Muslims back to the mentality of the middle ages. Now, let's try to understand Islam and its relationship with peace.

What about the relationship between Islam and peace?

Peace is the origin of the understanding of Islam as a religion as well as in the Arabic language. It is the base of the relationship between Muslims and others. Peace is also the back-bone of the Jihad laws in the Quran.

We start with the understanding of the word [Iman] or "Belief":

According to the Quranic terminology and its particular language, the word "believing" [Aaman], has two meanings in Quranic along with the Arabic language; you can believe *in* (Aamana be...) or you believe or trust others (Aamana le).

The first definition is related to faith as in the verse "The messenger believed in what was descended to him from His Lord and the believers. All believe in God, His angels, His books, His Messengers" (2:285). Thus to 'believe in' means to have a deeply rooted faith in your heart concerning the relationship between man and God.

People have had diversified faiths, even within the same religion or even within the same sect or school of thinking. The Quran confirms that people will be judged for the diversity of their faiths by God alone and only on Judgment day (as found in verses 2: 113, 3:55, 10:93, 16:124, 5:48, 39:3, 7:46).

The second meaning is the relationship between people, namely believing or trusting others, and implies that when someone is safe and secure people trust him. He is also called a 'believer' because he is trusted by the people, [Aamana laho al naas; Ma'amoun al janeb]. This meaning is repeated in the Quran especially in the Quranic stories concerning the Prophets. For example, in the story of Noah, the arrogant ones told him "Shall we trust you [An'omeno Laka] while it is the meanest that follow you?" (26:111). Meaning how can we trust you and feel secure with you seeing that you are followed by the lowest of the people! This meaning of 'believing' that is trusting someone is repeated in the story of Abraham (26:29), Joseph (12:17) Moses (44:21) and (23:47) and also in the Quranic Narratives of the life of the prophet Mohammed in Medina (3:37) and (2:57).This meaning of believing is found in other subject as well.

When somebody behaves in a trustworthy manner, he becomes safe and secure as seen from his outward behavior. According to the Quranic terminology, this person is called 'a believer' regardless of his religion or Faith. For that matter, he/she can be a Buddhist, Muslim, and Christian, Jew or an atheist. It is a private matter between the individual and God, that no creature has the authority to judge. It is reserved for God alone on Judgment Day.

The two meanings of the term 'belief' are simultaneously expressed in God's verses concerning the prophet Mohammed that says "He believes in God, has faith in the believers [Y'omono bellah wa y'omeno Lel m'omeneen]" (9:61). In the Arabic language and in this Quranic verse, the word Y'omeno means the two meanings: believe in and trust. Thus, this verse shows that to believe in God is to worship Him alone, and to believe in others is to trust them. To believe in God is to acknowledge that He is the one and only. The evaluation of this faith, which many people dispute, is to take place in Judgment Day. Therefore, what concerns and should only concern humans among themselves is to live in trust, safety, security and peace.

Therefore faith in Islam is equivalent to peace among people, and at the same time, being a believer means being a man of God and a man of peace and trust. This is the understanding of faith in the religion of Islam.

What about the word [Islam] itself in Arabic Language and in the religion of Islam?

The understanding of Islam in the Quran, as was the case with the word 'believe', has an outward meaning concerning the dealing with people and inward meaning concerning the relationship with God .

The inward meaning of Islam is to succumb and submit to God alone, pledging allegiance and obedience to Him and Him alone (6:161-163).

This meaning of Islam is the same message that came with all the prophets in all divine messages and in all ancient languages until it finally appeared in Arabic in the final divine revelation of the Quran. God doesn't accept any other religion different from the submission to Him alone as the only God. This is the meaning of the verse "The religion before God is islam ..." (3:19). Note that the word Islam is not capitalized on purpose to show that the Quran is describing an attitude or a mode of being and not a specific religion. Another verse says ("Whoever desires a religion other than islam, never will it be accepted of him and in the hereafter he will be in the rank of those who had lost") (3:85). Here, it describes about his future on the Day of Judgment where only God will judge all of mankind.

Islam means submitting to God alone in any language, time or place and in all divine messages. Alas unfortunately, in our culture, Islam was transformed into an Arabic description of a definite group in a specific epoch.

God is uninterested in the titles and divisions that people choose for them such as Muslims, Jews, Christians and Sabiens.

For this reason, God confirms in two verses that those who believe in God alone as the only God, believe in the Day of Judgment as the divine day of absolute justice and maintain peace and perform righteous deeds as a proof of their belief in the last day, they are the allies of God whether they are the followers of the Quran or the Old and New Testament (2:62, 5:69). These two verses confirm the other two verses: "The religion before God is Islam" and "Whoever desires a religion other than Islam, never will be accepted of him" (3:19 & 85).

These verses imply that he who believes in God, the last day and performs righteous deeds in this world will be considered a Muslim in the sight of God on the Last Day regardless of the title he/she had in this world. It is up to God alone- not to us - on the Day of Judgment – not now- to judge the faith. Any one that claims this right to him/her is claiming divinity upon himself.

The real meaning of the inward face of Islam is submitting to God only and succumbing to Him alone with the language of hearts. It is the universal language that leaves no room for discord among people or believers, and based on this language all people will be judged on the last day. This is the inward meaning of Islam in dealing with the Almighty God, the Creator, or the inner meaning of the faith that lies inside the heart which will be judged by God alone on the Last Day.

God alone is the One who can monitor the real feelings of the human heart in this life, and the only one who- on Judgment Day- will tell us of our religious disputes. It's up to every human to choose monotheism, paganism or atheism; it's his freedom of belief and he will be responsible before God alone on the last Day. This describes Islam in dealing with God, or the inner meaning of Islam.

In Islam, outwardly dealing with people is directly related to the safety and security expressed and practiced among people, no matter how different their inner believes are. God says: "O you who believe enter peace wholeheartedly" (2:208). Thus God ordered the believers to enter peace .We remember here that the salutation of Islam is peace "Alsalamu alikum" or "Peace be upon you" and that peace is one of God's holy names, As-salam. All of this expresses the confirmation of peace in Islam and it confirms the fact that belief also means safety and security.

Peace and security in Paradise will be for the peaceful believers:

The person who expresses and demonstrates his belief in goodness in his dealings with people and gains their trust and at the same time has true belief in God alone, deserves security, and will be secured and protected by the Almighty God on the Last Day. He will be rewarded in the hereafter for being trusted by people and for having a sincere belief in God alone in this life. This is the meaning of belief in Islam and its reward is in the Last Day.

The same is true with he who practices 'Islam' in his dealings with others, is peaceful, and practices 'Islam' in his relationship with God by submitting his heart and his behaviors to Him. This person is also entitled to 'peace' in the hereafter.

On this subject God says "It's those who believe and confuse not their beliefs with wrong, for them there is a security, and they are truly guided" (6:82). This means that those who believe in God and at the same time have gained the trust of others, will enjoy safety and security as a reward on the last day. Their reward is nothing but the outcome of their deeds, and God describes their place to be in paradise in the hereafter. Their greeting upon entering paradise will be "Enter ye here in peace and security" (15:46) and about paradise, God says that "for them will be a home of peace in the presence of their Lord" (6:127).

Thus, peace and security in dealing with others plus submission to believe in One God along with obedience to Him alone leads to peace and security in paradise. Such is the Islamic formula as presented by the verses of the Quran. On the other hand, transgression and injustice inflicted on others and on God leads only to Hell.

Muslims and peace in history

Now that we have clarified the relationship between the notion of peace, the understanding of "Islam," and its belief and faith according to the Quranic and Arabic languages, let's turn to the relation between "peace" and the real Islamic legislation or 'Shareah' according to the Quran alone. Let's examine the rules of 'peace' between Muslims and non-Muslims.

First however, lets suppose that early Muslims in the time of the prophet Mohammed were against peaceful Islam. Does this, however, make it right to ignore the peaceful nature of Islam because of its Muslim human behaviors? Religion is just rules and commandments and should be applied by its believers. If those believers ignore the fundamental teachings of the religion, it is their responsibility, and they are the ones to blame, not their religion. Religion should only be held accountable for the teachings according to its Holy message, and not due to its follower's human deeds.

It's not only an Islamic problem, but it's also the problem of Christianity and Judaism. We need only to remember what the religious Jews and the Christians did in the Middle Ages and modern history, for example. Therefore, it's imperative to make distinctions between the religion itself and its human believers whose deeds are mixtures of good and bad. However, we will discover that with Islam and its early Muslim followers, something different needs to be explained.

Recording Islamic History two centuries after Mohammed widened the gap between the Quran and Muslim Tradition:

The recording of Muslim history was started and established in the Muslim empirical periods that followed the footsteps of the Persian and the Roman empires. Thus the writing of their history was shaped by the concepts of power and influenced by the Middle Aged culture of fanaticism. For that reason, the gap between the Quran and the Muslim tradition was widened in terms of legislation and even in beliefs and faith.

As far as our subject is concerned, we find a clear gap between what the Quran says about the early Muslims during the period of the prophet Mohammed and what was said in the recorded history of the Prophet and also, in the' As-sirah An-nabaweiya,' the history of early Muslims and their battles.

The history of the prophet Mohammed was recorded two and more centuries after his death during the Abbasid Empire. The 'sira' written by Ibn Ishaq, Ibn Hisham, Ibn Shad, AlTabary, and others mainly concentrated on the Muslim violence in the battles during the ruling of the prophet Mohammed.

Those old historians rooted the concept that Islam was spread by the sword. They gave violence to the history of the prophet Mohammed to reflect the violent history of the Muslim rulers who succeeded him and gave Mohamed the image of a great conqueror who invaded the other nations establishing the great empire. In the third empire, the historians wrote the Muslim history of their time beginning with the history of the prophet Mohammed tens of decades after his death according to their culture, and created a gap between what was actually recorded in the Quran and their accounts. Those historians were also religious scholars invited to respond in their time by religiously legitimizing the expansion of the Muslim Empire.

Yet, what is found in the Quran is something entirely different from what is recorded in history. The starting point goes back to the Quranic term 'those who believed' and its original meaning being 'those who choose safety and security in their dealing with others even if they were persecuted and harassed by them. They are believers even if their faith does not respond to the Islamic monotheism.' We understand better the intended meaning of 'those who believed' from the verse that says ("Oh you who believed! Believe in God and His messenger, and the scripture which He sent before. Any who denies God, His Angels, His Books, his messengers, and the Day of Judgment, has strayed far away'. (4:136). Thus, God calls upon the believers, i.e. the peaceful ones to have a belief and faith in God, his prophets and his holy books. In other words, he calls upon those who chose peace to add to it the inner belief in God, His prophets, and His books.

The expression 'Oh you who believed' does not implies any particular religious group. It addresses those who choose peace as a way of life and calls them to accept religion because He said, 'Oh you who believed!' In other words, the belief in security and peace needs to be complemented by true sincere belief in one God, His books and His prophets, so that one is able to reach the blessings of paradise, namely peace and security, in the hereafter,.

The early Muslims were peaceful.

The peaceful believers who joined the prophet Mohammed in Mecca insisted on peace and on tolerating persecutions.

While they were in Mecca suffering, the Holy Quran revealed the aspects of their coming Muslim state which includes belief in One God, trust in Him, obeying Him, keeping prayers to Him and giving alms and conducting the direct democracy among them. God said explaining the other aspects: "And those who are oppressed can take revenge, the recompense for an evil is an evil; but whoever forgives and makes reconciliation, his reward is with God. Verily, He likes not the oppressors. And indeed whosoever takes revenge after he has suffered wrong, for such there is no blame against them. The blame is only against those who oppress people and resort to wrong in the earth unjustly; for such there will be a painful torment. And verily, whosoever shows patience and forgiveness that would truly be from the best commandments." (42:36-43).

This verse was revealed to prepare them to be ready for the future when they would have to defend themselves and retaliate, or to forgive and reconcile according to the future's circumstances.

Because of severe persecutions, early Muslims had to emigrate twice to Abyssinia [Ethiopia], and then immigrated to Yathreb or Al Madina, their final immigration where they established their own state led by the prophet Mohammed and the revelations of the Quran.

Biased historians ignored the peaceful nature of the early Muslims.

After they migrated to Medina, they were continuously attacked by the Quraysh to force them to go back to their previous idolatrous religion. It is an unknown historic fact mentioned in the Quran only and ignored by old Muslim historians and scholars. No Muslim scholar in our time knows that the mighty tribe of the Quraysh used to attack Al Madina and fight the peaceful Muslims living inside who did not defend themselves because they did not have permission from God.

If it were not for the Quranic verses descended which allowed them to practice self-defense, they would have been destroyed. Yet, the old Muslim scholars and historians during the middle ages did not allow these verses to be taken rationally, because rationalizing about these verses would bring out meanings that they preferred to be silent about.

The verse says, "Permission to fight is given to those are fought against because they have been wronged and verily God is most powerful for their aid" (22:39). This verse gives permission for self-defense in case of persecution and injustice regardless of what the religion is. God encourages self-defense and brings victory to the victims who do so.

The old Muslim scholars were oblivious to the generalization of this verse because it gave the right to any one to fight for his/her freedom of religion. Since this meaning is not exactly what the Middle Ages were about, it was better to disregard it. They also neglected a major factor of the verse. Since the followers of the prophet Mohammed were facing a dangerous enemy, if they had not been allowed to defend themselves, they would have easily been completely massacred.

The Quran demonstrates here a historical reality disregarded by the historians of the Abbasid Empire. The fact is that unbelievers of the Quraysh repeatedly raided Al Madina, often killing the habitants, but the peaceful Muslims would not take action because they were not yet allowed to do so. It was not until they received the permission to fight that they began to defend themselves.

The following verse is another case where the old Muslim scholars chose not to rationalize. The next verse talks about those peaceful early Muslims and states, "Those who have been expelled from their homes unjustly only because they said 'God is only Our Lord'. For had it not been that God checks one set of people by means of another, monasteries, churches, synagogues and mosques, in which the name of God is commemorated in a abundant measure would surely have been pulled down." (22:40).

We understand from this verse that not only did the victims face a threat of genocide, but the reason for their expulsion from their homes was the commemoration of God's name as their only God and Lord.

In Islam: One should fight to defend the churches, monasteries, synagogues and mosques.

Due to the religious fanaticism during the Abbasid Empire, the religious scholars chose to overlook the main point of this verse, namely that all followers of the Divine messages pray to the same God, and thus, all the houses of prayers are equal in God's eye. If the believers had not defended themselves altogether, their houses of prayers would not have stood up. The verse clearly mentions without differentiation the places of worship of the Christians, Jews, Muslims and others, all united by the act of 'constantly commemorating God's name'. What is of extreme importance here is that the Quran assures the need to protect and to respect all these houses of prayers regardless of the disputes among all of their followers, because in spite of disputes, these houses of prayers are shelters of peace and security, or it should be so.

It is very important also to note that the mosques – of the Muslims - are mentioned last. Had the Quran been biased for Islam only, the verse would have said 'In which God's name alone is constantly recited ...' but since there are non-Muslims who have attached other saints and names beside God, these are also taken into account even though they clash with the Islamic monotheist faith of 'there are no Lord but God' La illah illa ALLAH. Therefore the aim of this verse is to put all houses of prayer belonging to all faiths under protection from any violation, making it religiously accepted for any of these groups to defend themselves and their places of worship even if blood has to be shed.

It is clear here that the only reason for the fight is to protect the freedom of belief which God grants to all mankind, no matter what the religion is, as long it is a peaceful one void of any violence or transgression. Every person who builds a house of prayer has his own view and perspectives about God and worships Him accordingly. By all means, these houses and the people praying in them must enjoy safety and peace regardless of the differences among them. God is the only one who will judge them on the Day of Judgment. This Islamic truth was clearly disregarded by the old scholars.

Encouraging the peaceful Muslims to defend themselves.

In the same sura, God said to them and to all mankind, "Those who immigrate in the cause of God and after that were killed or died; surely, God will provide for them a good provision. And verily, it's God who indeed is the best who makes the provision. Truly, He will make them enter an entrance with which they shall will be pleased, and verily, God indeed is all- Knowing, Most Forbearing. That's so. And whoever has retaliated with the like of that which he was made to suffer, and then has again been wronged, God will surely help him. Verily, God indeed is Oft- Pardoning, Oft- Forgiving." (22:58-60). The early Muslims were in need of such encouragement to overcome their passiveness.

Be ready to defend yourself to achieve peace.

When the permission to fight was granted for the early Muslims, it was expected that they would rejoice with the idea of retaliation, but the opposite occurred. They had grown accustomed to passiveness and toleration of pain, and hated the new legislation concerning Jihad. Note that Jihad here implies holy war in terms of self defense. They were oblivious to the fact that they needed to fight to defend themselves and to achieve peace. They didn't realize that their enemy would seize to attack them once they showed some resistance.

The only way to defend oneself from his/her enemy is to be ready to defend themselves from attacks. It is the Quranic policy of "deterrence". God said to the early Muslims and to every peaceful state, "And make ready against them all you can of power, including steeds of war to terrify the enemy of God and your enemy…", "And if they incline to peace you must incline to it. And put your trust in God, Verily, He is the All – Hearer, the All-Knower", "And if they intend to deceive you, then, Verily, God is All- Sufficient for you ."(8:60-62), In this way, one can stop any potential attack against themselves and save not only their people, but also their enemy's.

These verses emphasize that the Quranic policy of 'deterrence' means to serve peace, not to encourage violence, especially when read in the context of all the rules of war specified in the Quran. In the Quran, the purpose of war is only to defend, not to attack.

Beside the basic reason of self defense, God revealed in the Holy Quran other rules of self defense and condemned transgressions against peaceful people, even if they are ardent enemies.

The early Muslims hated to defend themselves.

In spite of all these rules and their critical situations, the early Muslims in the time of the prophet Mohammed hated the permission to fight. Because of this reason, God addressed them in the Quran saying, "Fighting is prescribed upon you, and you dislike it. But it is possible that you dislike a thing which is good for you and that you love a thing which is bad for you. But God knows while you know not" (2:216). Here, God tells them that even though they hate the idea of fighting, it is good for them because they need to defend themselves. Even though they liked to be silent and passive towards raging war, God knows that it is dangerous for them.

The problem the early Muslims faced was that they had gotten accustomed to patience and peace, but conditions had reached a degree that threatened not only their religion, but their existence as well.. The Quranic clarification was not enough to change their attitude and to push them to prepare for defense. A group among them rejected the legislation for fighting and even raised their voices asking God to postpone His command. So God answered, "Have you not seen those who were told to hold back their hands from fight but established regular prayers and spend in regular charity? When at length the order for fighting was ordained to them, be hold! A section of them feared men as-or even more than-they should have feared God; they said 'our lord! Why have you ordained for us to fight? Would that you had granted us respite for a short period?" (4:77). In Mecca they were ordered to refrain from self-defense and to consecrate their time and effort in praying and spending in charity. The fact that a group rejected the order to fight and asked for it to be postponed showed the extent to which they were devoted to peace and hateful towards bloodshed.

Early peaceful Muslims in battles.

The battles during the period of the prophet Mohammed were the biggest proof for tendency of the early Muslims towards peace and their hatred for fighting, even in self-defense when it was forced upon them. We shall demonstrate from the Quran their peaceful attitude during three main battles: Badr, Alahzab, and Al Osra.

The battle of Badr:

This was the first and the most famous of the battles. In order to understand the real causes of this battle, we must first understand the terms (Eelaaf) or trade agreement of the Quraysh, which is mentioned in the sura of Quraysh (106:1-4). In its four verses, God said that because of His sacred Mosque located in Mecca, the Quryash tribe had its Eelaaf or trade agreement. They used to send their trade caravans between Syria and Yemen in peace during the winter and summer, and lived without hunger or fear, while the other tribes suffered hunger and continuous wars. The same meaning was repeated in other verses (29:67, 28:57)

The Quraysh traded with Syria and Yemen, exchanging goods once in the summer and once in the winter. They had obtained a covenant of security outside Mecca, safeguarding the caravan during their journeys between Mecca and Yemen, and between Mecca and Syria. Inside Mecca, there was another type of covenant among the inhabitants. The Quraysh tribe had to participate in financing both of the winter and the summer caravans. The budget needed was divided into shares which the Quraysh people invested in. At the end of the year, they calculated the profits of the shares and each one took his earnings. When the Muslims were forced to leave Mecca and go to Madina they lost their investments and the 'unbelievers' confiscated all of their homes and belongings. The Muslims did not dare ask for their money from their enemy who chased and attacked them for their beliefs.

Upon receiving the right to fight, the Muslims claimed their due share of the profits back from the Quraysh. It was for this reason that they raided the caravans which traded with their money. They hoped to get their money or the caravan without having to fight. However, on their way to meet the caravan, the

Muslims were promised that they would either take over the caravan or that they would win over their enemy. They went for the caravans, but soon enough, an army from the Quraysh came to save the caravans and kill the Muslims who happened to be few in number.

It was clear that since there were no caravans, they would surely win the battle as was promised by God. Nevertheless, some of the Muslims were frightened to face the enemy in battle. The Quran described this situation as follows,

> 8:5-6   "As Your Lord caused you to go out from your home with the truth, and verily a party among the believers disliked it. Disputing with you concerning the truth, after it was made manifest, as if they were being driven to death while they were looking."

. It's clear that the Muslims hated fighting, that they were honest about their position even though God promised to support them, and when they were ordered to engage in war, it was as if they could actually see death coming to seize them.

We need to mention here that what the Quran says concerning the battle of Badr contradicts the stories written about the Prophet during the Muslim Empire. In these stories, the old historians confirmed that all of the Muslims of Badr were anxious to fight and none of them were doubtful about it. If it was not for the Quran, we would not have known the reality of the situation.

The real situation confirms that the early Muslims were not blood thirsty fanatics willing to die for the cause of "Holy War." They were peaceful people who wanted to worship God and glorify Him in peace. However, the stories have been twisted around in order to depict the early Muslims 'incorrectly', to justify using violence under the name of God. The contemporary Islamic culture has until now ignored these verses for the same cause, so most of the Islamic reality is missing and continues to be so.

The battle of Alahzab, [The Allies]

The Unbelievers (which in Quranic terms means those who attack peaceful people) surrounded Al Madina to destroy it and to exterminate all the Muslims who were strongly overtaken by fear and terror. It's enough to see what the Quran has said about their state of mind, "When they came from above you and from below you, and when your eyes grew deviating, and the hearts reached to the throats, and you were harboring doubts about God. There, the believers were tried and shaken with a mighty shaking."(33:10-11). We also understand from these verses that the term of 'believers' has nothing to do with the faith, because they harbor doubt about God in this critical time. The only meaning here is the peaceful people who hate violence even if it is to defend their lives. The fear was so great that some of them ran away and called others to give up. On the other hand, others maintained great courage. (33:12-23).

The battle of Alosra:

This was the last of the battles. The Muslims were still not eager to defend themselves against the aggressive tribes to the north of Al Madina. Here, the Quran became more reprimanding in certain verses (9:13-16) and also, when God said "Oh you who believed: Why is it when you are told to mobilize in the cause of God, you become heavily attached to the ground?"(9:38). Therefore the lack of motivation that they felt in the beginning remained with them until the end of the Prophet's life.

The Quraysh tribe converted to Islam:

The nature of the daily lives of Arabian tribes of the time can help us understand why the Quraysh tribe converted to Islam to keep their interests. Violence is the key word that describes the life of the Arabs. In the Sacred Mosque in Mecca, every Arab tribe had its idol under the custody of the Quraysh. The Quraysh controlled Mecca, the sacred Mosque, and the pilgrimage. They lived in peace and prosperity while the other tribes lived in continuous blood shed for any and no reason. This made the Quraysh the most powerful tribe. The new religion of Islam threatened the religious trades of the Quraysh and its political and social situation. To keep its power, the elders of the Quraysh persecuted the followers of the new religion who were peaceful, helpless people from their and others' tribes. It was daunting for the helpless believers to face the mighty powerful tribe of the Quraysh. Thus, the only way to save the new converts of the faith from potential genocide was to encourage self defense.

Many people from numerous tribes converted to Islam, and helped others realize the nonsense of worshipping sacred tombs and statues, and from submitting to the Quraysh because of their false idols. Some of them wanted to get rid of the Quraysh, reducing its power and its hegemony, and to help the new Islamic state. This threatened the Quraysh's trade routes. The elders of the Quraysh reconsidered their situation. To keep their political and economical interests, they converted to Islam to use it for their continuous hegemony, especially since the active people inside the Islamic state were from the Quraysh tribe, including the Prophet Mohammed.

The elders of Quraysh quickly and easily surrendered and converted to Islam before the Prophet's death. After about twenty years, they became the new leaders of the Islamic state and led new kinds of war and a new way of life. They established powerful Muslim empires which ignored the fundamental rules of Islam and its peaceful nature. The empire lasted six centuries under the rule of the children of Qurayshy elders.

The disappearance of peaceful Islam after Mohammed's death.

After the Prophet Mohammed's death, the other Muslims from the different tribes who converted to Islam found themselves once again under the hegemony of the Quraysh. They revolted under individuals from inside their tribes who claimed prophecy. This was the war of apostasy which was the perfect chance for the elders of the Quraysh to maintain the leadership of the Islamic state after the death of Mohammed. The Quraysh tribe, consisting of the new Muslim converts along with the early Muslims, - led war against the other tribes who revolted against Islam and the Quraysh. By defeating them, the Quraysh became the real leader of all the Arabic tribes.

To avoid other tribal revolts, the Quraysh led all the Arabic tribes to fight two super empires: the Romans and the Persians. By defeating them both at the same time, the Quraysh established the powerful mighty Muslim Empires which influenced world history in the Middle Ages and ruled most of the world in that time according to the culture of the Middle Ages, and not according to the real values of Islam. So, the Islamic values were ignored, including the fundamental concept of peace.

During the time of the Muslim Empires, the true Islamic rules of Jihad were changed to attacking other peoples just to establish wealth, power and empire, while using the name of Islam. Here, we have to explain the real meaning of jihad in Islam.

Legislation of jihad in the Islam: -

According to Quranic terminology, jihad is the striving of the soul, money, and energy to please God by all means. It includes giving money to the poor regardless of their religion and faith, peaceful discussion with unbelievers, and to fight them only to defend oneself. (29:8) (8:2; 25:52).The Quran sets the legislation for jihad, its commandments, its principles and its final aims.

Generally, Quranic legislation is based on commandments which serve principles, and those principles in turn serve the basic Islamic aims and values. Regarding jihad, the commandment: "fight" is based on principles of self-defense in response to violent attack, or in the Quranic term, "fighting in the cause of God." This principle serves the final aim/value of fighting which is to assure religious freedom and prevent religious persecution. The greater value of jihad in Islam is to allow every person to follow the religion of his or her choice without any persecution. The Muslim state has to fight to prevent persecution and to defend itself and its freedom of belief and speech for the value of jihad. In this way, every one has the freedom of choice in the realm of religion and he or she will be responsible before God only on the Last Day based to his or her freedom of choice. In this life, one is responsible only before society if he or she violates the rights of other people. Examples that demonstrate the correct rules of jihad include when God said,

"And fight in the cause of God those who fight you, but transgress not the limits. Truly God loves not transgressors" (2:190). Here the commandment is to fight and the principle is "in the cause of God those who fight you, but transgress not the limits. Truly God loves not transgressors." To fight for the cause of God means to fight according to His legislation which forbids transgression. God repeated and confirmed the same meaning, "...Then whoever attacks you, you may attack them to inflict an equivalent retribution." (2:193). The ultimate goal of this legislation in His saying is, "and fight them until there is no more oppression."(2:193). Therefore, the prevention of oppression is the essential aim for the legislation of fighting. Oppression in the Arabic and Quranic language is represented by the word 'fitnah,' which is used in the Quranic terminology to refer to religious persecution committed by the unbelievers in Mecca against the early Muslims. That persecution included the continuous fight against the peaceful early Muslims even after their escape to Al Madina. God says, "And oppression is worse than slaughter. And they will not cease fighting you until they turn you back from your faith if they can" (2:217).

By allowing religious freedom and preventing oppression in religion, everyone deals with God alone, obeying or disobeying him, and every one will be responsible for his or her deeds only before God on the Day of Judgment. None has the right to take upon oneself God's sovereignty or judge other people's faith or to persecute those who hold different religious opinions. This makes the realm of religion belong to God alone without any kind of human religious authority. This is precisely what the Quranic verse calls for when it says, "Fight them until there is no more oppression and all the religion will belong to God alone." (8:39). God may forgive them if they refrain and stop transgression and persecution, and the Muslims have no right to attack them; otherwise they become transgressors themselves as God says, "And fight in the cause of God those who fight you, and transgress not the limits. Truly, God loves not the transgressors... But if they cease, then God is Oft- Forgiving, Most Merciful. And fight them until there is no more oppression and the religion will belong to God. But if they cease, let be no more transgression except against the transgressors only." (2:190 to 193) This is confirmed in other verses (8:38-40).

This legislation concerning fighting agrees with what is understood from the term 'Islam' which means submission and peace, and protects peace from any animosity or transgression.

Peace and freedom

Jihad assures religious freedom. It's enough here to remember that the Quranic principle states, "There shall be no compulsion in religion; the truth is now distinguishable from falsehood." (2:256). Moreover, God said to the Prophet Mohammed, blaming him, "And had your Lord willed, those on earth would have believed, all of them together. So, will you then compel mankind until they become believers?"(10:99). This confirms the Quranic fact that religion belongs to God alone without any human religious authority, and that the Prophet Mohammed does not have religious authority over mankind, as it's the will of God alone that let people exercise their freedom of choice and be responsible for their beliefs before Him alone on the Last Day. Freedom in religion is the key of democracy, as is the freedom of thought and speech.

63

Rules of alliance

For the first time in the Arabic Peninsula, some Arabs established a real state according to our modern definition of state. It was the first –and maybe the last- Islamic state in the time of the Prophet Mohammed. The new Islamic state had its border, people, and government. It had also allies and enemies.

Any believer in the Arabic desert who wanted to be a member of this state had to immigrate to it and live inside its border. All the believers inside this state were allies to each other against the enemies who attacked the peaceful state. The Quran stated to them that the believers outside the state should immigrate to be a part of the state. If believers outside the Islamic state asked for protection, the state was obligated to defend them unless there a treaty between the Islamic state and those who attacked these outsider believers existed. So, all believers were to be allies to each other inside their state to stand firm against the unbelievers who were united against the Islamic state. (8:72 -73)

Inside the state, there were different groups of oppositions who were against the state and its religion. The Quran called them the hypocrites. They enjoyed the freedom of speech and belief, and also the freedom to consipire against the state. The Holy Quran used to expose their plots and their inner thoughts, but at the same time, order the believers to avoid them, turn aside from them as long they did not fight the state. Details can be found in the following suras: (2:8 to 14 & 204 to206), (3:118 to119 & 155 to 158 &167 to168), (3:60 to 69 & 81 to 83 & 105 to 115 & 138 to146), (5:52), (8:49)(9:42 to 68 & 73 to 87 & 93 to 98 & 101 & 107 to 110 & 124 to 127), (24:11 to 26 & 46 to 54), (33:1 & 12 to 20 & 24 & 48 & 57 to 61 & 73), (37:16 & 20 to 30); (48:6 & 11 to 16), (58:7 to 22), (59:11 to 16) (63:1 to 8) (66:9)

Although the hypocrites inside Al Madina were under control, there was another kind of hypocrites who lived in the desert and used to come to the Islamic state claiming belief in Islam, with an inner goal of deceiving Muslims. Some of them offered to become allies to the state while in reality, they were enemies to the Islamic state. These hypocrites were a real danger to the Islamic state, so the Quran ordered Muslims not to ally with them until they immigrated to the state. If they refused to emigrate, then they were to be treated as enemies in the battle field. However, if they did not emigrate but did not attack the state, the Muslims were not allowed to fight them. (4:88-91). God described most of those Arabic Bedouins as the "worst in disbelief and hypocrisy and more likely to be in ignorance of the God's Legislation." (9:97).

Most of them controlled the routes north and south of the new Islamic state, and had a good relationship with the Arab Christian and Jewish tribes in the Arabic Peninsula. The Christian and Jewish tribes united together against the new Islamic state. Some people inside the Islamic state – including the hypocrites – had a good relationship with those allies in spite of their enmity. So, God ordered the Muslims not to take the hypocrites as allies as long as they fought the Islamic state. If they did not fight the Muslims, the hypocrites were to be allies and a part of the Muslim state. (5:51-58).

The Islamic state had to defend itself against the attacks of Christian and Jewish tribes. God ordered the Islamic state to fight them as they violated God's commandment until they paid expiation as a punishment for their aggression. (8:29). It means not to occupy their land, nor to force them to convert to Islam, but only to retaliate towards their aggression as our modern international legislation deals with any country attacks other country and is finally defeated. These rules of alliance protected the new peaceful Islamic state against all of its enemies who surrounded it.

Generally, God makes clear rules in dealing with the non-Muslims who are out of the Islamic state:

> [1] Muslims should deal kindly and justly with those who do not fight them, nor drive them out of their homes.

> [2] Muslims are not allowed to be allies to those who attack and fight them because of their religion, those who expelled them from their home, or helped the unbelievers in driving the Muslims out of their homes. (60:8-9).

Rules in battle field:

Not only does the Quran establish a clear relationship between the terms 'Islam' and 'peace' and the legislation of war, it also presents other legislations in order to confirm the main value of peace and to leave no ground for ambiguity or intended misuse.

1- A clear-cut example is presented in sura 4 which talks about the prohibition of killing a peaceful and safe believer. The verse states, "It's not for a believer to kill a believer except by mistake." (4:92) This means that it is unjustifiable, that a true believer would intentionally kill another. The verse goes further in talking about the compensation due in such a case and the rules related to it. Then, verse 4:93 talks about the divine punishment awaiting the killer of a peaceful person or a believer, for that matter doesn't make a difference. The verse says, "And whoever kills a believer intentionally, his recompense is Hell, to abide therein forever, and the wrath and the curse of God are upon him and a dreadful punishment is prepared for him." (4:93) Thus, whoever kills a peaceful believer faces eternity in Hell, wrath, curse, and great suffering. These are stated in the Quran as separate punishments each. Yet, it seems that the person who commits such a dreadful crime deserves all of these punishments added together.

Sura 4 continues as verse 94 declares the right of life to any peaceful person regardless of his or her inner belief, it says, "Oh you who believed! When you go to fight in the cause of God, investigate carefully and say not to anyone who greets you 'You are not a believer'." Thus in times of war, the believers must carefully investigate to make sure that they aren't committing the crime of killing a peaceful man, who by misfortune happens to be in the battle field. God gives everyone on the other side (the enemy) a constant right to be saved simply by pronouncing the words, "peace be upon you," or the Islamic greeting. If the enemy says so, it then becomes unlawful to kill him or her. He/she even becomes a peaceful believer regardless of his/her inner belief and his /her strange presence in the battle field. If he/she is killed, the killer will deserve the punishments mentioned in the verse 93. Therefore, any peaceful person is a Muslim and a believer even during war time and in the battlefield. If he/she is killed, then the killer deserves the abode in Hell, the great suffering, and God's curse and wrath.

2- It was a common practice of that time to kill the captives, enslave them, or free them for money or ransom. God blamed the Prophet Mohammed when he set free all the captives of Badr Battle for money, as the main mission of the Prophet was not to seek the vanity of this life, but be a good example to people. God ordered the prophet Mohammed to tell them that He would forgive them if they had any good in their heart, "O Prophet say to the captives that are in your hands, 'If God knows any good in your hearts, He will give you something better than what has been taken from you and He will forgive you, and God is Oft-Forgiving, Most Merciful.'" (8:70). God ordered the prophet Mohammed and the Muslims only two choices in dealing with the captives: to either set them free or exchange them as prisoners of war (37:4). Under all circumstances, the prisoner of war after release becomes Ibn Al Sabeel, or a guest as long he is in the Muslim State, and should be given charity and alms and shelter until a safe return home. (76:8; 2:177 &215; 4:36; 8:41; 9:60; 17:26; 24:22; 30:38; 59:7).

These Quranic laws about the captives were ignored by Muslims during their history, and captives were killed as it was a bad habit in the Middle Ages.. This used to happen during the battles between the Muslim Empire, the Roman Empire, and other nations, along with domestic wars inside the Muslims civil wars. Moreover, killing the captives or enslaving them was accompanied by enslaving women and children. It was the culture of the dark Middle Ages which made Muslim traditions and history full of these aspects that manifested defiance to the real Islamic values.

3- In the case of a warrior fighting against the Muslims who decided to cease attack, he/she only has to seek an asylum. When he/she does so, his/her life is safe and secured. He/she should be allowed to listen to the Quran, and to choose to believe in it or not, and also, to have no excuses before God in Judgment Day. The Muslims are ordered to escort him/her to a safe place, or a home, in security and peace. That is precisely what the Quranic verse says, "If one amongst the unbelievers seeks protection from you, grant it to him, so that he may hear the word of God, and then escort him to where he can be secured, that is because they are without knowledge." (9:6)

The truth is that most Muslims are also without knowledge. The proof is that Islam is a religion of peace. Peace is in its origin and in its legislation, but because of the behavior of the Muslims of the past and the fanatic Muslims of our time, Islam has become accused of fanaticism, fascism and terrorism. This leads us to identify the meanings of "infidel" and "unbeliever." Is he/she anyone who is non – Muslim as most of Muslims believe?

Two meanings for the infidel and unbeliever

Islam means to submit oneself to One God – in dealing with Him- and to be peaceful in dealing with people. God alone is the only one who has the power to judge our belief. The society in this world has the right to judge the individuals regarding the relationship among them. Therefore, any peaceful one is Muslim regardless of his belief, and any honest, safe, and faithful person is a believer regardless of his/her inner faith. On the other hand, anyone who transgresses the limits, wrongs others, or attacks and terrifies them, is an unbeliever or an infidel regardless of any religion or title he claims.

The Quranic language has many descriptions for infidels and disbelievers to characterize them regardless of time or any religion they claim. It's up to the One God alone to judge their inner belief, but it's up to us as human beings to recognize them according to their transgression.

Al Zolm

Al Zolm is the first description of the action an infidel or a disbeliever. It's an Arabic term which means to do wrong, to commit outrage, to tyrannize, to be unfair, unjust, to oppress, or to attack innocent people. This term, with its derivatives, is repeated in the Quran 260 times as it is the main aspect of the disbelief and infidelity. For example, see: 2:254; 31:13; and 2:165; 4:75 & 168; 6:45;10:13 &52; 11:37& 67& &94& 102 & 116; 14:44 & 45; 21:13; 29:49)

The unbeliever chooses to wrong the One and Only God by adding partners to Him, but God is the only one who will judge him/her concerning the realm of faith and religion. If this unbeliever lives peacefully, he is a believer according to our limits in this life as we are concerned about living in peace, safety, and justice in terms of dealing with each other.

Every one believes that their faith is the real truth, so it's against pure justice to judge each other in faith and belief. It's a pure justice to leave this to God Himself to judge us as we all have different faiths concerning Him. So He is the only one who will tell us the real truth on the Day of Truth; see: 2:113; 3:55; 10:93; 16:124; 5:48; 39:3, 7, 46). Our concern should only be to live peacefully and justly and not to allow anyone to violate this peace in the name of God while he/she is wronging God and disobeying His commandments. It's the most outrageous deed to disobey God and proclaim himself a person of God by killing people in His name.

This is an example of the Quranic Islamic culture contradicted by the early Middle Ages. A much greater contradiction was the culture of the Arabic Peninsula, where the Arab tribes used to live in continuous bloodshed, glorifying raiding each other as a sign of honor and courage. Those Arab tribal incursions meant killing men of other tribes and enslaving their women and children, thus and giving the other tribe the right to retaliate. This bloody culture was faced by Islam and its peaceful nature. The new Quranic language made transgression wrong, and attack and assaults the characteristics of disbelief in the One God.

The Quran discusses Al Zolm about two hundred times, making it a sign of infidelity and disbelief. In the Quranic context, another Arabic Quranic word 'transgression' is given the same meaning, and used in the same context regarding the unbelievers and infidels. Twice in the Quran, God says, " ...and transgress not. Verily God loves not the transgressors." This is mentioned in sura (2:190) to refer to the rules of fighting, and in sura (5:87) to confirm the absolute right of God alone in revealing Divine legislation. This was a serious warning to the believers not to prohibit the good things that God has permitted.

God mentioned two kinds of aggressions, one of them being made by infidels against peaceful people. Regarding them, God says, "It's they who are the transgressors." (9:10) Read also: 50:25; 68:12; 83:12. The other kind of aggression is made against God, His revelation and His legislation. See: 4:154; 7:163; 2:229; 4:14; 65:1; 5:94& 87; 23:7. It's up to God alone to judge those who violate His image, His revelation and legislation. But it's the responsibility of society to stand firm against those who violate human rights, especially the right of life.

To face this Zolm (transgression) and oppression, God ordered Muslims to be patient. Patience or al sabr is a Quranic term mentioned in the Holy book about one hundred times and is a great Islamic value meaning forgiveness, tolerance, forbearance, perseverance and endurance. Muslims have to uphold al sabr all throughout their lives, seeking to please the Almighty Lord in every stance of life. One has to have sabr in forgiving those who insult him/her, and to have sabr if he/she has to fight to defend his/her life or freedom of belief. It's a positive Islamic value meant to protect peace and to confirm tolerance and forgiveness. It is the middle ground between being totally passive as was the case of the peaceful, early Muslims, and the others who were active in aggression and transgression.

The terrorist is the worst criminal.

Some unbelievers possess the two kinds of transgression, one of them being killing innocent people in the name of God. The Muslim terrorists of our time are clear examples of this case. It's imperative to face them from inside Islam to prove the contradiction between their behavior and the true teachings of Islam and its jurisprudence. The simple criminal kill's one person or few people without any religious justification, but the other criminal kills thousands of innocent people believing it's his/her religious duty to kill those who have different religious beliefs. In this case, the terrorist does not kill the person, but also the real values of the Divine religion. In these circumstances, the killer is not the only criminal; the scholars and religious authorities who preach such bloody culture as religious teachings that should be obeyed are criminals as well.

The basic rules of terrorist religious culture:

1- The Historic roots.

Terrorists and their religious leaders and scholars claim the rank of the Almighty God; they monopolize the Divine right of God to judge and punish humans. They set up the Day of Judgment in this world before the Day of Resurrection and judge other people, accusing them to be enemies of God and believe they should be killed as a jihad or crusader. This was acceptable during the Middle Ages in Muslim and Christian sides, but it is an outrageous violation of human rights and the core of the Divine Religion of God.

The most important question to ponder is, if Islam is the religion of peace, why do we find the Muslim culture to be of violence and terrorism? The key word is the Quraysh, the mighty Arab tribe during the time of the Prophet Mohammed, who persecuted him and his peaceful followers in order to protect their political and economical interest in the Arab Peninsula. They finally converted to Islam to keep their political and economical interest and developed it in the name of the new religion, using its followers.

The Quraysh were the master of the known world trade of their time. They carried Indian goods from Yemen to Syria and the Roman Empire. The Quraysh has its allies among the Arab tribes which belonged to Yemen and in Syria as well. Those Yemeni tribes controlled the routs inside Syria and Yemen while the other tribes of Najd- which belonged to the same lineage of the Quraysh-controlled the other routes between Mecca and Yemen. The Quraysh controlled the Christian Yemen tribes by mutual economic interests and controlled the other wild tribes of Najd by keeping their idols in the sacred Mosque in Mecca. They also controlled the Arab religious pilgrimage. The Quraysh had inherited the pilgrimage from the religion of the prophet Abraham, the father of the Quraysh and all the northern Arabic tribes.

The true religion of Abraham was changed by the Quraysh according to their own interests. The Holy Sacred Mosque in Mecca was built by Abraham and his son Ishmael. When the Arabs converted to worshipping idols, the Quraysh put their idols in the sacred Mosque to control the idol worshippers. Mohammed was sent to revive the religion of Abraham and to separate it from business. Thus, Islam became a danger to the Quraysh and their religious trade. In its war against the prophet Mohammed and his peaceful followers, the Quraysh used their allies from the northern Arab tribes of Najd and the Christian Yemeni tribes. These wars brought about a lot of debate regarding the Quran and its intellectual debate concerning the true meaning of the idols and the sacred tombs. For that and other reasons, Islam had new followers who made the

Quraysh change their mind and decide to convert to Islam to keep and develop its political and economical benefits.

God confirms in the Quran that the Quraysh and all the Arabs in that time used to worship the only God, but at the same time, idolized saints in tombs and images of sacred stones just to bring them near to God 39:3; 7:194 &195; 16:20& 21; 23:84& 92). The Quraysh used to create and set up these stones in the Sacred Mosque, realizing the nonsense of worshipping human made idols. However, they prevented these Arabs from believing in the guidance of Islam and continued to disbelieve in the Quran for their economic benefits (28:57; 56:81& 82). It was therefore, easy for the Quraysh to convert to Islam after about twenty years of ardent enmity.

Soon after Mohammed's death, the elders of the Quraysh who were ardent enemies of Islam restored their influence in the Islamic state in the name of Islam. They suppressed the Arab movements of apostasy and reached a compromise with them to mobilize towards the rich lands around the Arab Peninsula to invade them in the name of Islam and jihad. It was a practical change in the Islamic Jurisprudence, "to fight in the cause of wealth and the vanity of this life" instead of "fight in the cause of God".

However, the Arab tribes had a religious justification from the Quraysh to invade and occupy the lands of others and to enslave them and steal their wealth in the name of Islam. To give these wars an Islamic face, the Arab leaders invaded other lands after offering three options before attack: to be Muslim like them, to pay tribute, or war. The real option was the only one of war. In this way, the Quraysh established their mighty Arab Empire under the name of Islam and against its real values and jurisprudence.

As it was war in the cause of wealth; not in the cause of God. Wealth was the real reason of political disputes between the Quraysh and the wild tribes of the north, who revolted before in the apostasy wars then returned to Islam and were active in invading the two super powers and occupying Syria, Iraq, Iran and Egypt. These political disputes became the cause of great civil wars among Arab Muslim tribes, dividing the Qurasy and the Arabs into many political parties, giving leadership to the Umayyad family to establish their dynasty, even though they were the former ardent enemies of the prophet Mohammed and early Muslims. All of this happened five decades after the Prophet Mohammed's death.

The Umayyad Empire fought Arab Muslims inside the Empire while it continued to invade India central Asia in east, North Africa, the Mediterranean Sea, and Spain in west. After about seventy years of civil wars and outer wars against Minor Asia, Africa, Europe and Central Asia, the Mighty Umayyad Empire collapsed under great pressure from another Quraysh movement led secretly by the grand children of Al Abbas, the old uncle of the prophet

Mohammed. The Abbasid Empire lasted in power for five centuries, fighting outside its borders and inside it as usual until the Mongols destroyed it.

2- Muslim Tradition Is The Source of Fanatic Discourse.

During the long years of wars, inside and outside the Arab Empire, Muslims in the Umayyad and Abbasid dynasties had many different cultures and political parties which produced many new religious sects and cults. Each one of them tried to establish its arguments by choosing certain verses from the Holy Quran, and twisting their meanings to serve its purpose. It was during this time that they invented the concept of the hadeeth, or sayings attributed to the Prophet Mohammed, some centuries after his death to confirm his alleged thoughts.

Muslims in our time inherit all these traditions and most consider the human tradition to be a part of Islam, in spite of the total contradiction between the Quran and most of this tradition. It was produced in response to the culture of the Middle Ages, not to Islam.

This Sunni tradition is kept and defended by Al Azhar in Egypt, the Saudi State, and its Wahabi agencies. Any Muslim scholar who dares to discuss this tradition is destined to persecution and accused to be the enemy of Islam and the Prophet Mohammed. Muslim communities in the U.S and in the West are followers of these seminaries in Middle East. Reform in Muslim communities needs to start with reforming the roots in Egypt and the Saudi States.

The leaders of the fanatic Muslims in the West and in the Middle East use the same fanatical discourse and tactic. In talking with the West, they preach Islam as religion of peace using some verses from the Quran, but inside their mosques and centers, they accuse the West to be the ardent enemy of Islam. They accuse all Christians and Jews and all those who are not Muslims to be infidels. Even those who usually curse Osama Ben Laden, could not criticize his religious discourse which he usually releases in his tapes because it's also their own discourse. The only difference is in their tactic. Osama Bin Laden is frank and direct, while the others are hypocrites and conceal what Osama releases.

All those Muslim terrorists, including Osama, –believe in this tradition as the basic part of Islam revealed to the Prophet Mohammed directly from God. This is what they were taught in schools and mosques. For most ordinary religious Muslims, these terrorist are faithful Muslims while the well known Sheikhs and Imams are just hypocrites who serve corrupted rulers. It is actually that the corrupt rulers are servants of America, and for them, America and the West are the enemy of Islam.

The Fourth Jihâd

Richard S. Voss, Ph.D.,

Prefatory Note

This essay is the brainchild of Mukhtar Jamaluddin Voss, hence this biographical note: Mukhtar is an Emory University student in business, minoring in Arabic, recipient of the 2007 Ameen Rihani Scholarship, member of the Emory University Student Government Association and College Council, violist on the Emory University Symphony Orchestra, and founder of Emory University's pro-Palestine student organization. Mukhtar declined to accept a byline for this article, as he felt that he had not personally contributed enough to its writing, but he was happy to be acknowledged for the ideas that it contains.

Introduction

Muslims today usually recognize either two or three levels of jihâd. Many Muslims hold to the first position, that there are a greater and a lesser jihâd. Others recognize a third type that is peculiar to the challenges that Muslims face by living in non-Muslim societies. Within each of these three types there are subdivisions according to some traditions, which will be addressed briefly in due course. Meanwhile, for the sake of simplicity, it is sufficient to describe the three most commonly held types. The greatest or highest level of jihad involves the struggle toward self-betterment, to seek ever purer attributes of transcendental faith and the evolution of our identity with the higher purpose to which God directs us. This is the greater jihâd <al-jihâdu~l-'akbaṛu> [الجهاد الأكبر], which corresponds mainly to the traditional category of <jihâdu~l-nafsi> [جهاد النفس], striving of the soul. We can call this first level al-Jihâd al-Akbar. The least, or most mundane, level involves the struggle to take up arms in self-defense or in defense of persecuted peoples. This is the lesser jihâd <al-jihâdu~l-'aṣghaṛu> [الجهاد الأصغر], which corresponds loosely to <jihâdu~l-kuffâri wa~l-munâfiqîna>, striving (against) those who oppose faith and those who dissemble. However, the traditional definition is broader, as undertaking armed

72

struggle against an active foe is only a subset of this category. We will adhere to the common category instead, which we can call al-Jihâd al-Aṣghar. As for the middle level that results, this would therefore be the struggle to maintain piety against the relentless pressures of living in a non-Muslim society. For the sake of simplicity, we can call this the middle jihâd <al-jihâdu~l-'awsaṭu> [الجهاد الأوسط], or al-Jihâd al-Awsaṭ. This corresponds loosely to <jihâdu~l-shayṭâni>, striving (against) Satan, although the traditional category does not specify the condition of living in a non-Muslim land. Al-Jihâd al-Awsaṭ is closer in character to al-Jihâd al-Akbar than is that associated with warfare, but restricted to a particular circumstance like al-Jihâd al-Aṣghar. A fourth traditional category, referring to jihad against the promoters of injustice, innovation, and evil deeds, also exists. In practice, the terminology varies from source to source, and it is sufficient to note that the Qur'ân does not provide any kind of breakdown that truly resembles what has emerged in traditional quarters. For our purposes, our discussion will consider only the three popular types just listed. The inclusion of the intermediate level is logical if we follow the tradition of Muslim thinkers of dividing the world into two zones, the Domain of Islâm which we can call Dâr al-Islâm, and the Domain of <dâru~l-'islâmi>> [دار الإسلام], or Dâr al-Ḥarb. These are not Qur'ânic concepts, <dâru~l-ḥarbi War> [دار الحرب], so they must be accepted with some degree of caution. Nevertheless, they are influential to formal Islâmic thinking (disregarding for the moment that proper Islâmic thinking should be Qur'ânic by definition). If we accept the premise that there are distinct zones, then in them belong two different styles of struggle, jihâd, in the broader sense. In Dâr al-Islâm, harmful pressures from a dominant, non-Islâmic culture ostensibly do not exist, so the Muslim is free to pursue higher self-development. Dâr al-Ḥarb, by contrast, would be an environment of maximal pressure to abandon religious piety and sink to a level of base existence. Thus, Dâr al-Ḥarb presents a type of jihad that should appear new and unfamiliar to people in Dâr al-Islâm. While believers in the latter domain can understand al-Jihâd al-Aṣghar and al-Jihâd al-Akbar very well, they cannot understand al-Jihâd al-Awsaṭ.

If Muslims experience a more difficult challenge in pursuing taqwâ in Dâr al-Ḥarb than in Dâr al-Islâm, then the standard of taqwâ in Dâr al-Ḥarb is lower than in Dâr al-Islâm. This means that an earnest Muslim of an identifiable level of religious sensibility and drive toward self-betterment should attain a higher level of taqwâ in Dâr al-Islâm than in Dâr al-Ḥarb. Therefore, the standard of taqwâ is different in the two domains. If, by contrast, it is possible to show that there is indeed no difference in the standard of taqwâ between Dâr al-Ḥarb and Dâr al-Islâm, then a concept of al-Jihâd al-Awsaṭ necessitates a corresponding concept in Dâr al-Islâm.

Taqwâ

as *right conduct*, *guarding* [تقوى] <Yûsuf 'Alî and M. H. Shakîr translate <taqwâ (of oneself or against evil), *piety*, (what is) *right*; *righteousness*, *self-restraint*,

<and *fear of Allah.* Verse 47:17 provides the source of taqwâ by saying <'âṭâhum
God) *grants them* (the believers) their taqwâ, as a product of Guidance.), [ءاتهم]
Believers do not achieve it by pursuing it; they receive it from God as an
affirmation of their virtuous striving. Taqwâ is a distal goal of the believer,
toward which he must strive, in hopes of being gifted it. Once gifted, taqwâ
belongs to the believer and emanates from him. This is made explicit at 22:37
<minkum>, *from you,* while 22:32 <taqwậ~l-qulûbi>, *the taqwâ of the hearts,*
indicates that it really resides in the believer's unconscious sensibilities, not
conscious reason. From there, it pervades the believer's identity, as the
possessive pronoun <-hâ> in the word <taqwậhâ> (91:8) refers to the soul
mentioned in the preceding verse. Finally, the connection back to God is made
clear at 22:37, with <yanâluhu>, it *reaches Him.* In essence, the human choices
that lead to the gifting of taqwâ begin by necessity in the conscious realm, but
once taqwâ is gifted, it resides in the unconscious. Taqwâ is therefore a higher
aim of the conscientious believer. The muttaq moves toward taqwâ by striving in
the Path of God, not by trying to obtain taqwâ. No Qur'ânic reference to taqwâ
suggests qualities or dynamics conditional to circumstance. The believer's
striving toward taqwâ incorporates the same range of challenges, whether in Dâr
al-Ḥarb or in Dâr al-Islâm. Every facet of the challenge must have an analogy in
the other domain. If it is logical to contemplate al-Jihâd al-Awsaṭ in Dâr al-Ḥarb,
then its analogy in Dâr al-Islâm is waiting to be found.

A review of references to jihâd in the Qur'ân is appropriate to pursue this topic
further. While such an analysis must consider the distinction between Dâr al-
Islâm and Dâr al-Ḥarb, in fact the Qur'ân never uses the phrase <dâṛu~l-'islâmi>
<or <dâṛu~l-ḥarbi>. Therefore, this analysis will first identify the root <ḥ-r-b
[حرب], referring in its basic form to war and derivatives suggesting boundaries,
referring in its basic forms to fighting or in its more intensive [قتل] <and <q-t-l
forms to killing, and how the Qur'ân might present these roots in association
with forms of <j-h-d> [جهد], from which jihâd is derived.

Al-Ḥarb

The word <ḥarbuń> [حرب], *war,* only occurs in four verses in the Qur'ân, plus
two verbal forms, for a total of six references to war *per se* in the entire Qur'ân
(less than one-tenth of one percent of all Qur'ânic verses). Of these, only one
instance refers to an act of striving: Verse 5:33 uses <yuḥâribûna> [يحاربون], *they
wage war,* and explains that *those who wage war against God and His Apostle,
and strive with might and main for mischief through the land* (merit) *execution.*
Yûsuf 'Alî translates *strive* with the whole phrase *strive with might and main,*
which is also how he translates <jihâd> as a verb. However, the Qur'ân does not
actually say jihâd here. It uses the ordinary verb <yas'awna> [يسعون], for *strive,*
not <yujâhidûna> [يجهدون]. This verb may be used in either positive or negative
senses, but it happens that the three occurrences of the precise form <yas'awna>
in the Qur'ân (5:33, 5:64, and 34:38) all refer specifically to striving *against*

74

Islâm or God's Signs. In each case, the context completes the idea to clarify .intent, so <fasâdàṅ>, *being corrupt*, rounds out the meaning at 5:33 and 5:64

Al-Qatl

One hundred twenty-two verses contain some form of the triliteral root <q-t-l>. None of them contains any form of the root <j-h-d>. Eight verses use the command <uqtulû>, *slay*, in the imperative mode, of which only half of these say to slay opponents of Muslims in wartime. Those four verses addressing the opponents of Muslims in wartime include *the Hypocrites* in the context of breaking the truce to which Sûrah 9 is devoted (9:5), *those who fight you* (2:191), and those who join the ranks of the enemy in wartime and then become renegades (4:89 and 4:91). The remaining four verses address slaying *oneself* (2:54), and then quote those who sought to kill Joseph (12:9), those who sought to kill believers (40:25), and those who sought to kill Abraham (29:24). Lastly, verse 4:66 uses <uqtulû>, but it is a condition, not a command. Fourteen verses contain the command <qấtilû> ("fight!"), of which two quote others who want to fight against believers (3:167, quoting the Hypocrites' command; and 5:24, quoting the people who addressed Moses and his master). Five of these address the truce-breakers in Sûrah 9 (9:12, 9:14, 9:29, 9:36, and 9:123). Of the remainder, verse 2:190 addresses *those who fight you* and adds "but do not transgress limits." Verses 2:244 and 4:84 refer to fighting *in God's Path*. Verse 49:9 refers to fighting against any party of believers that turns against another party and breaks an arrangement of reconciliation previously worked out by the community. Verses 2:193 and 8:39 cite fighting *until there is no more tumult or oppression*. Verse 4:76 addresses fighting *against the Friends of Satan*. Lastly, verse 2:191 also contains the form <qấtalûkum>, but this is conditional, not imperative.

The fact that the radical <q-t-l> never occurs in the same verse as the radical <j-h-d> might suggest that no evidence at all exists to tie jihâd to fighting, but it is observed that some verses that contain the phrase <fî sabîli~llấhi> also contain <q-t-l>, while others that contain that phrase also contain <j-h-d>. Perhaps the requisite linkage between jihâd and armed struggle, hence al-Jihâd al-Aṣghar, can be revealed in an analysis of the phrase <fî sabîli~llấhi>.

In God's Path

Eighty-one verses cite God's Path <sabîluṅ>. Some form of <q-t-l> occurs in twenty-two of these. In exactly two verses, believers are told directly <wa-qấtilû fî sabîli~llấhi>, *and fight in the Path of God*. In the first case (2:190), a warning not to go too far, <wa-lâ ta'tadû>, *but do not commit excesses*, follows the order. This makes clear that when attacked, Muslims must react. In the second case (2:244), the order is followed by "and know that God is Hearing, Knowing." Juxtaposed, these two verses are parallel by virtue of their opening, *and fight in the Path of God*, making them unique in the Qur'ân. Hence, what follows that opening, namely, the reference to the circumstance of righteous defense on the one hand and the imperative of God-consciousness on the other, is equivalent. In fact, the validity of inferring equivalence from the parallel structure as it influences the interpretation of the second instance is reinforced two verses later (2:192), *but if they cease, God is Oft-Forgiving, Most Merciful.*

No verse at all refers to *killing* or *slaying* one's enemies *in the Path of God*, only *fighting*. This is a critical distinction, as some critics claim that Muslims are commanded to kill their enemies. They are not, nor have they ever been. As noted above, Muslims are merely told to *fight* those who fight them, and in so doing to restrain themselves and to cease combat as soon as the enemy relents. There are, nevertheless, several verses that refer to the possibility that Muslims will *be slain* in the Path of God. A total of seven verses contain such wording (2:154, 3:157, 3:169, 3:195, 4:74, 22:58, 47:4). By contrast, it is equally noteworthy that one verse that refers to the Path of God in one sense does indeed indicate that believers might find themselves having to *slay* someone, but that reference itself does not include the phrase *in the Path of God*: "they fight in His Path and slay and are slain" (9:111). Here, only *fighting* <yuqâtilûna> is defined as occurring *in the Path of God*, while *slaying* and *being slain* are simply given as probabilities in a dangerous environment in which believers courageously confront a violent enemy, the kâfirûn.

Jihâd

The Qur'ân's references to jihâd and related terms come in 17 forms. Restricting our analysis to the most relevant grammatical form, the second-person plural imperative <jâhidû>, *strive!*, we have a total of four cases in the Qur'ân (5:35, 9:41, 9:86, and 22:78). Of these, one case includes the phrase <fî sabîli~llâhi>, *in the Path of God* (9:41), while verse 5:35 uses a shorter form, <fî sabîlihî>, *in His Path*, and 22:78 uses a unique form, <fî~llâhi>, *in God*. In addition to these four verses, verse 25:52 is important because it uses the terminology of striving against the kâfirûn "with an utmost striving" <jihâdàn>, but it also explains precisely how to do this. Specifically, it says to do so <bihî>, "with it," referring to the Qur'ân. In no case does a reference to jihâd tell Muslims to kill disbelievers, even though the kâfirûn of the time were carrying out a campaign of violent opposition against the Muslims. Instead, jihad referred to the difficulties that the Muslims faced by leaving their homes in oppressive towns and migrating, in the face of the constant threat of attack, to freedom.

In light of the evidence, jihâd was never meant to refer to warring, fighting, or slaying. The Qur'ân does indeed instruct believers to jâhid (strive) against those who actively oppose the Muslim community. Were the Qur'ân intent on equating jihâd with warring, fighting, or slaying, whether as its primary meaning or its secondary one, this equation would reasonably occur in the Qur'ân itself, rather than only exist in the minds of some theologians who may have taken it upon themselves to draw such inferences.

Lastly, in an interesting reflection of the terminology of the present day, the Qur'ân makes an important distinction between those who "sit at home" (or more accurately, "occupy the base") are distinct from those who are undertaking jihâd with wealth and self (4:95). The term for those who sit at home is <al-qấ'idûna>, which is the correct term for the adherents of the terrorist organization al-Qâ'idah. The term appears three times in that verse, while other verses are consistent in this attitude (5:24, referring to despondent Israelites who wanted Moses and Aaron to fight enemies "while we watch"; 9:46, referring to the Hypocrites, who were afraid to venture out with the believers to perform the pilgrimage at the risk of violent opposition; and 9:86, referring to wealthy property-owners who want to stay behind in safety, rather than go out and join the Prophet in spreading the Word). Thus, applied to persons, <al-qấ'idûna> is always a term of disparagement. Jihâd is anathema to <al-qấ'idûna>. The plural term <qawâ'idu>, in fact, is translated "old women," who stay at home (24:60). In reference to structures *per se*, it means "foundations" (2:127 and 16:26). From this perspective, one has to wonder whether the famous terrorists actually read the Qur'ân. If so, perhaps they might have selected a different moniker.

Conclusion

The term "fight in the Path of God" strikes some readers as explicitly connecting jihâd with fighting, because a characteristic of jihâd is that it must likewise occur "in the Path of God." By this logic, any action to which the Qur'ân refers using the phrase "in the Path of God" must be a variety of jihâd. That this is not the case is made clear, however, in one particular verse that highlights the phrase's true and frankly plainer meaning of "in a manner consistent with God's Will" (4:89, "until they take flight in the Path of God"). This verse refers to the Hypocrites <al-munâfiqứna>, a classification of people who first pretended to be among the believers but then turned against them when they thought the believers would in fact be defeated by the pagans. The phrase "take flight in the Path of God" refers to joining the believers in their flight from oppression to safety, a common reference in the Qur'ân. This action cannot equate to performing jihâd, because Hypocrites who decide to undertake the journey do so reluctantly, not out of a sense of duty to God. That jihâd cannot be undertaken reluctantly is part and parcel of its inherent meaning. Thus, the phrase <fî sabîli~llấhi> "in the Path of God" encompasses a subtype of the action referenced, the opposite of which refers to performing the same action out of line with God's Will. While it is consistent with theological principles only to promote jihâd "in the Path of God" and call it hypocrisy of effort is put forth contrary to God's Will, it does not follow that undertaking something "in the Path of God" makes it a type of jihâd.

It is clear that jihâd is defined in the Qur'ân as a category of intensive, virtuous action involving one's property and oneself. As a virtuous category of action, it exists by definition only "in the Path of God." Jihâd never refers to warfare, slaying, or even fighting. Meanwhile, neither warfare nor slaying is ever described in the Qur'ân as occurring "in the Path of God." Only "fighting" is, and it is acknowledged that fighting may lead to believers' sometimes slaying their enemies and sometimes being slain by them. That fighting should so often be associated with the phrase "in the Path of God" is consistent with the necessity to specify it as such. That is, jihâd is never described as something in which either the opponents of Islâm or the Hypocrites themselves could ever engage. A Hypocrite, more specifically, cannot engage in jihâd until he becomes a *bona fide* believer. By contrast, fighting can be undertaken by believers or opponents of believers. Therefore, it is more often necessary to specify the motivation of the fighting, that of the believers being precisely "the Path of God," that of the opponents of the believers being "the path of evil." That fighting does not apply to Hypocrites is part and parcel of their hypocrisy, as they are motivated by fear of loss and injury, not by belief. Significantly, the word for Hypocrite has nothing to do with belief, friendship, hatred, or enmity, but in fact with the idea of selling oneself. The root is <nafaqa>, which refers to the salability of market goods.

If it can be argued that al-Jihâd al-Akbar is valid, then it must refer to the only kind of jihâd actually mentioned in the Qur'ân, namely, applying one's property and oneself in an intensive, virtuous effort of some type. The risky decision to leave one's town due to oppression is the most common reference in the Qur'ân. That al-Jihâd al-Aşghar exists is a more difficult argument, but it may be an acceptable concept, even though the Qur'ân never mentions this. The very difficulty theologians would have in attempting to answer the question of whether fighting is indeed a type of jihâd would naturally lead to the conclusion that if it is, it is certainly of a lesser or less central variety than that which the Qur'ân actually describes. If we are therefore to accept it, we must qualify it in this way.

The question of whether al-Jihâd al-Awsaţ is a valid concept, as some theologians have argued, involving one's struggle to grow and evolve in a non-Muslim society, likewise revolves around how the Qur'ân itself has described jihâd. The environment that the Qur'ân describes is in fact a non-Muslim society. Therefore, jihâd in the Qur'ân is indeed described as corresponding to the struggle to evolve in a non-Muslim society. To justify this third type, therefore, it is necessary to argue that the Qur'ân directly describes only a virtuous struggle using one's property and oneself, not a virtuous struggle against an environment of temptations, but that the latter type of condition constitutes a reasonable subtype of the pressures against which effort can indeed rise to a level that can be called jihâd.

However, the question of whether a Muslim society is inherently devoid of the pressures against which a Muslim must travail in order to grow and evolve remains. In the early years of Islâm, the intellectual growth of the Muslim society suggests that there can indeed be this type of environment. However, it does not follow logically that every society that calls itself "Muslim" is in this category. Indeed, what does it take for a Muslim to explore the truth of his faith without being bridled by pressures to conform that emanate from Muslim dogma itself? Perhaps the term "Muslim dogma" is blasphemy in some eyes, as it suggests that there may be a set of tenets that Muslims are not permitted to question, but which are not necessarily thoroughly Islâmic. But in which type of society is the Muslim freer to explore the full range of Islâmic ideas without fear of breaking the rules of the dominant worldview? Is this kind of exploration more feasible in the environment characterized by al-Jihâd al-Awsaṭ, or in the self-described Muslim environment?

Non-Muslim societies are often freer than self-described Muslim societies today, so they actually invite freer exploration into Islâmic ideas than the latter. Opponents of this view may object, saying that Muslim societies have the answers to all questions that Muslims might ask, so it is not necessary to engage in such exploration at all. Therefore, inquisitive Muslims should focus their attention on pursuing perfection in religious practice (al-Jihâd al-Akbar). But to what extent can a Muslim truly engage in the highest form of jihâd if he must accept an interpretation of Islâm without question? To what extent does the natural yearning in the manner truly characteristic of jihâd permit resisting questioning man's interpretation of scripture?

True jihâd does not permit accepting man's interpretation of scripture at all. In true jihad, the Qur'ân is beyond question, but no one can dictate to anyone what it must mean. Exploring the true meaning underlying any passage in the Qur'ân tests the fragile limits of what others, in their specific times and places, might have conceived. The Qur'ân actually assumes that the reader lives in a non-Muslim society. What, therefore, is the special challenge confronting Muslims who today live in a self-described Muslim society? It is in fact that of breaking through the limitations on thinking that such a society naturally espouses. True belief does not fear questions; in fact, it should invite questions, for the truth will not only prevail through the constant testing of ideas. The believers' understanding will evolve in strength as can only occur when the same body of truth is exposed repeatedly to the tests of logic and stands up to them with ever newer nuances of understanding. Is it more difficult to explore the Qur'ân freely and thereby seek self-betterment in a self-described Muslim society than in the freer environments of the industrialized nations of the world? Yes, it is. This by itself is justification for recognizing that a fourth type of jihâd must exist, if the first three types are at all legitimate. This Fourth Jihâd must involve applying one's property and oneself in an intensive, virtuous effort against the pressures of Muslim dogma, to break through the limitations of that dogma and rise to new heights of understanding, which that dogma would only have obstructed. If it deserves a name, perhaps <jihâd~l-'aqîdati>, *striving* (against) *dogma*, or Jihâd al-'Aqîdah, will do.

Islamocapitalism:
Islam and the Free Market

Mustafa Akyol

Is Islam compatible with modernity? This has become a hotly debated question in the past few decades. Much of the discussion focuses on issues relating to political liberalism — democracy, pluralism and freedom of thought. Another important dimension of modernity is, of course, economic liberalism and so we should also ask whether Islam is compatible with it, i.e. a free market economy, or, capitalism.

Most Islamists would reply to this question with a resounding "no!" Since they perceive Islam as an all-encompassing socio-political system, they regard capitalism as a rival and an enemy. The struggle against both communism and capitalism has been one of the standard themes in Islamist literature. Sayyid Qutb, the prominent ideologue of the Egyptian Muslim Brotherhood, wrote a book titled *Ma'arakat al-Islam wa'l-Ra's Maliyya* (The Battle Between Islam and Capitalism) in 1951. At an Islamic conference held in the Spanish city of Granada on July 2003, attended by about 2,000 Muslims, a call was made to "bring about the end of the capitalist system."

However such radical rejections of the capitalist economy don't seem well-suited to the theological attitude and the historical experience of Islam towards business and profit-making. As a religion founded by a businessman — Prophet Muhammad was a successful merchant for the greater part of his life — and one that has cherished trade from its very beginning, Islam can in fact be very compatible with a capitalist economy supplemented by a set of moral values that emphasize the care for the poor and the needy.

Business, *Zakat* and the Koran

This interesting compatibility between Islam and capitalism has been studied extensively. A classic work on this theme is Maxime Rodinson's famed book, Islam and Capitalism (1966). Rodinson, a French Marxist, by appealing to the textual analysis of Islamic sources and the economic history of the Islamic world, demonstrated that Muslims had never had any trouble with making money. "There are religions whose sacred texts discourage economic activity in general," said Rodinson, "[but] this is certainly not the case with the Koran, which looks with favor upon commercial activity, confining itself to condemning fraudulent practices and requiring abstention from trade during certain religious festivals."

It is true that the Koran has a strong emphasis on social justice and this has led some modern Muslim intellectuals to sympathize with socialism and its promise of a "classless society." A careful reading of the Koran would work against such "Islamo-socialism." The Muslim Scripture takes it as a given that there will be rich and poor people in society and, in a sense, assures that disparity by actively supporting the rights to private property and inheritance. However it persistently warns the well-off to care for the deprived. *Zakat* is the institutionalized form of this compassion: Every rich Muslim is obliged to give a certain amount of his wealth to his poor brethren.

Zakat is a voluntary act of charity, not a collectivization of wealth by a central authority. According to scholars John Thomas Cummings, Hossein Askari and Ahmad Mustafa — who co-authored the academic paper, "Islam and Modern Economic Change" — "*Zakat* is primarily a voluntary act of piety and a far cry from what most modern-day taxpayers experience when confronted with increased income levies or complicated regulations." Moreover, they add, "there is no particular Islamic preference for [a] Marxist emphasis on economic planning over market forces."

Indeed, when Prophet Muhammad was asked to fix the prices in the market because some merchants were selling goods too dearly, he refused and said, "only Allah governs the market." It wouldn't be far-fetched to see a parallel here with Adam Smith's "invisible hand." The Prophet also has many sayings cherishing trade, profit-making, and beauties of life. "Muhammad," as Maxime Rodinson put it simply, "was not a socialist."

The conceptual openness of Islam towards business was one of the important reasons for the splendor of medieval Muslim civilization. The Islamic world was at the heart of global trade routes and Muslim traders took advantage of this quite successfully. They even laid the foundations of some aspects of modern banking: Instead of carrying heavy and easily-stolen gold, medieval Muslim traders used paper checks. This innovation in credit transfer would be emulated and transferred to Europe by the Crusaders, particularly the Knights Templar.

So central was trade to Muslim civilization that its very decline may be attributed to changes in the pattern of global trade. When Vasco de Gama rounded the Cape of Good Hope in November 1497 — thanks in part to the astrolabe invented by Muslims — he opened a new chapter in world history, one in which global trade would shift from the Middle East and the Mediterranean to the oceans. Consequently the Arabic Middle East, which had been scorched by the Mongols two centuries before and could have never recovered anyway, entered deadly stagnation. The Ottoman Empire would excel for a few more centuries, but decline was inevitable. The loss of trade also meant the end of cosmopolitanism; this was followed by the rise of religious bigotry. While the early commentators of the Koran cherished trade and wealth as God's bounties, late Medieval Islamic literature began to emphasize extreme asceticism.

Muslim Calvinists?

If things had not gone wrong, the business-friendly character of Islam could have well put it into the historical place of Calvinism, which, as Max Weber persuasively argued, spearheaded the rise of capitalism. Weber himself wouldn't have agreed with this comment — he saw Islam as a religion of conquerors and plunderers, not hard-working laborers. According to Weber, Islam was an obstacle to capitalist development because it could foster only aggressive militancy (jihad) or contemplative austerity.

However Weber, in his Confucianism and Taoism (1915), argued that China could never breed a successful economy, because its culture was too nepotistic. He was pretty pessimistic about Japan's potential for economic success, too! His analyses of these non-Christian civilizations failed because he assumed the perpetuity of their forms, and, in part, misread their histories. One of the greatest Turkish sociologists, Sabri F. Ülgener — both a student and a critic of Weber — wrote extensively about how he, despite his genius in analyzing the origins of capitalism in the West, misjudged Islam and overlooked its inherent compatibility with a "liberal market system."

Stuck on Usury

However this compatibility is not entirely unproblematic. Among the aspects of modern capitalism, there is one particular bone of contention with Islam: interest. "Allah has permitted trade", the Koran commends, "and He has forbidden riba." And riba is generally translated as taking interest from money.

That's why modern Muslims have developed "Islamic banking" as an alternative to interest-based banking. This is, in fact, a transplantation of "venture capital" as it has been developed in the West; aspects of Islamic banking are adaptations of related services like leasing, partnership, mark-up financing and profit-sharing.

While Islamic banking allows capitalism without interest, some Muslims go further and ask whether riba really includes reasonable interest. This liberal interpretation dates to the 16th century in the Ottoman Empire. During the reign of the Suleiman the Magnificent, his Sheik-ul Islam (Head of Islamic Affairs), Ebusuud Effendi, granted permission for the collection of interest by foundations working for the betterment of the society. In modern times, there are many Muslim scholars who have reinterpreted riba. Imad-ad-Dean Ahmad of the Minaret of Freedom Institute, for example, argues that the term actually means any unconscionable overcharging, whether on an interest rate or a spot price. Charging a market rate of interest, he holds, does not constitute riba.

Whether reasonable interest is allowed or not, Islam's theological and historical attitude towards business is undoubtedly positive. "The alleged fundamental opposition of Islam to capitalism," as Maxime Rodinson put it, "is a myth."

Synthesis?

If this is so, whence comes "the battle between Islam and capitalism" as envisioned by radical Islamists like Qutb?

The answer lies both in the asceticism of late Medieval Muslim thought, which remains alive today among many ultra-conservative Muslims, and in the un-Islamic origins of Islamic radicalism. The latter was born as an anti-colonialist, reactionary movement; its main aim has been to create a socio-political system to challenge and defeat the West. Since the West was built on democratic capitalism, Islamic radicals argued that its opponents must adopt an alternative political/economic vision. That's why the founding fathers of radical Islam — such as Qutb and Mawdudi — borrowed heavily from what Ian Buruma and Avi Margalit call "Occidentalism" — an ideology with its origins in Heidegger's criticism of the West, adopted by Japanese fascists, the Nazis, the Khmer Rouge and, more recently, Al Qaeda and their ilk.

Yet for those Muslims whose lives revolve not around Occidentalism but around personal religiosity and a natural human desire for the good life, democratic capitalism seems quite well-suited.

Some striking examples of this phenomenon have emerged in Turkey in the past two decades. Turkey is not the richest country the Islamic world, but it is arguably the most developed. The richest are the oil-rich Arab nations, most of which, despite their petro-dollars, remain socially pre-modern and tribal. Regrettably, oil brings wealth, but it does not modernize. Modernization comes through rationality, which can be achieved only through organization, order, exchange, and risk-taking in pursuit of goals. The late Turgut Özal, one of Turkey's wiser Presidents, once said, "we are lucky that we don't have oil; we have to work hard to make money."

Özal was a pro-Western politician and a Muslim believer. His revolutionary, Reaganesque reforms during the 1980s transformed the Turkish economy from quasi-socialism to capitalism. In this new setting the conservative Muslim masses of Anatolia have found fertile ground for a socio-economic boom. Thanks to their astounding successes in business, they have been called "Anatolian Tigers." They constitute a new class that rivals the long-established, privileged, highly secularized and utterly condescending "Istanbul bourgeoisie."

The European Stability Initiative (ESI), a Berlin-based think tank, conducted an extensive study of the "Anatolian tigers" in 2005. ESI researchers interviewed hundreds of conservative businessmen in the central Anatolian city of Kayseri. They discovered that "individualistic, pro-business currents have become prominent within Turkish Islam," and a "quiet Islamic Reformation" was taking place in the hands of Muslim entrepreneurs. The term they used to define these godly capitalists was also the title of their report: "Islamic Calvinists."

The incumbent Justice and Development Party (AKP), seems to be a political echo of this rising "Islamic Calvinism" in Turkey. Most AKP members come from business backgrounds and the party has been quite pro-business from its very first day. Its leader, Prime Minister Erdogan, has repeatedly welcomed foreign direct investment from all countries — including Israel. Recently, in a speech given at an international Islamic conference, Mr. Erdogan called on Arab leaders to redefine the Islamic ban on interest and warned that Islamic banking could turn into a "trap" that might hinder development in the Muslim world. The more such voices are raised by Muslim leaders, scholars and intellectuals, the freer markets — and minds — will become in the broader Middle East.

Recalcitrance

Still, many Muslims — in Turkey and elsewhere — despise capitalism and perceive it as something both alien and destructive to Islam. Yet this is a misdirected disdain. When you look at anti-capitalist rhetoric in Muslim circles, you will see that it is focused on sexual laxity, prostitution, drugs, crime, or the general selfishness in Western societies. Yet these are not the inherent elements of capitalism, they would be better explained by the term "cultural materialism" — the idea that material things are the only things that matter. Most Muslims who abhor capitalism simply confuse it with materialism.

Such worried Muslims would be quite surprised to discover that some of the most outspoken advocates of the free market in the West are also staunch defenders of religious faith, family values and the healthy role of both in public life. Unfortunately, the synthesis of democratic capitalism with Judeo-Christian values — which is basically an American, not a European phenomenon — is not well known in the Islamic world. The America of churches and charities is poorly represented in the global mass media. Quite the contrary, what most Muslims see as standard Americans are the unabashed hedonists of MTV and Hollywood.

In other words, not all capitalists are of the flock of Mammon. The more Muslims realize this, the less they will fear opening their societies to economic development and the more they will remember the Koranic command, "spread through the earth and seek God's bounty and remember God much so that hopefully you will be successful."

Then the world will be a much safer place — for a morally-guided quest for capital is way more peaceful than a hate-driven "battle" against it.

The Pursuit of Knowledge and the Pursuit of Piety

Ruby Amatulla

With the very first revelation in the Quran, God is commanding humankind to read:

> 96:1-5   "Read in the name of your Lord who has created. He created the human being from an embryo. Read, and your Lord is the Generous One. The One who taught by the pen. He taught the human being what he did not know."

What is this 'reading', and 'use of the pen' God is implying? This cannot be simple reading and writing in the ordinary sense. Because if this Message is for humankind as declared in many places, most of humankind at that time and still now, did not know how to read or write. It must be much broader in scope and deeper in meaning: On the grand scale of human knowledge and understanding, the 'reading' implied here may be the 'reading' of the reality: deciphering God's truth (haqq) inscribed in the reality through the signs (ayats) He has deliberately put it for a human to note, ponder and figure: This ability to note a sign and where it points to is wisdom. That is why in all religions, wisdom and righteousness are synonymous. Wisdom penetrates the veil of illusions and appearances of reality to find truth in life, in nature, and in the seen and the unseen Universe.

And the 'the use of the pen' may mean retrieving, preserving and spreading knowledge in all its forms and dimensions.

How important is the pursuit of knowledge in Islam? The Quran in many places in many ways implying that there is actually no difference between righteousness and wisdom [hekmah]: these are synonymous. A truly wise person cannot fail to be righteous and a truly righteous one is wise. One's faith and piety is as good as one understands it to be.

Knowledge and wisdom delivers the understanding of God's moral law and the true pattern of causes and consequences that help shape one's conviction. And piety and actions emanate from conviction: higher the wisdom and understanding deeper the conviction. On the other hand piety helps increase one's wisdom that act on acquired knowledge and information to transform to higher level of awareness and appreciation. These two factors are deeply interdependent and mutually reinforcing.

For example, in the Quran, the sky is compared with a "canopy", the function of which is to protect and to provide shelter. To an uninformed person the sky appears like a canopy and he/she appreciates it that way. But to an informed person, that canopy consists of the ozone layer and the magnetic field to save life from harmful rays and discharged particles from the Sun. The level of understanding and appreciation of God's Mercy among these two groups cannot be same. Knowledge and piety help one to achieve higher levels of spiritual existence through higher understanding and appreciation.

There are two kinds of knowledge: the one is the inherent knowledge that is wisdom -- the capacity or ability to know and distinguish right from wrong and to see God's truth -- implanted in nature ['fitra'] at the time the Creator created humans (Quran 30:30). Each one of us possesses this inherent capacity: it is like the unseen umbilical cord between a human and the Creator. The purer it remains in its nature, the higher is its capacity to receive God's guidance to see His signs [ayaat] in reality and understand things better. This capacity is inherent but latent in every human being until he/she acts on the acquired knowledge. If one attempts to be sincere and righteous this latent capacity becomes more and more manifested as he/she acquires information. Therefore it is the paramount duty of a Muslim -- all throughout his/her life -- to practice piety and to acquire knowledge both. Both of these drives would lead to closer and closer to God.

One's piety sharpens the capacity to understand while knowledge enlarges this capacity. Righteousness can emanate only from the right understanding of God's Will and His moral Law and the active submission to this Law. That is the essence of Islam. Without the right understanding righteousness is not possible. However, the pursuit of right understanding requires both practice of piety and search of knowledge and this intertwined process leads to the core of Islam.

Wisdom is the frame of mind in which the information is sorted, placed, looked at, and understood. Information is like a tree, but not the forest, merely dots in a pattern but not the whole pattern. Wisdom, however, is the ability to see the forest, to know the pattern, and to comprehend the truth. Wisdom leads one to pursue the right goal, to set the right priorities, and to do the right things in life to be truly successful. Righteousness essentially is the result of wisdom. Therefore the objective of knowledge is to achieve wisdom. The Quran exhorts the believers to pray for knowledge because ultimately true wisdom and understanding come through God's guidance. One could avail this Guidance only when one pursues to be pious and pursues to be knowledgeable.

In the Quran [4:162], God says "..those from among them who are deeply rooted in knowledge, and the believers who believe ....these it is unto whom We shall grant a mighty reward." The Quran then exhorts the believers to ask knowledge from God.

The purpose of the Quran, as the Book proclaims, is to Guide, to warn and to give glad-tiding to humankind. If one does not know or understand the Message of the Quran how then this Book could help fulfill these purposes?

To understand the Quran one needs to remain conscious of one's allegiance to God. That is the highest allegiance that supersedes all other consideration or loyalty or commitment in life: such as the loyalty to a leader, an imam, a scholar, a group, a sect, a tribe or even family members. There is no blind following in Islam. One is responsible for one's conscience – the capacity to discern right from wrong – that God has empowered a human being with.

Therefore one must remain committed to the pursuit of knowledge and understanding to his/her utmost sincerity and openness in order to receive God's guidance to wisdom. Any blind following may lead to wrong ideas and wrong things. The Quran warns that – on the Day of Judgment – followers will not be able to absolve their respective responsibilities by finger-pointing at the leaders who mislead them. Each human being remains responsible for his/her understanding and action because God has given him/her the inherent ability to know, understand and do the right thing if one chooses to do so.

The way knowledge can be pursued is by using the faculty of 'reason' ['aql'] on the acquired information. The faculty of reason is the vehicle through which wisdom can be achieved: The Quran lays down the things that can corrupt this faculty of 'reason': arrogance, ignorance, and addiction to the illusions of life. If the true 'nature' can be kept purer by complying with God's Laws, then 'reason' transforms the acquired information into wisdom.

This enormous endowment of 'reason' is the reason why one remains accountable to the Creator for one's attitudes and actions. This is an enormous gift and an enormous responsibility. For this ability a human is given 'the burden of choice' and a god-like status: God commanded the angels to bow before a human because of this faculty of 'reason and knowledge': "And He imparted unto Adam the names of all things [asmaa sing. 'ism']" (2:31)

What are these 'names? The Arabic word "ism" used here also implies "the knowledge [of a thing]". That is to know and to identify the elements and components of the reality. One has to apply 'reason' on the 'acquired information' to know these components: the forces and matter and their nature and interaction patterns, and the nature and the interaction patterns of living things, etc.

Responsibility always equates ability and empowerment: God knows the ability of this endowment He has granted to humans. So God has placed the highest responsibility of representing Himself on human beings. How? What is this responsibility? The answer clearly is to take care of God's creation similar to the way He Does: with truth and justice, with care and compassion, with restraint and balance, and with patience and wisdom.

This life, therefore, essentially is a test of 'reason': choices made on the basis of sound reasoning of considering the whole reality and purpose or on the basis of flawed reasoning obstinately ignoring the truth. The Quran refutes the assertions of the European 'enlightenment' period that 'faith' is not based on reason, and that faith exists when reason fails. In Islam faith cannot be achieved without 'reason', and this process of reason is to attempt to see the bigger picture: the entire panorama of existence and its purpose.

God has provided us with this reality with full of signs for us to deduce truth. And He has endowed us with the ability of reason to reflect upon this bewildering creation. At every level of knowledge and understanding one can see the profound signs of His Presence all around: in the process of procreation and propagation of life and vegetation and in the process of balance and harmony in the nature, the messages are there for one to see the Truth. Everything in it is pointing toward the Existence of a Supreme Planner, Creator and Sustainer.

It is not a coincidence that we constantly and consistently find corollaries or parallel ideas between the physical laws and the spiritual laws, the physical phenomena and the behavioral phenomena, the nature of matter and the nature of mind: as if the seen phenomena is reflecting the deep unseen phenomena through a veil of parallel images.

The most complex and incomprehensible ideas can be presented and intuitively understood through parallels of expressions. That is why the Quran uses allegories and parables to present deep seated truth for human perceptions.

The Quran is full of exhortations such as: "so that you may think", "so that you may know", "so that you may become wise", etc. These are appeal to that faculty of 'reason' the Creator has gifted us with in our 'true nature'. Following that 'true nature' is the true religion [Quran 30:30].

Understanding the spirit of the Quran and the Prophet the sincere followers embarked on a journey to search truth by acquiring information and applying 'reason'. This pursuit with an open mind helped landed them on the Golden age of Islam. Threatened by the openness, free thinking and analytical reasoning [ijtihad] the then orthodoxy along with the power of the state sealed the door of "ijtihad' in the 10-11th century. It is no wonder that since then there is a parallel decline of the Islamic Golden age ultimately into the dark age when the Muslims are subjugated and colonized. The Europeans, on the other hand, by picking up the torch of analytical thinking from the Muslims brought about the era of "Enlightenment" and progress that dominated the world ever since: The inevitable consequences of the failure to understand and follow the Quran.

We still take enormous pride in the success and glory of the Golden age of Islam, however do we reflect upon enough why we slide down the path towards degradation, why we lost the glory and the eminence? The failure to pursue knowledge with openness, objectivity and free thinking led to the path of blind following that has dragged Muslims to centuries of degradation and subjugation. Instead of being leaders the Muslims have become insecure reactionaries. In spite of God's enormous gift of the possession and control of the 76% of the oil reserves of the world the Muslim world, at large, has remained subjugated and down trodden mainly because we have failed to be wise and knowledgeable: our mindsets are wrong, our priorities are wrong and our lifestyle is wrong. Again if we fail to take the responsibility of our own failures and always tempt to finger-point at others for our failure we would not learn the lessons of history the Quran often exhorts the believers to do so diligently.

On the other hand Islam rejects a narrow definition of reason Europe promoted during the period of Enlightenment and since. Faith is based on reason, a deeper reason, a reason which incorporates a broader angle of vision than the process of empirical proof/disproof on the basis of detection and measurement.

It is interesting to note that even in science a broader angle has to be applied in order to understand the mysterious phenomena that exist in the physical universe. The most advanced theories of physics such as the Quantum Mechanics and the String Theory that try to explain the fundamental workings of the Universe, acknowledge that there are things that are not provable and determinable: the 'Heisenberg Uncertainty Principle' and the undetectable existence of String particles clearly demonstrate things that are beyond human ability to know and to prove something so substantial and fundamental that can explain the universe. Being compelled the scientists take a rather imaginative approach of understanding toward these concepts because these help explain the universe better.

If the scientists can recognize and accept things that are not detectable and measurable, yet use them to explain the reality, then why is it so difficult to accept the existence of the Ultimate Reality [Haqq]? Does not this idea of the Supreme Cause and Presence gives the best possible explanation of this immensely complex yet highly coordinated reality? Billions of related and unrelated factors are synchronizing continuously with billion others to render this reality. To see this phenomenon as a purposeless, meaning less succession of endless coincidences itself defies reason and wisdom.

This is paradoxical that the most advanced minds of science today in a more advanced state of knowledge are compelled to accept things that they cannot prove in order to explain the entire physical phenomena. This I believe is not a coincidence: this makes a mockery of those who seek to rely on a narrow process of empirical proof in the pursuit of knowledge.

The meaning of Islam is peace. It is said that one of the highest forms of duty to God is to help establish peace within oneself and among fellow human beings. But peace cannot be achieved without justice. And justice, in turn, cannot be established without the knowledge of truth. Therefore, the pursuit of knowledge is absolutely essential for achieving peace as well. Injustice thrives on people's ignorance, prejudice and falsehood. Therefore, wrong inclinations such as arrogance, hatred, greed, envy, excessive fear etc. which distort truth and obstruct justice also hinder peace. Only through knowledge, reason and piety can one conquer these wrong tendencies to deliver fairness and justice to all. Only then is true "peace" possible.

Salafism: Greatest Obstacle to Muslim Integration

Ghayasuddin Siddiqui

Research has highlighted three major obstacles to human development within Arab countries. They are: absence of freedom; gender inequality; and knowledge deficit. Although these findings relate to Arab countries, they apply to all Muslim societies.

History of integration of all minorities in Britain has followed a certain pattern – whether they be Jewish, Irish, Afro-Caribbean or others. Initially, they are despised because of their history, language, culture or colour. They are treated as a threat to British values, even a fifth column or enemy within. They are told who is in charge, and what their place in society is. Minorities adjust to these pressures, begin to engage, build bridges and begin to find a space. For Muslims it is too early to be definitive as to why the Muslim community has become an "odd one out" and not following the same pattern. The purpose of this presentation is to highlight possible obstacles in their integration into British society. The three shortcomings highlighted by the Arab Human Development Report (2002) were good enough reasons to ensure the Muslim community was going to take longer to adjust and integrate into British society. But the presence of ideology of extremism and confrontation has made it difficult for the community to understand British society, learn from the experience of others, and carve out a space for them within the British ethos, where they may also have freedom to pursue their own community goals.

Until the 20thC Islam was understood to be a religion of peace, justice, compassion, pluralism and gender equality promoting tolerance and creativity. However, writings of scholars like Maududi, Syed Qutb et al have changed the goalpost. Now, according to their interpretations of Islam, the priorities of Islam are to re-create the seventh century society of Arabia, establishment of an Islamic estate, or the global Khalafa, and pursue jihad for the re-conquest of the world for the application of shariah, the Islamic law. An opportunity to fulfil this dream came when the Soviet Union invaded Afghanistan in 1979. The CIA, British Intelligence Services, Pakistan Intelligence Services, and Saudi Intelligence got together and created an alliance between godfearing corporate America and the Salafism against the godless communism. The war of liberation was turned into a religious war. As a result a dramatic development began taking shape - salafism, which was itself a minority ideology within Islam became globalised and militarised. Thousands of young men were attracted to Afghan jihad where they were trained the by CIA and British Intelligence Service to make explosives among other things. This, equipped with radical Islamic literature, they found themselves setting Muslim agenda globally. These Islamists with new narrative of Islam also had a well oiled and well organised infrastructure. Now, people who believe in salafism in any form are the ones who are occupying the main ground within the Muslim communities in Britain, although they are no more than 15% of the Muslim population.

It is known that Muslims are at the bottom of all piles: social, economic and educational. But for the salafist leadership the hijab, the jilbab and foreign policy are the main Islamic issues. None of them talks about social exclusion, marginalisation and racism. They do not realise that a socially excluded community cannot influence foreign policy of any country but a community, which has a clout due to its excellence in the society, might.

Whether Islam came to create a society or a state is an internal debate. Muslim scholars and societies ought to decide what is the right course of action. The salafists push the foreign policy argument to increase their internal legitimacy within the Muslim groups without realising that this approach is further marginalizing the community. Politicians are good at using external conflicts to distract attention from real issues on ground and salafists are politicians of highest order!

There ought to be open discussions on these issues within the Muslim communities. But this is not happening. Whatever debate and discussion that is taking place is within religious settings. As long as these draw backs are not understood Muslim integration will remain slow. They will defy the normal pattern of integration and continue to provide ammunition to the rightwing groups.

The salafists have managed to turn the war on terror into war on Islam. I see it as a war on resources and markets. If we look at the history of the US since the second world war, they have killed far more Christians than Muslims in their war of hegemony. But Muslims have a very limited memory of the world events. They suffer from victimhood. They think that the whole world is against them. We need to explain this to our younger generation to win their hearts and minds so that they understand how dangerous this ideology is! Research on this is needed, and should be done by Muslims themselves, so that the research is not misunderstood. Unless we liberate ourselves from this ideology, there will be no peaceful future for us.

[This paper was presented at a workshop on Comparative study of Jews and Muslims in the UK, organised by Royal Holloway, University of London, on 29 November 2006]

Religious Freedom in Indonesia before and after Constitutional Amendments

Mohammad Mova Al Afghani

1. Introduction

The Indonesian Constitution is unique in terms of its church and state relationship. It is stated there that the state is based "...on the belief in the One and Supreme God"[1] but at the same time, the Constitution never explicitly mentioned the name of any established religion in the world. The word "Allah", which connotates with the Islamic term for "God" appears once on Article 9, which regulates the formal oath for elected President. The word Allah also appeared in the Preamble of the Constitution, which stated that Indonesian independence could only occured *by the grace of Allah Almighty*. The preamble also contained the state ideology Pancasila (The Five Pillars). The first pillar reiterates that the State is based *on the belief in the One and Supreme God*.

Religious freedom is acknowledged under Article 29(2) which stipulates that *the state guarantees each and every citizen the freedom of religion and of worship in accordance with his religion and belief*. In addition to that, the second Constitutional amendments in (*) radically modified the human rights chapter under Article 28 of the Constitution. Those which are precisely relevant with religious freedom are Article 28E (1) and (2) and Article 28I. These Articles incorporates basic freedom as normally found in modern Constitutions, namely the freedom to worship and to practice the religion of his choice, the freedom to have convictions and to practice it in accordance with their conscience, including the freedom of thought, belief and expression.

However, blasphemy and deviant religious teachings are criminalized in Indonesia under Presidental Enactment 1/PNPS which were enacted in 1965. Article 1 of the enactment prohibits "deviant interpretation" of religious teachings and delegates authority to the President to dismiss any organization practicing the deviant teachings. Article 3 of the law provides 5 years imprisonment for those who – after a formal prohibition from the government under Article 1– still practices its deviant teachings. Meanwhile, Article 4 of the enactment modified the Indonesian Criminal Code through Article 156a which contained a criminal provision of 5 years of imprisonment for those "who deliberately, in public, which in essence sparked hostility, insulting or abusive views towards religions with the purpose of preventing others from adhering to any religion based on God."

---

[1]   1945 Constitution, Article 29 (1)

This paper will focus itself on the issue of criminalization of (i) *deviant religious teachings* (ii) abusive or insulting expressions towards religion whose purpose is to drive people away from their religion and weigh the two cases against the "original" and "amended" Constitution. When I wrote *original*, I intended to describe the 1945 Constitution as enforced on the 18th of July 1945 and the 1945 Constitution valid through Presidential Decree 5th of July 1959. *Amended* is meant to describe the 1945 Constitution after being modified and is declared valid by the People's Consultative Assembly.

First, the church and state relationship under the original 1945 Constitution will be elaborated, by taking into account its historical background. Second, the legal consequence of such relationship into blasphemy delicts is argued. Third, the paper will discuss Constitutional Amandments and its implication towards blasphemy delicts.

2. Church and State relationship under the *original* 1945 Constitution

    a.   Religion and God

The *original* Indonesian Constitution consisted of a *preamble*, 37 Articles, four transitional provisions and two additional provisions. The terms God, Allah and Religion appeared several times under the Constitution, namely in the preamble, Article 9 and Article 29 and they all survived Constitutional Amendments.

The Preamble of the Constitution stated:

"Whereas the struggle of the Indonesian independence movement has reached the blissful point of leading the Indonesian people safely and well before the monumental gate of an independent Indonesian State which shall be free, united, sovereign, just and prosperous. By the grace of Allah Almighty and urged by the lofty aspiration to exist as a free nation, now therefore, the people of Indonesia declare herewith their independence..."

This part of the preamble affirmed that the Indonesian independence can never occur without the will of Allah the almighty. This paragraph is an expression of gratefullness (*syukr*) to god that the nation has finally obtained its independence. Meanwhile, in another paragraph it is stated:

"...which is to be established as the State of the Republic of Indonesia with sovereignty of the people and <u>based on the belief in the One and Only God</u>, on just and civilized humanity, on the unity of Indonesia and on democratic rule that is guided by the strength of wisdom resulting from deliberation / representation, so as to realize social justice for all the people of Indonesia."

The five main ideas on the paragraph above is known as the state ideology Pancasila (The Five Pillars) and the <u>*belief in the One and Only God*</u> is placed as the first pillar. The first pillar of the Pancasila corellates with Article 29 of the Constitution:

1) The state is __based on the belief in the One and Only God__. (2) The state guarantees each and every citizen the freedom of religion and of worship in accordance with his religion and belief.

Thus, the __belief in the One and Only God__ will be a very important aspect of this paper.

Meanwhile, Article 9 stated:

(1) Prior to taking office, the President and the Vice President shall take oath according to their religion, or to make a solemn pledge before the MPR or the DPR as follows:

The Oath of President (Vice President):

"I swear by Allah to fulfill the duties of President (Vice President) of the Republic of Indonesia to the best of my capabilities and in the fairest way possible, to uphold the Constitution by all means and to execute all laws and regulations as straightforwardly as possible as well as to dedicate myself to the service of the Nation and the People."

It is clear from the passage above that it will not be possible for a declared atheist to hold presidential or vice presidential office, since the Constitution requires the candidate to take oath in the name of god. This conclusion is also paralel with other provisions and preamble of the Constitution which mentioned God, Allah or religion. It would be unthinkable for a state which is based on the belief of one and only God to be led by an atheist. This is indeed a form of discrimination, but it should be seen merely as an incorporation of political reality rather than a violation of human rights provision.

Certain primordial prerequisite for Presidential candidacy is quite common in Constitutions of other states (*). They normally require its President to be of a certain ethnicity or origin. (*) This was acceptable in the past as it was perceived that there is a connection between ethnicity or origin with nationalism. The former Indonesian Constitution even requires the President to be a "true" Indonesian, meaning that Indonesian which has immigrant origin (Chinesse or Arabic or Dutch) would not qualify as Presidential candidate.[2] This provision has been abolished and is replaced by the phrase "….has to be an Indonesian citizen from birth".[3]

b.   "Allah" and the __belief in the One and Only God__

Where do the idea of Allah and the __belief in the One and Only God__ came from? Do these terminologies reflect a preference towards a certain religion?

Some lawyers argued that the word Allah and the __belief in the One and Only God__ came from Islam and thus reflects the true relationship between the Indonesian Constitution and the religion of Islam. Commenting on the idea of God during the drafting of the Constitution by the BPUPKI

---

[2]   Article 6 of the original 1945 Constitution
[3]   Article 6 of the 1945 Constitution, the Third Amendment

(Committee who were authorized by Japan government to draft the Indonesian Constitution in 1945), the late Professor Hazairin said:

Where does the phrase belief in the One and Only God came from? Is it from the Christian side, the Hindu, the descendant of the "Foreign East" (Chinesse) who participated on the Committee? Impossible! The phrase belief in the One and Only God can only be created through the brain, wisdom and faith of an Indonesian Moslem, which is a translation of the phrase Allahu al wahidu al-ahad, under verse 2:163 and 112 of the Qur'an, and chanted through the Kanzu al Arsy prayer, line 17.[4]

However, Soekarno – who was also involved in the drafting of the Constitution and is regarded by some as the father of state ideology *Pancasila* -- had a different interpretation on the idea of God. Resorting to the 5-stage evolutional perspective in Marxism, Soekarno opined that the idea of God shifted overtime. In the first stage, hunting and gathering, God was perceived to be of natural objects such as moon and rivers. In the 2nd stage, animal domestication, God is represented by animals. And in the 3rd stage, God is manifested into anthrophomorphical deities, such as Dewi Sri (the Goddes of rice) in Java and in Sundanesse as Saripohaci. Soekarno said: "*Is God changeable? No! God does not change. The essence of God does not change. What is changeable is the perception of human beings*".[5] Soekarno further argued that someday people might enter the 4th and 5th stage of God-perception. The 4th being the era of the division of labor, whose God is invisible and intangible and the 5th being the era of industry, where human beings regarded themselves as "god" since they could do things previously considered the works of "god".

With regards to the phrase Allah, while it might be true that the word "Allah" and the phrase *belief in the One and Only God* originated from the Islamic representatives at the BPUPKI, it can neither be inferred that Islam is the state religion of Indonesia, nor that the Constitution favors Islam over other religions. As explained by Nurcholis Madjid, the word "Allah" is a generic term used by many religions and tribes in the world. Even long before Muhammad came to Arabia, the traditional Arabic tribes has already used the word "Allah", and so does some tribes in the ancient Egypt, the Christians and the jews.[6]

The *belief in the One and Only God* may appear as a statement of *tawhid* (monotheism), does this means that other religions such as Christianity, Buddhism and Hinduism is excluded from this conception? From the Islamic perspective alone, Islam does not claim exclusivity over monotheism. Nurcholis explained that Islam recognizes the teachings of Moses and Jesus as a form of monotheism. Under the Qur'an, sincere followers of Christianity and Jews are termed "the People of the Book"

---

[4]   Hazairin, Piagam Jakarta
[5]   Sukarno, "Pantja Sila Dasar Falsafah Negara", in Tjamkan Pantja Sila!: Pantja Sila Dasar Falsafah Negara (Jakarta: Departemen Penerangan, 1964), p. 92.
[6] Nurcholis Madjid, Islam, Doktrin dan Peradaban p. xciv

(*ahl-al-kitab*).[7] Other well known Islamic scholars such as Muhammad Rasyid Ridla even extend the term "the people of the Book" into some people in India, China and Japan.[8] Muhammad Yusuf Ali in its Tafseer (interpretation of the Qur'an) extends the understanding of "the people of the book" into the sincere followers of Zoroaster, Veda, Budha, Confusius and other "great masters".[9] Nurcholis Madjid explained that the stand of these scholars is consistent with the teachings of the Qur'an that Allah sent some messenger (*rasool*) for humanity for the purpose of teaching the *tawheed* (monotheism), some of the stories are informed to Muhammad, some are not.[10]

Thus, under this interpretation, even if the statement of *belief in the One and Only God* is originated from Islamic teachings, it does not in any way exclude other religions under its conception as Islam itself claims no exclusivity over monotheism and some scholars even regard non-semitic religions such as Confusianism as a form of monotheism. It must be emphasized that representatives from other religions on the BPUPKI do not object to the word Allah and the phrase *belief in the One and Only God* and Article 29 was passed with a consensus, without any vote.[11] This signifies that the word Allah and the phrase *belief in the One and Only God* have a neutral character, acceptable to various religions and moral teachings known by the Committee members during the drafting of the Constitution.

c. Some historical background: the "Jakarta Charter" and the Islamic clauses

Piagam Jakarta (*Jakarta Charter*) is the original draft Preamble of the 1945 Constitution and thus, a document underlying the current state ideology *Pancasila*. It consisted of five principles: *the belief in God with the obligation to perform sharia for its followers, just and civilized humanity, the unity of Indonesia, democratic rule that is guided by the strength of wisdom resulting from deliberation / representation, and, social justice for all the people of Indonesia.*

The charter is a political compromise as a result of a very long debate by the founding fathers. However, shortly before the opening of a meeting on August 18, 1945, Hatta proposed several important changes on the draft of the Constitution, namely that (i) the word *mukaddimah* (an Indonesian word derived from Arabic) in the preamble was substituted with the word *pembukaan* (an original Indonesian term for preamble), (ii) the phrase "*the belief in God with the obligation to perform sharia for its followers*" on the preamble is altered into "*The Belief in the One and Only God*", (iii) Article 6 should read "the president of the Republic of Indonesia should be a native-born Indonesian," and the phrase "and an adherent of Islam" is removed from it and (iv) article 29 came to read "the State based on Belief

---

[7] Nurchlis, p 189
[8] Muhammad Rasyid Ridla,
[9] Muhammad Yusuf Ali,
[10] Nurcholis,
[11] Risalah Sidang BPUPKI

in the One and Only God" while the words "with the obligation to practice the sharī'a for its adherents" is omitted.[12] This modified Constitution is finally approved and since then is known as the 1945 Constitution.

With the omission of Islamic clauses, the 1945 Constitution becomes religion-neutral. The 1945 Constitution lasted only for several years. In 1949, Indonesia adopted the Republik Indonesia Serikat (RIS) Constitution, as a part of its dealing with the Netherlands. In 1950, Indonesia adopted the Undang Undang Dasar Sementara (Temporary Constitution) and the *Konstituante* (Constituent's Assembly) at that time was designated as the body authorized with the drafting of the Constitution. However, in 1959, Soekarno felt the need to consolidate his power, so through the Presidential Decree dated 5 July 1959, he dismissed the *Konstituante* and decided to return to the original 1945 Constitution. Under the "Considerations" (*konsiderans*) part of the Decree, Soekarno emphasized that "...*the Jakarta Charter dated July 22 1945 inspires the 1945 Constitution and is part of the chain of unity with the aforementioned Constitution*". Until the end of Soekarno's presidential term and its succession to Soeharto, the Constitution has never been amended. During the New Order era, Presidential Decree of the 5th of July 1959 has always been regarded as a source of law which embodies the Constitution.

Thus, prior to the amendment, there is a clear link between the 1945 Constitution and the Jakarta Charter, namely through the Presidential Decree. Although quoted only in the *Konsiderans* and not the dictum itself, the decree brings legal implication that the interpretation of the Constitution must weigh the Jakarta Charter. After the amendments, the 1945 Constitution was enforced directly by the People's Consultative Assembly (MPR), hence its

d. Is Indonesia a theocratic or a secular state?

The effect of the relationship between church and state towards structural norms has been examined by Winfried Brugger. Brugger examined six models of State-Church relationship:

1	2	3	4	5	6
Aggressive animosity between state and church	Strict separation in theory and practice	Strict separation in theory, accommodation in practice	Divisin an cooperation	Formal unity of church & state, with substantive division	Formal substantive unity of church and state

Source: Brugger

The first type (*aggressive anymosity*) is practiced by Albania under the 1976 constitution which recognizes no religion and supports a materialistic and scientific worldview instead. In the former USSR and

---

[12] Yamin, ed., *Naskah*, vol. 1: 400-410.

some other communist states, anti-religious propaganda is allowed and obtained a Constitutional guarantee. The second type (*strict separation in theory and practice*) is the US under the "wall of separation" doctrine as reflected in the *Everson* case.[13] The third type (*strict separation in theory, accomodation in practice*) is reflected by the US in the *Lemon* test, which allows weak or marginal organizational entanglements or supports towards religions as long as it is not the primary objective. The fourth type (*division and cooperation*) is reflected by Germany through Article 4 (1) and (2) and 140 (which correspond to Articles 137, 138 and 141 of thw Weimar Constitution) of the Basic Law. For example, under Article 137 the state supports churches by witholding tax for its adherents and by allowing other previleges in zoning law. The fifth type (*formal unity of church and state with substantive division*) is practiced by Great Britain, Israel and Greece (under the 1975 constitution). In UK, the monarch is the "supreme governor" of the Church of England and ratifies the appointment of bishops. In Greece under the 1975 constitution, orthodox Church is established as a state church. In Israel, Rabbinical courts have jurisdiction over family law. In addition to that, a significant discrimination is provided by the Law of Return and elsewhere, giving more facilities to adherents of the Jewish religion.[14] Lastly, the sixth type (*Formal and substantive unity between church and state* or "theocracy") is practiced by Iran and Saudi Arabia. In this model, legal obligation is a part of religious duties and a violation thereof is sinful. Brugger concludes that type 1 and 6 would likely be illegal under most modern Constitutions.

Which type is Indonesia? Brugger himself told that there is no hard-and-fast rule. The US is somewhere in type 2 and 3 while Germany could be between 3 and 4. Clearly, the Indonesian model does not follow the US "strict wall of separation" (type 2) as *the state is based on the belief of the One and Only God* (See Chapter 2.a.,b and c above). At the same time, Indonesia is not a theocratic state with formal union between a particular religion (type 6) as the laws are enforced and created independently from clerics and the role of religious laws are only in inspiring positive law. It is also difficult to categorize Indonesia under type 5, as states under this type have state's religion under its Constitution. Categorizing it under type 3 will not be possible as type 3 only permit weak support for religion while in Indonesia religions must be supported. Categorizing Indonesia under type 4 (such as Germany under Article 140 of the Basic Law) will also be difficult given the fact that the Indonesian Constitution does not specify any religion that it would assist while in Germany, the Constitution specifically assists Christianity. However, it can still be argued that the Indonesian Constitution assists not only a specific religion but *all*

---

[13] Justice Black of the US Supreme Court in the *Everson* decision explained that the state is "neutral" towards religion, in the sense that the state may not – among other -- establish a church, pass law to aid some or all religions, prefer one religion over another, influence to or not to attend religion, punish persons for his belief or disbelief and participate in the affairs of religion.

[14] For example, right of return is given to non converting Jews. Another example is that exemption from military service is given to teenagers who studied Talmud

religions. This may position Indonesia under type 4, but with a variant that *all religions* are supported.

Nevertheless, although the German Constitution aided Christianity, elsewhere it is stated that Germany is *neutral* with respect to worldviews and religion. It even put _worldviews_ under the same position with _religion_. This is different from the Indonesian Constitution. The Indonesian Constitution values God and Religion, but without detailing which God and which religion. The Indonesian constitution is not neutral towards religion or worldviews like the US or Germany, it is "pro-religion" in the sense that it prefers and supports a theistic worldview rather than the non-theist/atheist worldview, but is nevertheless neutral on which theistic view it prefers the most. This fact brings me to the conclusion that the Indonesian Constitution existed somewhere between type 4 and 5 of the Brugger's typology.

3. Religious Delicts and the *original* 1945 Constitution

a. Religious delicts and the _belief in the One and Only God_

As explained above, Indonesian Law criminalizes of (i) *deviant religious teachings* (ii) abusive or insulting expressions towards religion whose purpose is to drive people away from their religion. Is the criminalization of the actions above consistent with the Constitution? Some scholars who lived in the 60s would answer "yes": a state which is based on the _belief in the One and Only God_ would be justified to penalize any actions deemed to be detrimental towards religion, its teachings, doctrines and symbols. The late Criminal Law expert Professor Oemar Seno Adji, who was also a former State Attorney, Minister of Justice and Chief Justice of the Supreme Court during the Soekarno era wrote in his book (translated):

> *"Religion in this state which is based on God is not only protected from "attacking" statements which undermines or insult religions, but also from all sorts of propaganda and agitations which has the purpose of omitting, lessening, weakening or encroaching one's belief towards religion, these needs to be dealt with criminal sanctions"*[15]

He further argued that those who confess as a prophet of an *acknowledged* religion, or those who perform rituals of an *acknowledged* religion with defiance could also be accounted for crimes, insofar as they may lessen, weaken or encroach one's belief towards religion.[16]

---

[15] Seno Adji, Oemar. Hukum Acara Pidana Dalam Prospeksi. Penerbit Erlangga, Jakarta. Cetakan Keempat, 1984. p. 138

[16] *Ibid.* p. 138 and p. 81. The word acknowledged is italicized as Prof. Seno Adji actually admitted that it would be difficult to define "religion". Penpres 1/PNPS/1965 according to him also did not attempt to define any religion, its elucidation is merely meant as a "Constatation" (See p.140). He also argued that the 1945 Constitution invoked a non-preferential treatment towards religion, which means that no religion is to be favoured over another (See p. 125).

Thus, Professor Seno Adji is of the opinion that a state which is based on the *belief in the One and Only God* is permitted to criminalize all the three actions mentioned at the beginning of this chapter.

b. Some theories underlying religious delicts

Religious delicts are justified in general, based on two motives: (i) public order and (ii) non public order reasons. Within the public order reason lies the *Friedenschutzstheorie* (The Protection of Peace Theory) and the *Gefühlschutzstheorie* (The Protection of Feeling Theory). On the contrary, religious delicts which are not based on public order reasons stood independently of those theories above, which mean that they can be triggered irrespective of any disturbance to peace and irrespective of any feelings that is injured by the action, this is known as *Religionschutzstheorie*. We shall elaborate the three theories above and categorize the position of Indonesian religious delicts under the theories.

Under the *Friedenschutzstheorie*, an action is criminalized if it disturbs peace. Most of the articles in Book II of the Indonesian Criminal Code would be justifiable under the *Friedenschutzstheorie*. Meanwhile, *Gefühlschutzstheorie* protects the feeling of other people. Most criminal provisions about defamation or insults would be justifiable under the *Gefühlschutzstheorie*. Both the Friedenschutz and Gefühlschutz usually contain a restrictive clause before in can be triggered, namely that the *public order* has to be disturbed.

On the other hand, *Religionschutzstheorie* requires no public order to be affected. A delict constructed under this theory would be triggered irrespective of whether the public peace is disturbed or not or whether someone will be offended or not. The *Religionschutzstheorie* protect the religion, its symbols, practices and shrines. Thus, it sees not whether the community will be affected or not. It automatically perceives any action harmful towards religion to be punishable as it protects religion as itself: "*religion in itself, has a legal interest which must be protected.*"[17] Under this theory, religion is perceived to be a part of the State, as a common spiritual possession of the nation. The state is obligated to maintain religion because of its function in supporting order and tranquillity.[18] An example of *Religionschutzstheorie*, as put by Prof. Seno Adji, is the insult towards God (known as Gottlästerung in German or Godslastering in Dutch). According to the Professor, God should be protected by the state not because someone or a group of society will be offended by the

---

[17] Seno Adji, Oemar. Hukum Acara Pidana, p.88

[18] "Het gaat dan om godsdienst als staatsbelang, als gemeenschappelijk, geestelijk bezit van de natie. De godsdienst heeft geen morele waarde, maar is functioneel omdat zij de orde en rust in de staat moet handhaven." See Ingeborg Middel, Een onderzoek naar het nut van de strafbaarstelling van smalende godslastering anno 2007, Doctoraalscriptie, Faculteit der Rechtsgeleerdheid van de Universiteit van Amsterdam, augustus 2007 p.13

statements, nor because it will disturb the public order or security, *but because God is God.*[19]

Religionschutzstheorie has been criticized as the protection of religion by the state would not be impartial.[20] It would be difficult for the state to define religion and finally accord protection of such religion.

The German Criminal Code recognizes the protection of religion under Chapter 11. § 166 (*Beschimpfung von Bekenntnissen, Religionsgesellschaften und Weltanschauungsvereinigungen*) protects religion, faiths and philosophies of life from insults, to the extent such insult disturb the public peace. § 167 (*Störung der Religionsausübung*) protects rituals from being disturbed. § 167a (*Störung einer Bestattungsfeier*) protects funeral services from being disturbed, meanwhile § 168 (*Störung der Totenruhe*) protects burial sites and corpses from being damaged.

§ 166 of the German criminal code above has a very important conditional clause, namely that it will be active only if the insult is performed in a manner which disturb the public peace (*die geeignet ist, den öffentlichen Frieden zu stören*). With such conditionality, activation of the blasphemy accusation will depend on the evidentiary process which proves that the action in question really has disturbed the public peace. It is required that the "manner and content" of that insult must be such that a reasonable person could assume that his action would disturb the peace of those who share the insulted belief. Thus, the element of "intention" would be very vital in this case. The § 166 provision is actually a development of an old provision which protects God and his institutions. The older provision has been more conservative and leaned toward *Religionschutzstheorie* while the current § 166 is more liberal as it is more based on *Friedenschutzstheorie* and *Gefühlschutzstheorie*.

There has been proposal to wipe out the phrase *in a manner which disturbs the public peace* above so that § 166 could be triggered irrespective of whether public peace is disturbed. This proposal has been rejected as it might be contrary to Article 103 para. 2 of the German Constitution.[21]

c. Nature of the Indonesian Blasphemy Provision

Article 156a of the Indonesian Criminal Code contained a criminal provision of 5 years of imprisonment for those "who deliberately, in public, which in essence sparked hostility, insulting or abusive views towards religions with the purpose of preventing others from adhering to any religion based on God.". This Article has been ambiguous with

---

[19] Seno Adji, Oemar. Hukum Acara Pidana, p.88
[20] Middel, Ingeborg, p.13.
[21] Esser, Albin. Schutz von Religion und Kirchen im Strafrecht und im Verfahrensrecht. Joseph Listl (Hrsg.): Handbuch des Staatskirchenrechts der Bundesrepublik Deutschland. 2., grundlegend neubearb. Aufl. Berlin: Duncker & Humblot. Bd. 2 (1996), S. [1019] – 1045, p. 1032

respect to its criminalization theory as there are doubts as to whether it is motivated by *Religionschutzstheorie* or public order reasons. Judging from its position in the Criminal Code, Article 156a is placed in Chapter V of the Criminal Code which regulates the crimes against public order, along with Article 156 which criminalizes those who spark hatred against others. However, if seen from the content, the Article does not contain any condition which suggest that it will be activated only if carried out *in a manner which disturbs the public peace* such as the German's § 166. Thus, Article 156a could be enforced irrespective of whether the insult caused public peace to be disturbed, or whether it would injure the feeling of religious adherents or not. To give a concrete example, Article 156a could be activated although the offence is conducted before persons who are not an adherent of any religion.[22]

The ambiguity of Article 156a has been acknowledged by Prof. Seno Adji with him proposing it to be reformed so that it can fully protect religion. It was proposed that Article 156a should be reconstructed and removed from Chapter V as it is clear that its content is in protecting religion, irrespective of public order.[23] However, even without this modification, in practice Article 156a has been very extensively applied so as to cover cases involving both public order and non public order. With these facts, it can be inferred that the interpretation and application of Article 156a leaned toward *Religionschutzstheorie* rather than *Friedenschutzstheorie* or *Gefühlschutzstheorie*.

d. Constitutionality of Blasphemy Law under the *Original* 1945 Constitution

It is argued that the wide protection -- for example by allowing the blasphemy provision to be applied irrespective of feelings or disturbance toward public peace –accorded by Indonesian Criminal Law to religion is a manifestation of the unique state-religion relationship in Indonesian Constitution, which is based *on the belief of the One and Only God* (See Chapter 3a above). I disagree with this conclusion. The reasons are as follows:

First, although Indonesia is based *on the belief of the One and Only God*, it does not necessarily justify overreactive protection towards religion. As discussed in **Chapter 2d** above, I have concluded that Indonesia may existed somewhere between type 4 and 5. Brugger stated that in general, the more accomodating a state towards religion (moving to the right side of the typology) the higher its standard in identifying infractions against religious liberty clauses in its Constitution. In any event however, punishment for deviant religious teachings is not likely to occur on typology 2-5, it can only occur in theocratic states (type 6). Thus, it would be mistaken to conclude that Presidental Enactment 1/PNPS/1965 Article 1 and 3 (regulating deviant sects) is justifiable under the *original*

---

[22] Seno Adji, Omar. P. 86
[23] *Ibid*

103

Constitution. State in typology 4-5, such as Germany, do not have any law punishing "deviant" sects.

States within typology 3-5 may have blasphemy laws, but most of these laws are constructed for public order reasons. Thus, it would be arguable that blasphemy laws which are independent from public order reasons such as Article 156a (which is constructed and interpreted under *Religionschutztheorie*) can gain justifications.

Second, the phrases *the belief of the One and Only God* on the Constitution does not refer to any specific religion. Article 29 (2) specifically guarantee the rights of the people to worship and perform their rituals in accordance with their respective belief. Both Article 29 (1) and (2) does not provide any authority for the state in order to preserve the "purity" of any religion. Thus, the state has no authority to declare a certain sect to be "deviant".

Third, even under the *original* Constitution, Article 28 already guaranteed the freedom of expression and opinion. This Article has similar authority with Article 29.

4. The *amended* 1945 Constitution and its influence towards religious freedoms

As discussed by Brugger, Human Rights Conventions which protects the freedom for all religious and philosophical beliefs—although such pacts do not have the authority to replace internal constitutional order-- have an effect on the structural relationship between church and state as they exert a certain amount of pressures.[24] Indonesia has adopted the International Covenant on Civil and Political Rights (ICCPR) and invoked the ICCPR as its internal law[25]. What makes it more interesting is the fact that the Human Rights Chapter in the amended constitution is directly inspired by human rights convention which has been ratified by Indonesia.[26] In fact, many of the sentences on the Human Rights Chapter of the Constitution (Chapter V) strikingly resemble the words used in Human Rights Covenants. Due to these facts, there has been suggestion in order to interpret the Human Rights Provisions of the Constitutions in line with the interpretation of International Conventions.

a. The effect on State-religion relationship

The influence of state-religion relationship to structural norms can be evaluated from two perspectives: (i) liberty side and (ii) equality side.[27] From the liberty side, more emphasis on religious liberty is provided by the amandments of Article 28:

---

[24] Brugger
[25] Law No.
[26] Memori Penjelasan
[27] Brugger

Article 28E

(1) Each person is free to worship and to practice the religion of his choice, to choose education and schooling, his occupation, his nationality, his residency in the territory of the country that he shall be able to leave and to which he shall have the right to return.

(2) Each person has the right to be free in his convictions, to assert his thoughts and tenets, in accordance with his conscience.

Article 28I

(1) The rights to life, to remain free from torture, to freedom of thought and conscience, to adhere to a religion, the right not to be enslaved, to be treated as an individual before the law, and the right not to be prosecuted on the basis of retroactive legislation, are fundamental human rights that shall not be curtailed under any circumstance.

From the liberty side, Article 28 E (2) can also be interpreted as a guarantee towards non-theist worldviews. From the equality side however, it appears that there has been no change with respect to the rights of non-theist followers. This would mean that the state is under obligation to protect their conviction, but is not obligated to provide material supports. Conversely, for theist followers, the state is obligated not only in protecting them, but also in providing supports.

b. Constitutionality of Blasphemy laws

i. Prohibition of "deviant" teachings

Under the *original* 1945 Constitution, religion and god is not clearly defined. The Constitution does not refer to any specific organized religion nor deities when mentioning them. The interpretation of religion, god and Allah under the *original* Constitution will have to refer to the writings and conversations of the founding father during the drafting of the Constitution. If Soekarno's understanding of God and Religion is to be taken (see **Chapter 2b**), then it will cover even the gods of the ancient tribes in Indonesia under animism. Such a liberal interpretation would mean that the Constitution does not prefer mainstream religions over minority religions or sects. Thus, the right of "deviant sects" to profess their beliefs remains protected by the State.

The *Amended* Constitution, especially Article 28 E (2) explicitly guaranteed everyone's right *to be free in his convictions, to assert his thoughts and tenets, in accordance with his conscience*. Thus after Constitutional Amendments, the structural norms undergone a modification: more emphasis in the liberty side is being placed. Prohibition of "deviant" sects would therefore be incompatible with Article 28 E (2).

ii. Article 156a of the Criminal code

Under the *original* Constitution, there is confusion as to whether it would be permissible to enact anti-blasphemy regulation by basing upon the *Religionschutzstheorie*. The argument is anchored on the state-religion relationship on the 1945 Constitution: a state which is <u>based on the belief of one and only god</u> would be allowed to enact laws which would enable penalization irrespective of public order reason. As has been discussed above, this argument does not necessarily hold true: even states which has stronger ties with religion in its Constitution is currently moving towards the abolition of blasphemy laws which are based solely on *Religionschuztstheorie*. Blasphemy laws remain the law of their land, insofar as it is useful to preserve public order.

Following the Constitutional *amendments*, the confusion should end. Article 28I placed the freedom of religion on the same level with the freedom of thought and conscience. This approach is consistent with the approach used in international HR instrument: freedom of religion is only a tenet of the freedom of thought and conscience.[28] Thus, the *amended* Constitution placed a greater emphasis with respect to liberty rights.

Does this mean that all blasphemy laws should be outlawed? No. Blasphemy laws can be permitted insofar as its aim is in preserving public order. Blasphemy laws which stood independently from public order reasons (such as those which are constructed under the *Religionschutzstheorie*) would have the potentiality to infringe major human rights instrument and the 1945 Constitution.

Article 156a of the Criminal Code does not contain any conditionality that it would only be imposed insofar as it it necessary to protect public order. In practice, the Article has also been applied and interpreted very extensively so as to cover both public order and non public order reasons. This article could therefore infringe Articles 28 E and I of the Constitution

iii. Limitations under Article 28J

Article 28J (2) of the Constitution put limitation as to the exercise of all rights and liberties within the Constitution[29]:

Article 28J

(2) In exercising his rights and liberties, each person has the duty to accept the limitations determined by law for the sole purposes of guaranteeing the recognition and respect of the rights and liberties of other people and of satisfying a

---

[28] General Comment 11 or 12?

[29] Article 28 J is to be interpreted so as to cover all articles within the Constitution and not just the Human Rights Chapter. Decision of the Constitutional Court

democratic society's just demands based on considerations of morality, religious values, security, and public order.

What remains a controversy is how *religious values* there should be determined. Religious values according to whose interpretation? The Constitution itself is silent with respect to the definition of "Religion". It is in my opinion that the interpretation to the word "Religion" should also refer to the interpretation of the similar word contained in Article 29 (2). If historical interpretation method is to be taken, then Soekarno's liberal interpretation of religion could be an authoritative source.

5. Conclusions

The following table will sum up the arguments made in this paper:

No.	Subject Matter	Before Constitutional Amendments	After Constitutional Amendments
1.	Linkage with Piagam Jakarta	Linked through the "Consideration" part of Presidential Decree July 5th 1959.	The link with piagam Jakarta is disconnected as the Constitution is enforced through MPR Decision.
2.	"Deviant Sects"	No clear definition of religion. No authority from the Constitution to declare a sect to be deviant or not. The right to worship is guaranteed by the Constitution.	The condition remained unchanged i.e. there is still no exact definition on "religon", however the amended Constitution emphasized more on liberties. So now the Constitution guaranteed: (i) freedom of worship, (ii) freedom of thought and (iii) freedom of conscience
3.	Insult towards religion (Blasphemy under Article 156a of the Criminal Code)	There is confusion: should a state which is based on the belief in the One and Only God not allowed to have laws which protects religion and its institutions from insults or from anti-religion propaganda? The mainstream opinion was that it should be allowed. Hence, a criminal provision under Religionschutstheorie was enacted, it has the capability to punish people irrespective of public order reasons or its intention in insulting.	Articles 28 E and I puts the freedom of religion on the same level with the freedom of thought and conscience. Thus, one must weigh between an insult towards religion against the freedom of thought and conscience. Criminal provision under Religionschutzstheorie will not be compatible with Articles 28 E and I. Blasphemy provision could still be allowed if its purpose is solely in maintaining public order. Article 156a could therefore become unconstitutional.

There are two ways of evaluating the influence of religion-state relationship towards structural norms, namely from the liberty side and from the equality side. It is true that the 1945 Constitution prefers a theistic worldview compared to non/a theistic worldviews. However, this discrimination can only occur on the equality side and not the liberty side: theistic worldviews could be given more previlege and state facilities or financial supports compared to non/a theistic worldviews. Conversely, on the liberty side – after Constitutional Amendments – no discrimination shall be made. This means that the right of "deviant" sects and the rights of atheist or non-theist shall be remain protected: they should be allowed to profess their beliefs. Constitutional amendments also emphasize the liberty in terms of the freedom of thought and conscience and put them at the same level as religions. Consequently, blasphemy codes will have to weigh the freedom of thought and conscience. Blasphemy codes which are too extensive could be declared unconstitutional.

Delusions of Liberation

Melody Moezzi

I've never fully understood how and why a simple piece of fabric, strategically placed on a woman's head, can be so frequently and easily misinterpreted as some sort of universal symbol of oppression. I have often heard American women express disgust at the notion of a woman who wears a "veil" to cover her hair. Many of these proud and self-proclaimed "feminists" seem to have the common collective belief that Muslim women who cover (that is, Muslim women who wear hijab) are all being forced to do so by some archetypal misogynistic husband or father. "No woman would choose that," seems to be the common interpretation. And it is the interpretation that I overhear one afternoon in some Starbucks attached to a bookstore I happen to have found my way into. Four young white women sit at a table, all picking at the same brownie, all sipping on a grande something-or-other, and all reading fashion magazines with what I assume they think are free and liberated half-naked starving women on the covers. One of them looks over at a black woman in a purple headscarf holding a baby in her arms. Ordering a tall mocha frappaccino, she looks far from oppressed to me, but one of the fashionistas clearly disagrees. "I would never let a man do that to me." I look around to see if maybe there is a man harassing a woman in the vicinity, but no. She is referring to this innocuous-looking woman with her child. Another girl chimes in, "I know, seriously. I feel so bad for those women. I would rather die than live like that."

I know all too well that these women were dead serious. I wonder how they all so readily share the same assumption, that in the middle of Atlanta in 2007, this woman is being forced to cover her hair by some evil unseen masculine oppressor. Of course, there is a possibility that the woman about whom the quartet is speaking is not freely choosing to cover her hair, but something about her makes me doubt this. At any rate, the question I find myself asking in the middle of all of this, as the debate in my head over carrot cake or chocolate brownie grows harder to resolve, is why none of these liberated modern women seems to recognize the evil masculine oppressor that is staring all of them right in the face. They look at airbrushed photos of models and actresses and heiresses, and they seem to believe that this two-dimensional farce is somehow the embodiment of the ideal contemporary woman, when she is in fact the carefully-constructed composite of several pathetically trite heterosexual male fantasies. They all seem to have bought into the idea that bikinis equal freedom, that lip-gloss equals empowerment, that low-rise jeans are a completely reasonable and comfortable substitute for real pants. These women are walking, talking testaments to the power of American advertising.

Meanwhile, the oppressed woman in lilac has been joined by a man who appears to be her husband. All signs seem to indicate that he is not, in fact, the devil incarnate. He comes pushing an empty pink and white stroller with one hand and carrying a plate of carrot cake in the other. He places the cake on the table in front of his wife, and she hands him the baby. As she comes to get a fork, she looks at me, apparently having noticed my inordinately long visit with the painfully well-lit dessert case.

"Why not just try one of each?" she asks me, laughing.

"I know," I tell her. "You'd think it were some big important decision or something, right?"

"Are you saying that cake isn't important? Shame on you!" she says as she walks away, again laughing. I laugh along with her and decide that I'll try the carrot cake too. Meanwhile, the quartet is getting up to leave. "I can't believe I ate nearly half of that entire brownie," I hear one of them say. "Relax," another responds, "I'm going to the gym later. You can come with if you want. Don't forget your purse."

From Christianity to Salafi Sect of Sunni Religion and Finally to Islam!

Chibuzo Ohanaja

While I am now a firm believer in Islam, I can not state that my journey to the true message of Islam was easy. My Journey to Islam represents a long and unwavering quest for truth and God that I encourage all people to take. This quest for truth is a quest that few people of my background embark upon and I would have never thought years ago that I would be in the state of mind that I am in today.

My parents came to the U.S about 30 years ago from Nigeria and are both doctors, my mother is an Optometrist and my father is a Neuropyschiatrist in Dallas, Texas. Growing up I considered myself a Christian not adhering to any particular sect since my father is an agnostic secular humanist but my mom's side of the family is Catholic. I was very active in sports in high school and was even active in Christian-Athlete study groups. Additionally, I was an avid reader of the Bible and would read Biblical passages every night before I went to sleep at night as a habit. I never had any type of exposure to any other type of faith and never thought of any reason to look in to any other religions. My first exposure to Islam occurred when I met my best friend in high school whose family is from Pakistan. His family was a traditional Sunni Muslim family and taught me a general knowledge of Islam that made me interested but not enough to revert.

After High School, I decided to go the University of Notre Dame, which I was encouraged to do by mother because of the strong religious environment that the school offered. Due to the fact that it is the biggest Catholic university in America, the catholic culture is very strong at the school. The curriculum is very much based around Christian theology and philosophy, particularly Catholicism. Nevertheless, I attempted to expand my knowledge during my college experience and took Arabic as my friend from home encouraged me that it was an interesting language to study. I discussed the decision to study Arabic with my academic advisor. I was surprised when he strongly discouraged me from studying the language but, regardless of his warning I decided to take the chances and ended up loving the language so much it became my second major. Once I learned the language I wanted to learn more about the people who spoke this language and ended up taking classes offered at my university on Islam. Although, the classes were very general I was able to expand my studies by doing outside readings and research and I became enamored with Islam. Although, I did not believe in many of the doctrines of Christianity my vast amount of study of Islam made me reflect about my own set of beliefs and outlook on life. I questioned my own beliefs and pondered about my purpose of existence in this world. This type of deep reflection led me to deeply study Islam based on its central authority the Quran and every other religion that preceded it and has claimed to supersede it, brought me to the conclusion that Islam was the most pragmatic and rational system of living that had ever come into this world.

I decided to revert at the age of 20 and even made a formal announcement on my 21st birthday at a local Masjid near my home in front of the community. From those months onward I continued to learn more Arabic and read more about Islam not only from a religious perspective but also from a political perspective as it is today. I started going to the mosque more often and for a while, I saw myself getting away from focusing on the Quran and instead focused on the rituals and sunnah (traditions) from hadith that so many Muslims, mostly mullahs and members of Tabligh-i Jamaat, at my local mosque were telling me were mandatory i.e. eating zabiha, sleeping on the correct side, doing zikr by reciting la illaha illa allah multiple times to attain higher taqwa, growing a beard, changing my name, removing all pictures and images from the walls of my room because I thought pictures were forbidden, eating with my right hand because Satan eats with his left ,belief in absurd hadith such as the miraj (ascension), referring to religious mullahs by the title of Maulana meaning "Our Lord" or "Our Master" which entails the grossly offensive act of shirk (associating partners to our only Lord) and so forth. From that point on I had become a blind follower of false tradition and did not even realize that I had gotten myself into a sect. I began to blindly accept the ignorant, irrational ideas of mullahs without reflection or self confirmation. The Quran warns mankind about blind following information

17:36   And you shall not follow blindly any information of which you have no direct knowledge. (Using your faculties of perception and conception) you must verify it for yourself. In the Court of your Lord, you will be held accountable for your hearing, Sight, and the faculty of reasoning.

It seemed like I had fallen into the same way of thinking before I reverted. Eventually, I began to come out of my shell when I studied abroad in Cairo, Egypt, during a summer in hopes of improving my Arabic and learning more about Islam. Although I met many people and made new friends during my time in Egypt, I began to start questioning many things from Muslims which I saw as non Quranic, such as, Muslim men wanting a dark spot on their foreheads (Zebibah) from prostrating so much on the ground, the poor treatment of women in the society, the lack of social action, large amounts of impoverished people, the lack of education of the majority of people and the widespread superstitious and irrational beliefs propagated by Mullahs in the media and in the mosques.

Before I continue, I feel that I must clarify what I mean by the term Mullah. By Mullah I do not mean to insult any person who has true knowledge of Islam but a specific mentality with some common traits. A mullah is extremely close-minded and is unable to engage in any rational discussion and takes pleasure in vain arguments. He is very arrogant despite being thoroughly ignorant. He has derogatory beliefs about women, and his knowledge is neither good for this world or the next. Thus, for these reasons I believe the Mullah mentality is a detriment to humanity.

I took a philosophy course taught by a professor who was a German-American whose observations of what he saw around the Muslim world were often the focal points of his lectures. The professor kept pointing out to the students about how irrational people mostly Muslims were in the county. Most of the time he didn't even bother to teach philosophy, he just made fun of the ignorance of Mullahs in the past such as (Al-Ghazzali) and present, Egyptian Muslims and religion in general since he was an atheist. His most harsh statement came one class after he made fun of some of the common statements and actions by Mullahs in Egypt and then boldly stated without any hesitation in front of the class that Islam ruined Egypt. I was surprised that the Egyptian students did not say anything in defense, but then I thought to myself how could they if they believed the nonsense that was taught to them by mullahs? How have the Muslims who were once staunch defenders of the use of reason rational and logic in religion fall into such ignorance?

After the program was over I came back home to the U.S. With a changed understanding about Islam I started to attend the mosque by my house more frequently and began to hear many irrational things preached during khutbahs: our Salafi Imam yelling loudly and frequently hitting his hand on the podium violating the Prophet's sunna which he claimed to uphold, and ascribing insulting statements to the Prophet Muhammad such as "Don't ever come to me and say you lost your wallet in the Masjid just like the hadith of the Prophet s.a.w.s 'If a man loses his wallet in the Masjid I pray to Allah that he never finds it'". After hearing that horrible hadith I decided to look more deeply into the so called saheeh hadith collections and found some of the most absurd things. I went to the Masjid one night with one of my friends to ask the Imam a few questions about the science of hadith especially since he had a lecture about it the previous night.

To start the discussion I asked him a few questions about some of the common ridiculous hadiths such as, the Planet of the Apes like hadith in which a group of monkeys stoned a monkey for committing adultery, Allah revealing his thigh to Muhammad, and Moses running bare naked after the stone that stole his clothes. I then began to ask him even harder questions and since he knew that these hadiths were ridiculous and were causing me to doubt belief in Hadith instead of accepting them he told a blatant lie to my face denying that they were even in the hadith collections. He then went on and started to yell saying "You know what! If somebody wants to tell me that there is something wrong with these hadiths and the sahih collections tell them to come here, and I'll tell them that they are stupid! I'll tell them they are stupid!" At that point, my friend and I were shocked about his behavior and reaction. In attempt to prove his case, then the Imam went on and told me step by step the science of hadith and the criteria for authenticity, which made his argument even worse. At the end of his rant he said "you know hadith are not perfect and it is possible to make mistakes but ultimately the system is good. You know there is one hadith that some scholars often deny but I don't see why? It says that Moses one time saw the Angel of Death in a cave and punched him in the face and ran away, I don't see why that can't be true?" At that moment I turned to my friend in even more awe, shocked at the ridiculous degree of gullibility of not only an Imam but a grown man. What I find even more surprising is that you would expect Imams such as him who have PhD's from here in the West to be from a different stock than what you find in the other parts of the world but the truth is they are not.

Even after arguing and pleading with him even more about why Mullahs choose not to remove such ridiculous hadiths especially since they inspire many orientalist works in the West invoking condemnation, humiliation and false propaganda on Muslim around the world he had no answer. He did not seem to care; he just kept on avoiding my questions and continued repeating "don't let it ruin your aqeedah!" At that point I was confused and turned to the Quran and was reassured by my research that many of the absurdities were not present inside and the and the ones that were inside were due to the misguided approaches to translations of the Quran that have been based on Hadith and Taqlid. The final straw came when I came back home and attended the local mosque for Friday prayer. The exact same Imam was there giving his typical hadith based khutbah, glorifying the hadith collectors of the past and neglecting the beautiful message of the Quran in his speech. He then came to a point in his speech where he discussed people in the Muslim Ummah who reject hadith and Sunnah outside the Quran calling them Kafirs-"infidels". I found this statement of his to be hitting too close to home and was directed at me and probably others people in the community who approached him with similar questions. The Imam then stated "Don't come to me and say that this is unreasonable and irrational. No, you see brothers and sisters those who reject the hadith, don't mind them. They don't have the mind to understand and grasp the Quran. Their brains are too small for them to understand the Sunnah they are too dumb". At this point, I was disgusted by this man's speech but even worse, no one else in the congregation was aware of the irrationality of his statements.

Suddenly, I realized that this was one of the sole reasons why Muslims are in the state they are in today. Through my research I realized that in the third century after Prophet Muhammad, the so-called Imams of tradition, history, Fiqh (religious jurisprudence) and Hadith (the most unreliable sayings of the exalted Prophet Muhammad, collected on hearsay centuries after his death) imposed a religious Martial Law on people. Thus, Muslims became bound by the same shackles the Quran so effectively broke, which liberated people from physical and mental slavery. The dynamic, rational and humane system of life for all of mankind in the Quran had been converted into a religion or Mazhab that entailed nothing but wishful thinking, empty rituals, fabrications and dogmas. The Quran rightly states "Do not ever lose heart, and do not grieve, for you are bound to

114

prevail if you are truly believers" (3:139). It further states, "God has promised that those of you who will believe in the Divine laws and strengthen human resources, He will make them rulers on earth, as He granted rule to the previous nations" (24:55).

Thus, the religious teachings prevalent today among Sunni and Shiite population, has little to do with the message of the Quran. The true Islam was implemented in the lifetime of the exalted Prophet Muhammad and his noble companions 14 centuries ago. No objective mind can deny the glory of humanity in that period in history. Human dignity, women's rights, rule of law, justice and equity, freedom of religion, speech, true democracy, and sanctity of human life, are well documented in the surviving golden pages of history by scholars and intellectuals.

I believe that many Muslims everywhere must have been asking themselves this question: is the Quran wrong? No, what is wrong is not the Quran. The problem is in the inherited false religious teachings that are made-up and promoted by the religious leaders. Muslims must turn back to the Quran. Now that I had seen the light of the situation everything started to make more sense. Since then I have felt a renewed sense of enlightenment and intellectual freedom based on knowing Islam rationally through the Quran. I have realized that the Quran grounds mankind kind in reality and much of the world's problems today are result of people being out of touch with the reality of their existence. I believe any distorted system or outlook on reality can have harmful effects and can misplace our judgment. Muslims must reform their understanding of Islam, their schools and reform their governments. Muslims must refrain from preaching the man-made dogmas and instead focus of the true Islam in the Quran. They will be doing a great service to Islam, Muslims, the West, and the entire world if they revert to the Glorious Quran.

After a long journey through much searching I have come to know the simple message of Islam and what it truly means to be a Muslim (one who submits or causes peace, balance and security with himself and God's creation). After much research, I have come to the same conclusion as many great modern Muslim scholars such as Dr. Edip Yuksel, Dr. Shabbir Ahmed and Ghulam Ahmed Parwez . I have come to a strong belief and conviction that only the true Islam embedded in the Quran can save mankind. But as the Quran states, "God does not change the condition of a nation until they first change themselves" (13:11). Thus, only when we as Muslims, change our way of thinking will Islam return as a beacon of light for all of humanity.[1]

---

[1]   BrainbowPress is interested in publishing a book containing stories like this (1000 to 3000 words). Please contact Edip Yuksel for more information.

Muslims and the Quran: Towards the Resurrection of a Civilizational Impetus

Farouk A. Peru

A. Introduction

The intent of this essay is to assert that the reason behind Islam's loss of its original civilisational impetus was the diametrical shift in its intellectual environment, thereby resulting in Muslim attitudes being negative towards intellectual growth, seeing it as a threat to their faith. We indicate this by analysing the syllabi of typical traditional Islamic education and obtaining some official views about intellectual activities. This essay further suggests that not only does the Quran obligate intellectual activities on the human being, it puts itself as the epicentre of those activities. As Muslims are said to be believers in the Quran by their own definition, they should therefore implement programs of this nature.

What is known as the 'Islamic Golden Age' was a time which, in the opinions of famed historians such as Lamartine and Briffault, the Muslims lead the way in taking humanity to new heights of achievement. While it is well known that they produced towering figures and achievements in science and technology, what should be more interesting to us is that humanist fields, such as philosophy and literature, had notable Muslim contributors. Some historians have noted elements of scepticism, secularism and liberalism in Muslim philosophical writings and a tremendous degree of imagination are found in their literature.

So what lead to this civilisational quagmire we see today? All over the world Muslims are seen to be opposing modernity and unable to appreciate freedom of speech and thinking. It is possibly due to media focus on these fundamentalists that we form such a perception but there's no denying that such Muslims exist from grassroot levels all the way up to national institutions.

While we cannot exactly determine the Quran's role during the Islamic Golden Age, we can certainly analyse the Quran in the present Islamic culture and may deduce that it isn't being allowed to fulfil the self-defined role for which it was meant. It has rather become an icon and its devotees have closed off possibilities of engagement with the Quran as a text and have instead become consumers to ready-made syllabi of education.

This essay then analyses the Quran itself through its own internal principles of reading to obtain a clear picture of the kind of society the Quran envisions, how it instructs its reader to achieve that society and whether this society is like the society of the Islamic Golden Age. Lastly, this essay hopes to show some means by which the Quran suggests its reader can rejuvenate the intellectual vitality that the Quran asserts leads to achieving the ideal society.

B. Definitions

In the world, we will find The Quran to be with the group of people known as the Muslims. The Muslims are a group of people of diverse ethnicities brought together by the shared inherited culture that began with the historical phenomenon of Muhammad and proliferated to what later became known as the Muslim world. The culture that emerged after the death of Muhammad became known as Islam. At various points in history, there were groups of people who adopted Islam as a religion possibly for reasons of faith or to cement political allegiances. Their descendants are now known as Muslims. Muslims also add to their numbers by conversions where people outside this inherited culture come to adopt Islam as their religion in the form of a cultural adoption.

The Muslims of today are divided into a few sects and the majority of Muslims belong to the sect known as the *Ahlus-Sunnah wal Jamaah* (informally known as the 'Sunnis'), a group of people who believe themselves the followers of the Prophet's Sunnah (lit. *well- trodden path*) or lifestyle. The Sunnis make up approximately 90% of the Muslims in the world. Therefore, when one studies Islamic culture, it is most likely that one is observing Sunni culture that has taken root globally. Similarly, when one studies introductory materials to Islam, it is also most likely that one is reading materials to the Sunni version of Islam. In this essay, we equate Sunnism with Islamic culture due to this aforementioned reason. When we say Muslims, we mean 'Muslims of a Sunni enculturation'.

C. The Traditional Education of Islam and The Case Study

The Muslims have a well-established culture of traditional education. All over the world, where Muslims live in communities, it is very likely that they would have established *madrassahs* or schools that conduct a basic education of Islam. These schools are usually run by personnel trained in traditional Islamic tenets and are meant to protect and perpetuate traditional Islam. Muslim-majority nations also institutionalise traditional Islamic education as part of their syllabus.

For the main case study of this essay, we chose Malaysia's formal Islamic education system conducted by its government. Malaysia has a population of 24 million people, approximately 60% of which are Malays who are by constitutional definition Sunni Muslims. All Muslims are required to take the subject of Islamic studies in government schools. From the ages of 7 through 17, every Muslim child would study various aspects of Islam for 180 minutes 5 days a week during the school terms. Muslim children also have the option of going to Islamic schools where the focus of education is almost exclusively Islamic studies. This formalised structure of education offers us tangibility of facts that is useful to discern whether or not Islamic education offers what the Quran considers to be Islamic education.

Through the official government website, www.japim.edu.my, we can see the official syllabi for the various levels of Islamic study. The overall philosophy of Islamic education, as stated by http://www.japim.edu.my/bkpim/falsafah.htm is as follows :

Islamic Education is an on-going effort to deliver knowledge, skills and appreciation of Islam based on the Quran and the sunnah to shape attitudes, skills, personality and world-view as servants of Allah who are responsible for the establishment of self, society, environment and country towards achieving benefit in this world and eternal peace in the hereafter.

This goal, as we will see in a later section of this essay, broadly fits with the goals envisioned in the Quran itself and seem to be concordant with the people produced during the Islamic Golden Age. In other words, the end as defined above broadly coheres with the worldly end envisioned in the Quran. What we need to compare now would be the means by which this end can be achieved.

We analyse the levels of KBSR (Integrated Curriculum for Primary Schools), KBSM (Integrated Curriculum for Secondary Schools) level and the level of PQS (Education of The Quran and Sunnah). The first two levels are normally taken while the third is taken as religious stream and taught in religious schools.

A analysis of the contents of the objectives of the three levels of Islamic education found in this web website, we can observe the following traits:

a. In the KBSR and KBSM levels, the study of the Quran as a text is far from total. Rather 'selected verses' are studied. Commendably, in the PQS level, the Quran is studied totally.

b. No comparative studies are mentioned. Rather the content of Islamic studies are studied in itself. We do not find that representatives of other faiths are being invited to these classes to explain their faith.

c. The concept of 'bangsa', translated as 'race' (as 'negara' is already translated as 'nation' or 'country'), is also given consideration. The teaching of Islam is interspersed with the dispensation of elements of racial heritage, in this case of the Malays. This further ossifies intellectual impetus.

d. No feedback is expected from the students. They are meant to master what is taught, not to offer any kind of criticism towards what is being taught. On the contrary, in Sunnism, it would even be tantamount to blasphemy to challenge what is being taught. Since Muslims in

Malaysia are not allowed to leave Islam, the 'no feedback' position helps to ensure that students do not express doubt towards being taught.

Before we continue, it also worthwhile to note the opinion of Muslim scholars towards philosophy. We have chosen philosophy in particular because philosophy is the field concerned with the nature of the human condition and as such, will require the full range of modalities of human thought. A good compilation of these opinions may be found on the url: http://www.islam-qa.com/index.php?ref=88184&ln=eng&txt=philosophy

The opinions compiled on this page can be described as hostile, making it forbidden to study philosophy and deplorable to admit its exponents as Muslims. Thus we can discern that scholars of traditional Islam have voiced negative responses towards the study of philosophy. Subsequent sections will help determine if this negative response is concordant with the Quran.

D. Our Methodology of Reading the Quran

We now use the Quran to measure Muslim thought. However, it is not enough to simply state the Quran as the yardstick without mentioning the methodology with which we read it. This essay employs principles of reading the Quran that are mentioned in the Quran itself, thereby fulfilling the intents of the author of the text. Those principles are as follows:

1.. In this essay, the Quran is being read as it declares itself, in the clear Arabic language (chapter 16, verse 103). This is in contrast with Sunnism's linguistic misappropriation of Quranic terms (misappropriation because it does not fit with the intent of the author of the Quran) which propose 'religious meanings' for Quranic terms. An example would be zakaat which has a religious meaning (ma'na fiqhi) that is 'religious tithes' but if one reads from the Quran, one would find that the word zakaat is means betterment or growth which is a straightforward linguistic meaning (ma'na lughawi) and which is contrasted with the word dassa which means to bury something, contextually, in the dust.

2.We accept in this essay, the stories of the personalities mentioned in the Quran are eternal lessons of the human endeavour (12:111). This is in contrast with notion in Sunnism that the personalities prior to Muhammad had each his own *sharia* (religious law) and their *sharia* have been rendered invalid with the coming of Muhammad.

3. Another principle that we adopted in this essay is the notion that through studying the use of any word throughout the Quran, we may thereby discern the meaning by comparing the contexts in which that word is used. This principle is attested by the Quran itself in verses (73:4-5) and is known as Tasreef al-Ayat

4. The arrangement of the Quran is also taken into account in our reading. We believe the assertion of the author that the Quran was arranged, verses by verse and chapter by chapter intentionally as stated in (75:16-19). Therefore, it is vital

to note what nestles a particular passage or verse in order to further elucidate what the said passage or verse means.

5. The last principle which we employ is the principle that the Quran is already complete in setting out the details of its teachings (6:114). This would mean that when we read any of its verses, we will not inject a meaning which is clearly not in the text nor try to restrict the meaning without justification from the text itself.

E. The Quran's Definition of an Ideal Society and The People who can bring about Such a Society

Two concepts from the Quran are vital for this study. One is the concept of *baraka* which is vital for understanding the ideal society the Quran envisions and the other is the concept of *ulil albaab* which vital for understanding the kind of person who will invoke *baraka*.

Baraka linguistically means to be 'blessed by stability, growth, rootedness and abundance'. The *ulil-albaab* are literally 'those of the core' showing that person has penetrated the outer reality of things and can perceive its utmost reality.

The Quran uses *baraka* as follows:

1. A natural understanding of '*baraka*' can be found in 41:10 in which Allah is the one who brings *baraka* to the earth. This statement is nestled by between the statement that Allah placed mountains on the earth as anchors of stability and the statement that Allah measured for the earth everything in due proportion therefore intuiting to us that *baraka* comes after stability then gives proportion to the created world. A second occurrence, this time of the word *mubarak* (something which brings *baraka*) in 50:9 tells us that the rain from the sky comes with *baraka*, as it brings about the fertilisation of gardens and harvests. The garden is used in the Quran to symbolise a state of heavenly bliss

2. In 11:48, we are told that, after the flood before which Nuh was given the inspiration to save himself and his followers in the ark, he was given the command to disembark from the ark in a state of peace and in which *baraka* is present. A cross-referencing of this passage, this time with 23:29 presents another rendition of this story in which Allah's descending of the ark with *mubarakan* is equated with God being the best one to perform the act of descending, therefore equating the quality of *mubarak* with the quality of being best.

3. In 21:71 and 37:113, we are told that Ibrahim's land after his exile was given *baraka*. Again with cross-referencing with the passage 14:35-41, we can see that Ibrahim founded God's system in a place which did not have it in place, established divine commands and was thus rewarded with fruits of this life. He was also given protection by God in this life and the next. In 3:96-97, we are told that God's system established by

120

Ibrahim was established in a state of extreme effort and difficulty but was in a state of *mubarak*.

4. The followers of Musa are said to be inheritors of the east and the west of the land in 7:137 which God has given *baraka* due to the patience and constancy. When we cross-refer this with another rendition of Musa's story, namely in chapters 26 and 10, we find that the Children of Israel inherited the treasures of the land and the critical moment came when they established the divine system in the land.

5. Isa in the Quran 19:31 claimed that he is in a state of *baraka* wherever he is before mentioning that he would be in constant connection with God and a constant bringer of growth.

6. The kingdom of Dawud and Sulaimaan who are said to be given the right judgment in matters of equality and given the right knowledge and judgment in all matters. Also subjected to Dawud are the powerful ones and the geniuses. Dawud was also taught the construction of armour for the protection against violence. For Sulaiman God subjected the unruly political winds to flow according to his command to the the land which was given *baraka*. This is found in the passage 21:78-81. From here we can see this civilisational epoch which was bestowed to Dawud and Sulaiman was to a land which was given *baraka*.

7. In 24:35, we are told that God's light is contained in a tree which is *mubarak*. Light in terms of the Quran has been used to contrast with darkness, symbolically referring to a state of loss.

8. In 24:61 we are told that we are told to give peaceful salutations in a *mubarak* manner before entering into a particular domain, that is in a manner of blessedness and a wish for growth and stability.

9. In 55:78, that we are told that there is *tabarak* (*baraka* giving) in actualising the name of God giving human beings lives of beauty and honour. So we can infer that by actualising the name of our Lord, we are bringing about the potential for this state of beauty and honour in human life.

From the readings above, we can see that *baraka* is a state which is indicative of God's' approval and blessings upon those who strive to establish his commands. The created world functions with this *baraka* resulting in the emergence of gardens, which in the Quran symbolises a state of heavenly fulfilment. The personalities of Nuh, Ibrahim, Musa, Isa, Dawud and Sulaiman, having established divine commands, were given also *baraka* in various forms. This *baraka* then resulted in a state of betterment, growth, stability and divine protection.

The Quran also mentions itself with respect to *baraka*, showing its reader that it can itself participate in this process of invoking *baraka* in human lives as we can see in the following examples:

1. The Quran mentions the event of its descent. In 97:1-5, it says that its descent comes with the descent of the spirit of inspiration and the angels, symbolising the power of God, bringing about a state of intrinsic peace. This night is called a night of *mubarak* in 44:3.

2. 6:92 tells us that the Quran's descent is with *mubarak* by confirming through its statements what is around it or in other words, acting as a constant prophecy. This is intimately connected with the preservation of the divine connection.

3. 6:155 tells us that again that the Quran's decent is with *mubarak* and following it and being mindful of God will lead to the acquirement of God's mercy. Interestingly, the preceding verse 6:154 which mentions Musa receiving the book in total which classifies everything for the human being which coincides the Quran describing this attribute for itself in 16:89.

4. 21:50 tells us that the Quran is a constant reminder which is *mubarak* and that we have no cause not to acknowledge it.

5. Finally, 38:29 tells us that the Quran is a book, of which its descent is *mubarak* and what we are to meditate on its signs as they will be a reminder for people of the core.

With 38:29, the last verse mentioned above, we connect *baraka* with the *ulil-albaab*. The *ulil-albaab* are the people who will take heed from a *mubarak* reading of the Quran. From the Quran, we find the following descriptions of the *ulil-albaab*:

1. They are those who understand that in the law of equality, whereby everything is given fair compensation, there is vivification for society (2:179)

2. They understand the nature of wisdom as a precipitator of overflowing benefit (2:269)

3. They understand the organic nature of God's system and how observations of signs in reality may give disclosures of this system (3:7)

4. They are those who study the creation/evolution of the heavens and the earth and deduce from it the need to remember God and seek His protection (3:190-191)

5. They understand the difference between what is wholesome and what is unwholesome (5:101)

6. They understand the stories of the messengers in the Quran on such a deep level that they may see them working in human society (12:111)

7. They understand the nature of truth and how from responding to it, they may attain what is good and beneficial for mankind. (13:17-19)

8. They listen to all available sayings and choose the best ones (39:18)

From this section, we can see the picture that the Quran, by using its concepts of *baraka* and *ulil albaab*, has clearly drawn and thereby expounded its notion of an ideal society and the characteristics of the people who can expect to realise it. We can understand the link to be as follows:

1. The Quran shows us examples from its stories and created phenomena about what *baraka* brings and how human beings can invoke it.

2. The Quran itself can bring a state of *mubarak* and the ones mentioned as heeding this *mubarak* reading are the *ulil-albaab*.

3. The *ulil-albaab* show characteristics that indicate they are people who study the world and what is around them. They listen and evaluate all opinions and follow what is best from that and yet, they are able to discern the deepest manifestations of the stories in the Quran in the world.

F. How the Quran Assists in Rebuilding an Intellectual Culture

From section E, we can elicit that the Quran centralises itself as a tool to understand and acquire the means to achieve the ideal society. In this section, we attempt to discover the mindset and tools that the Quran proposes for its reader in order to acquire the characteristic necessary to read the Quran in a way that can construct the ideal society.

1. The Quran does not shy away from doubt. In the passage (10:35-41), we find that the response to the suggestion that the Quran was forged by Muhammad (10:38) is to ask the claimant to bring about a discourse like the Quran itself. The Quran had already described the qualities to measure its divinity in (10:35-37) in which it says that it is guidance towards a permanent and life-giving truth, declaiming all other knowledge as conjecture and that it encompasses knowledge human beings have yet to encounter. It concludes by peacefully ending the intellectual exchange, asking the other person to work to his knowledge as the believer will work to his.

2. In the passage 25:32-33, we are told that the meaning of the Quran isn't revealed in totality. Rather, in order to invoke a wider meaning of the Quran, we must continuously bring the Quran more models of the human condition to which the Quran would offer us a more correct and meaningful model.

3. The Quran continuously enjoins its reader to seek more and more information (20:114) and (41:3) in order for its reader to see where the Quran points to and how the Quran classifies the phenomena its reader experiences.

From the above, we can infer that the Quran does not expect its reader to simply inherit the belief that it is of divine origin. Rather, it expects its reader to build an intellectual relationship with itself and acts as a tool to towards building knowledge and faith.

Conclusion

The Muslim world is currently stuck in a civilisational stagnancy. While there may be agendas to reframe the perception of the Muslim world towards a perception that generates hostility and disdain, the Muslims themselves have thus far failed to neutralise such a perception.

Further to this situation, we find that systems of traditional Islamic education to be far lacking in producing an environment in which Muslims can engage with the systems of philosophical thought existing in the world. This may due to the fact that the proponents of traditional Islamic education are largely concerned with the integrity of Muslim identity maintained by the preservation of the said education systems. Unfortunately, this also leads to traditional Islamic education being stagnant and unable to engage with modern thought systems.

On the contrary, the Quran expounds upon the concepts of *baraka* and *ulil-albaab* to respectively explain its notions of an ideal society and the people who can read it in such a way that acting upon such a reading would bring about that ideal society. The Quran then gives tools through which we may exercise our intellectual capacities to that end. We are required to deeply investigate the phenomena of our being and experiment with the various thought systems in the world. This is a diametrical opposition to the negative attitudes towards philosophy – which is in reality nothing but thought systems – which Muslim scholars have voiced.

Muslims would now need to deeply self-introspect and ask themselves if they wish to adopt the conceptual system of the Quran and act upon its program. Only by doing rejecting the negative attitudes and elements in the traditional Islamic education system that prohibit positive intellectual growth, the Quran asserts that they can reassume the role as humanity's prime movers and participate the evolution of our species.

Rules to Understand the Quran

F.K.[2]

(Dear Edip. The Quran as a guiding book has its own guidance about itself. It defines itself, and shows ways to consider reading it for best understanding. I have extracted 19 rules that one can follow. Also I would like to mention that I did not try to purposely discover 19 rules. It just happened. You may classify them differently if you want to. This is not ready for publication, but if you wish you may improve and publish it under your name.)

Rule 1: Do not abandon the Quran. Verse 25:30 is clear about that. From this verse we must conclude that the reading of The Quran is an obligation. It is *Fardh* as they say in Arabic. The Quran did not leave room for too much speculation about this rule. Verses 28:85 and 24:1 are further clarifications. Please read those verses and think about it.

Rule 2: It is easy to understand. Be sure that it is easy to understand. The divine reminder in 54:17 is repeated four times in chapter 54. It is easy. If you say it is difficult, indeed it becomes difficult. First, because you rejected God's repeated assertions about the Quran, and second, because of this prejudice you lost all the motivation and wits to understand even the simplest statements. Therefore, you must read it to understand and think about it. The Quran makes it clear that the messenger will not spoonfeed it to people. They have to figure it out on their own (38:29).

Rule 3: Best times to read it. You can read the Quran anytime that is possible for you. Read and reflect on it at nights. The best time for most benefit is early morning (17:78). When your mind is clean and ready to take in.

Rule 4: Trust it and be free of doubts on its authenticity. Trust it. It will clear out your questions and concerns (5:101). God's book is safe. No one can fabricate it and mess with it (10:37). Read it with no concern.

Rule 5: Be unbiased. Don't read it when you are biased with pre-established position. Be clean from your ego. Make sure you are not reading for your personal gains against it, or for it, or just use for manipulating others. The Quran makes it clear that it will be difficult or impossible for unclean to get in touch with it. See, 56:79. Yes, of course it is difficult to be clean from ego and hidden agendas. But, you must try your best. That is the reason why the Quran asks you to seek refuge to God whenever you read The Quran (16:98). You do not need to "say" some words, but you must think about it. Once you are neutral and have a clean heart, the Quran opens up to you. In another words, your mind opens up to the Quran.

---

[2] F.K. is a Kurdish-American (born in Iraq) monotheist with dozens of patents in computer hardware technology. He has a PhD in mathematics.

Rule 6: Listen to it whenever it is recited (7:204). You don't have to think about it and study it only when you yourself reading it. Sometimes when others read it, your mind will be free and can comprehend it much better.

Rule 7: Good reading, good habit of reading is necessary. Make sure you pay attention to it. Many people read books while their minds are not even there. Their lips move and sounds come out. Engage the verses with each other to close the gap in your understanding. Organize the verses well (73:4). Remember, the Quran is not organized in its chronological chain. This shows the flexibility for organizing in various studies as you see in this research. This leads you to be mentally active, not a passive follower of a good story.

Rule 8: Make sure do not mix cultural practices with the Quran (5:104). We learn things through culture and we think it is part of the Quran. Be careful not to reject the Quran because of the differences you see in norms.

Rule 9: It does not make your life miserable. Remember this Quran did not come to you to make your life miserable (20:2). It should drive you toward easy and happy life (87:8). The Quran leads you to be in peace with your intellect and nature. So if you find implementing certain verses makes your life miserable be sure that you do not have an understanding of its meaning. Stop there and re-read that verse and study it again according to all the rules until it clears out. The Quran is supposed to make your life good here and hereafter. This is a good rule to follow to understand the Quran.

Rule 10: Do not chop it. Do not chop or cut the verses. It is not fair to cut a verse and then use it for ill intentions. This is a bad manner and is not acceptable in any norm. You can't take a half sentence from one and use it against him/her (15:89-91). Make sure no one misleads and manipulate you and others through this common abuse of the Quran.

Rule 11: It is a complete universe. The Quran is detailed and its verses are packed together in a very intelligent way. As the planets and the stars are having effect on each other, the verses are the same. You can't understand a verse in isolation from rest of the book. Do not rush to reach conclusions until you see the entire the Quran (20:114) (Why verse number 114? Amazing☺). Once you see all the Quran and related verses to the subject verse, you will understand it better.

Rule 12: No contradiction in the Quran (4:82). This rule is very useful to give the reader a tool to clarify his understanding. Once you find a verse contradicts another one, you must stop at once with no conclusion. Back up and try to question every word, every verse until you reach a consistent understanding. God will not contradict himself. Many Muslim scholars made mistakes by ignoring this rule. For instance the verse 2:62 and 3:19 may look contradictory to each other on the surface. This caused great misunderstanding among Muslims. But, a careful debugging and verification of the word Islam will show that there is no contradiction. Once you clear that you understand the Quran better. It is great rule for verification and in depth understanding.

Rule 13: God teaches the Quran (55:2). Once you find yourself having difficulties understanding the true meaning of verse of a word, go through the entire Quran searching for that word and its uses in various forms in various verses. You will start getting clearer understanding slowly. God repeats some phrases and words for many reasons. One of the reasons is to teach us the true meanings. There are other ways but you must experience it on your own.

Rule 14: Use resources, including the Torah and Injeel (3:2, 4:36, 5:69, 4:135, 5:67). It is useful sometimes to look at these sources to understand better. But, be cautious. Also use specialists by asking them. Do searches through media.

Rule 15: The Quran is not a magic book. It is important to understand the Quran as a guiding book and not a machine to change people. God has given us the freedom of choice and He will not force people and does not allow any one use force (17:41; 2:256).

Rule 16: There are fixed verses and there are allegorical and multi-meaning ones (3:7). Make sure you pay special attention to those allegorical or multi-meaning verses. People can manipulate them. They require special reading and knowledge to follow them. If you can't, don't worry. They have their meanings planted in other verses. You will not miss their benefits.

Rule 17: Do not reject because you do not understand. Many people reject some verses of the Quran or any book if they do not understand them. Many years ago, if one said hands and legs will witness against people it would have been rejected (24:23). These days we know we can use lie detectors by monitoring skin, hand, face and so on. This knowledge is new. Imagine what we could do in a 1000 years from now. So do not reject things you do not understand. Ignorance does not prove nor disprove anything (10:39).

Rule 18: Group Study. Group study is a proven method to help understand, discover, and come to better understanding. When organizations want to find new fresh ideas and better understanding of issues, they perform brain-storming, which is done in group meetings. The Quran advices us to use group study whenever we reach a point were we can not understand it. See 34: 44-45. I think this method is useful even if you have an understanding so you find out if you make any sense

Rule 19: The Quran is a unique and interesting book, filled with prophecies and signs. If you do not follow the crowds, your peers or your ancestors blindly and if you search for truth continuously as it is instructed by the Quran (17:36), God will show His signs in your person and in the horizons (41:53). If you belong to the group that appreciate the Quran's prophetic sign (74:31) and became one of those who are described "progressive" (74.37), you are in minority. Against ignorant and arrogant people, be patient, and follow verse 39:18.

Muslim Identity Politics:
Contestation, Confusion and Certitude[1]

Eman M. Ahmed

Building on the Greek root of the word heresy--meaning to choose-- sociologist Peter Berger introduced the concept of the 'heretical imperative'(1979). According to Berger, the process of consciously choosing any set of values— even if they are orthodox values—is an act of heresy. Berger explains that modernity with its ethos of aggressive pluralism is an onslaught of choices (including between and among faiths), and hence heresy (choosing) becomes imperative. However, I argue that the forces of modernity, combined with other factors, have led to the rise of a monolithic and puritan religious ideology which is suppressing the diverse cultural expressions of Islam, and thus constricting an individual's ability to be heretical, to choose. This gradual erosion of the diversity within Islam has had an impact on Muslims identity politics and has led to a narrowing of the Muslim sense of self.

After a brief explanation of the key terms, this paper proceeds to examine the larger geo-political and socio-psychological contexts in which Canadian Muslim identity is being constructed. In doing so, one has taken into consideration the mounting global religious resurgence generally, and specifically within Islam,

---

[1]	The current article is based on research conducted for and published by the Canadian Council of Muslim Women, under the title *A Multitude of Solitudes: Canadian Muslim Women and Rising Religiosity*. The paper studies the presence of puritan Islam among Canadian Muslim women and the nature of rising religiosity among Muslim communities. It also explores issues of identity and engagement with the larger Canadian society. Both these foci are also contextualized within a global and rising Muslim religiosity and its impact on Canadian Muslims and thus, third, it indicates some areas of reflection requiring consideration of all Canadians irrespective of religious allegiance. Secondary and primary sources were used during the research phase, including 10 individual interviews with Canadian Muslim women. Although in the current article I do refer to some of the interviewees, due to space no biographical details have been provided. For more details see Ahmed, E. *A Multitude of Solitudes: Canadian Muslim Women and Rising Religiosity* in Muslim Women at the Crossroads: From Integration to Segregation?, CCMW, 2007.

and the increasing acceptance of puritan views. The impact, as illustrated through the example of language and clothing, has been a steady erosion of the socio-cultural diversity inherent within the religion. This in turn has led to a narrowing of religious identity at multiple levels.

Since the majority of Muslims in Canada are immigrants, one has also explored specific aspects of the evolution of Islam in Diaspora. It is suggested that, coupled with the pressures of (anti)globalization, the dynamics of Diaspora communities is leading to a homogenization and an essentialization of Muslims and Islam. Other contributing factors which have been discussed include the perceived threat to traditional values and the confusion within and without Islam about what defines a Muslim.

Key Terms

This paper employs the terms *puritan* and *moderate* as defined by the Islamic jurist Khaled Abou El Fadl (2005). In this framework, the hallmark of puritan thinking is not fanaticism or extremism but "the absolutist and uncompromising nature of its beliefs. ...it is intolerant of competing points of view and considers pluralist realties to be a form of contamination of the unadulterated truth" (El Fadl 2005:18). The puritan's vision is exclusive since those who do not fit their defined mould of Islam, are considered non-Muslims, deviant and heretics. In contrast, the moderate understanding of religion is inclusive and is based on the recognition of a hermeneutic relationship between the reader and the text, thereby allowing for a diversity of voices/interpretations. One can therefore argue that choice/heresy is integral to the moderate vision.

Another defining characteristic of the puritan orientation is its emphasis on The Text(s) (the Quran and *Hadith*) and its immutable nature. For the puritans, the text is a how-to manual that regulates every aspect of their life, and their ultimate objective is to (re)create a society founded 1400 years ago. Puritans enforce laws derived from The Text(s) without taking into consideration the larger socio-political and historical context of each revelation, and without accounting for the cultural and personal—including gender—subjectivities and biases of the interpreter/translator/reader.[2] By comparison, for the moderates, the Quran and *Hadith* were in response to particular historic circumstances and provide general guidelines rather than specific instructions or laws. The underlying aim of the original Texts is to establish a just and benevolent society, and this for moderates is the crux of the matter (El Fadl 2005:156).

---

[2] Although El Fadl does not discuss this, one can note that questions regarding the relative nature of modern knowledge and the bias(es) inherent to human subjectivity, including interpretation, are by now established facts in numerous disciplines such as anthropology, psychology, history, feminism, linguistics and literature, to name a few. For example, see *Umberto Eco*, (1995). *The Role of the Reader. Explorations in the Semiotics of Texts Bloomington*, Indiana University Press.

Thus, the issue is not simply, for example, that a purist is one who believes that Islam forbids abortion or that polygamy is a right for any Muslim man who can afford it. It is their attitudinal and ideological orientation, which is a text-centred normative particularism that leads them to otherize Muslim and non-Muslim alike

El Fadl and other specialists (Keppel 2004) also document how, from the 1980s onwards, Wahabism[3] and similar interpretive religious ideologies have had great influence on contemporary puritan theology and Islam.

The Problematics: Puritan or Moderate?

Within in this paradigm then, the moderates can be considered the heretics and the puritans the orthodoxy. However, we must acknowledge that at times the stand-point of some moderates can be equally rigid and monolithic as that of the puritans. For example, on the issue of veiling there are moderate Muslims and non-Muslims alike who see it as a sign of repression and are firmly against the practice. If the puritans deny women the *right not* to wear the veil, some moderates deny them the *right to* wear it. This denial of choice by the puritans and moderates makes them mirror images of each other and equally rigid.

Moreover, much like the larger concept of Islam/Muslims, the puritan and moderates are not homogenous and there is a blurring of boundaries within the terms. In the face of the potentially infinite variations in humanity, such blurring is perhaps inevitable. The problematics of the terms puritan/moderate are in a way similar to the use of the term 'fundamentalism'. As Karen Armstrong has correctly pointed out it is basically propagandist and misleading. On the other hand, one can also concur with her observation that "the term is not perfect, but it is a useful label for movements that, despite their differences, bear a strong family resemblance." (Armstrong, 2001: xii-xiii) Therefore, and also given the limited scope of this paper, the terms puritan/moderate have been used since they provide a useful touchstone to larger questions addressed in this article.

RISING RELIGIOSITY & NARROWING OF MUSLIM IDENTITY

This section contextualizes current Muslim identiy politics within a rising global religiousity, and specifically examines this trend and its influence within Islam.

---

[3]   Wahabism is "a Muslim puritan movement founded in the 18th century by Muhammad ibn 'Abd al-Wahhab. Members call themselves al-Muwahhidun, a name derived from their emphasis on the absolute oneness of God. They reject all acts implying polytheism, including the veneration of saints, and advocate a return to the original teachings of Islam as found in the Qu'ran and the Hadith. They supported the establishment of a Muslim state based on Islamic canon law. Adopted by the ruling Saudi family in 1744, the movement controlled all of Nejd by the end of the 18th century. It was assured of dominance on the Arabian Peninsula with the creation of the kingdom of Saudi Arabia in 1932, and in the 20th century — supported by Saudi wealth — it engaged in widespread missionary work throughout the Islamic world." (Britannica Concise Encyclopedia, 15/09/07).

In doing so, larger geo-political factors have been taken into account, such as cold-war politics and the Saudi Islamization project, and their impact on Muslim identity politics has been examined.

Global Religious Resurgence

Today, the reality of religion cannot be ignored, particularly its more strident and assertive expressions. In her book, *The Battle for God*, Karen Armstrong (2001) studies religious resurgence in Judaism, Christianity and Islam and concludes that it is equally and strongly present in all three. Similarly, by now there is a massive amount of research documenting this assertive resurgence in other major traditions.[4]

Many scholars, in the global North and South, have linked this rise of assertive religion to the forces of modernity[5], and to the rapid changes in socio-political-economic-cultural-religious structures that accompanied it. As Armstrong points out:

> "Western civilization has changed the world. Nothing – including religion – can ever be the same. All over the globe, people have been struggling with these new conditions and have been forced to reassess their religious traditions, which were designed for an entirely different type of society. All over the world, people are finding ... the old forms of faith no longer work for them ... as a result men and women are trying to find out new ways of being religious ... attempting to build insights into the past" (Armstrong 2001: xiv)

To understand this resurgence within Islam and its impact, we must be aware of these broader contexts including its particular historical links with global geo-politics.

Islamic Resurgence: the Rise of Wahabi Islam

While it is beyond the scope of this paper to go in to the detail of the broader global geo-political history and events, as well as their economic contexts, nevertheless, some basic coverage is critical to understanding current Muslim identity politics. These issues include for example, how superpower rivalries between the (defunct) Soviet Union and USA, turned societies such as Afghanistan and Pakistan into proxy battlegrounds based on strong religious subtexts. The 1970s and 1980s witnessed enormous financial support from the

---

[4]   For example, see Butler, J. S. (2006). Born Again: The Christian Right Globalized. Pluto Press; Almond, Gabriel; Appleby, Scott R; and Sivan, Emmanuel;(2002). Strong Religion: The Rise of Fundamentalisms around the World (The Fundamentalism Project); University of Chicago Press.

[5]   Some key features of modernity are economic production, urbanization, centralized bureaucratic states, the privileging of science and rationality over religious faith and a belief in progress based on science and technology. In the last century, it also includes women's rights and feminism.

West and the Saudis to Muslims during this conflict. These are well researched and acknowledged issues which in turn have larger links to the politics of oil in the Middle East and its significance in the global, especially Western, economies.

It is also around the same time that the Saudi Arabian monarchy, awash with oil money, started its global Islamization process. In an effort to appease religious conservatives and the *ulema* at home, and to counter the possible political impact of the Iranian revolution on its own legitimacy, the house of Saud gave Saudi Wahabi clerics increasing influence within the kingdom, and financially supported and authorized them to spread their hard-line brand of Islam abroad. The influence of Wahabi Islam backed by massive money at every level, including institutional, is well documented. Its impact is evident in almost every Muslim country and also extends to Europe and North America—including Canada.[6] Influential international Muslim organizations active in the West, such as the Muslim Student Associations (Dowd-Gailey 2004) on university campuses, Islamic Circle of North America (ICNA), and the Muslim World League, have been labelled by some as a Saudi 'apparatus'. (Middle East Media Research Institute 2002).

There is a high probability that if individuals have been influenced by such organizations, their views will be more puritan than moderate in nature. However, since the Islamization process has been steady and relentless for more than three decades, exposure to the Wahabi strain of Islam is no longer to be had only through mosques and religious centres. Rather, it has been deeply internalized by many across the global spectrum of Muslims. Given its strong bonds with financial support, particularly in the initial decades, the Saudi Islamization process can be summed up as a highly successful marketing campaign for one particular brand (among myriad) of Islam. So successful in fact, that many no longer see Wahabism as just another 'brand' but the *only* one. Wittingly or unwittingly, it has become the generic equivalent to a brand name and as a result, all other visions/choices/heresies have been weakened/delegitimized/overwhelmed.

i. The Impact: Cultural Displacement and Replacement

The history of Islam provides strong, one could even say self evident proof that the religion is deeply and inextricably linked to culture and as such, has historically had multiple expressions. If this were not the case, it could not have given rise to many great civilizations such as the Mughals (India) the Arab rule in Spain, the Ottomans (Turkey), the Persians (Iran), the Moorish (North Africa), to name just a few. All these civilizations were unique in terms of their cultural

---

6   See Middle East Media Research Institute, (2002). Saudi Government Paper: 'Billions Spent by Saudi Royal Family to Spread Islam to Every Corner of the Earth', http://www.memri.org/bin/opener.cgi?Page=archives&ID=SP36002, Accessed on 07/07/07.

expression—language, dress, architecture, cuisine, music etc.—yet they were all also distinctly Islamic. As Edward Said points out, strictly speaking there are numerous Islams and it is dangerous to simplify and reduce them to a monolithic idea (Said 2002).

Nevertheless, within less than 50 years, the ascendance of the puritan vision of Saudi-Wahabi Islam has been accomplished, at the expense of a parallel weakening and undermining of local cultures as well as of the legal, socio-political, and linguistic diversity inherent to what are actually numerous Islams.

The impact is visible in the seemingly innocuous but vital domain of culture which is inextricably (in)directly linked to identity construction.

a. Language and Identity

The attempted universalizing of bedouin Arab culture as the one true Islam is (in)visibly present at many levels. Consider the case of language which has strong bonds with culture and consciousness. For example, there is an increasingly popular trend among South Asian Muslims to use the farewell greeting "Allah Hafiz" as opposed to the long established custom of "Khuda Hafiz". 'Allah Hafiz' means may God be with you, 'Allah' being the Arabic word for God.[7] 'Khuda Hafiz' also means may God be with you, with 'Khuda' being the Persian word for God. Till the 1980s 'Khuda Hafiz' used to be the centuries old, standard, normative farewell greeting in South Asia. Today, it is a rarity, not only in Pakistan but among South Asian Muslims in Canada. Many individuals can recount anecdotes of being scolded by relatives for saying 'Khuda Hafiz': "Don't you know that is not how you refer to God? That is not one of His names".

While this may seem a minor matter of semantics, it can be considered symptomatic of an (en)forced alienation from one's cultural-linguistic heritage, which in the case of South Asian Muslims has appropriately been called Indo-Persian Islam. Pakistani academic Suroosh Irfani refers to this as the "Arabist shift" (Irfani 2004) which emerged in the 1980s, along with a tendency to "view the present in terms of an imagined Arab past with the Arab as the only 'real/pure' Muslim, and then using this trope of purity for exorcizing an 'unIslamic' present." (Irfani 2004) The result of the Arabist shift, Irfani points out, was that Pakistani's:

> "… lost the eclecticism and intellectuality that were the basis of a creative South Asian Muslim identity, and this has led to a hardening in the understanding of Islam as a result of imagining Pakistanis in Arabist terms" (Irfani 2004: 148).

---

[7]   Arab Christians and Arab Jews also regularly use the word Allah when speaking about God in Arabic, whether in prayer or in conversation.

Among the women I interviewed, one of the younger ones provides an example of the confusion unleashed regarding a situation of cultural displacement/replacement and variation: "I realized I had my own misconceptions since the Islam I practiced was a (names 'X' country) version of Islam … and (this) version mixes culture and religion …". In her description of her journey towards an Islam not influenced by culture, there is the assumption that the Islam she has adopted (i.e. a Saudi-Wahabi Islam) is somehow free of Arab/Bedouin cultural influences, and therefore 'pure'. Even if one argues that she did not subscribe to Wahabism, and in deed many of her views were not reflective of Wahabi ideology, she nevertheless remains implicitly convinced that religion *per se* can exist in a vacuum and have nothing to do with culture. This is only possible when there is an exclusive reliance on dogma based on/in the Text(s).

b. Clothing and Identity

In many parts of the world, clothing remains deeply linked with identity. The narrowing of Muslim cultural and religious identity is also evident in countries where traditionally veiling was prevalent but in a myriad forms. In her article titled "Veil-s" Marieme Hélie-Lucas observes the eroding of culturally specific religious expression and asks:

> "Where are the veils—and the non-veils—of my childhood? Where has their religious, geographical, cultural, social and political diversity gone? Into which grave of history? With what political consequences?" (Hélie-Lucas 2006)

Commenting on the variety of traditional forms of veiling that are no longer to be seen in Algeria, she refers to the white woollen veils worn by the women from Mzab which allowed only one eye to peep out, and to the colorful headscarves worn by the women of Kabylie, which were "an attractive blossom of colors elegantly perched on the head, tied in various ways, depending on villages or families—a far cry from the "Islamist nun outfit". The Islamist 'nun outfit' Helie-Lucas refers to is the particular style of hijab originating in the Gulf and Saudi Arabia, which is fast becoming the 'Islamic uniform'. Echoing similar concerns, Islamic scholar Riffat Hassan believes

> "My reading of the spread of hijab is that it is funded by Saudi Arabia. They want to impose their version of Islam, which is the Hanbali school, that is the smallest and most conservative school. What is binding in the Quran is modesty. Wearing a hijab today is a sign of submission to Saudi Arabia." (Ebrahim 2004)

In sum, the decades long campaign of promoting and privileging the Wahabi-Arabicized view has reached a point where Wahabist-Arabism is now increasingly perceived by many as 'official' Islam.[8] Consequently, when the younger generation does turn towards religion, what they are most often confronted with is an austere introverted Islam which is basically one among a myriad. Not only can this monolithic Islam, in some cases, justify alienation from ideas, values and people perceived to be 'western'; it also builds on an alienation from an individual's own rich and diverse non-Wahabi Islamic heritages/traditions, and thus leads to a narrowing of Muslim identity.

Supporting heresy is in deed one way of countering this push, thereby expanding and deepening the Muslim sense of self. It has been observed that heretics are "cross-cultural pollinators" and that their approach to religion is generally more inclusive:

> "To the extent that heretics do not draw rigid lines within and between religions, heretical consciousness can be considered hybrid, multi-leveled, ambiguous, refusing to adhere to some singular, pristine ideal of dogma. ...in its embrace of diversity it [heresy] not only doubly reinforces itself, but revivifies – even if through controversy – the traditions of which it partakes." (Ahmed 2002:18)

DYNAMICS OF DIASPORA COMMUNITIES & GLOBALIZATION

Accompanied by the dynamics Diaspora communities and the forces of globalization, Canadian Muslim identity is being further homogenized and chiselled down to a uni-dimensional one. Diaspora communities, in the process of adapting their religious views and practices to their new environment, distinguish between what is essential to the religion and what is not (Vertovec 2000). In the case of immigrant Muslims, this is done by excluding vernacular or cultural variations of religion, and restricting it to what they believe is truly Islamic, the literal word of the Quran and the Sunnah. As opposed to a community that is rooted in ethnic variation, reducing religion to the simplest common denominator no doubt attracts more members. At the same time however, the reduction of all Islams to the bare ritual basics, deprives the religion of its qualitative diversity and nuances, and is resulting in a homogenization of Muslims in Canada and elsewhere.

Again, it should be pointed out that the tendency towards religious homogenization in Diaspora communities is not peculiar to Islam.[9] When it

---

[8] "But Wahhabism did not spread in the modern Muslim world under its own banner. Even the term "Wahhabism" is considered derogatory by its adherents, since Wahhabis prefer to see themselves as the representatives of Islamic orthodoxy. To them, Wahhabism is not a school of thought within Islam, but is Islam. The fact that Wahhabism rejected a label gave it a diffuse quality, making many of its doctrines and methodologies eminently transferable."(El Fadl 2001)

[9] The homogenization of religion and religious practices, as a result of being developed away from the homeland, is not unique to Muslims and Islam. Similar dynamics are also evident in the Hindu community in Britain. See, Steven

135

comes to Islam, the question is, to what extent is the homogenization accepting of differences within a tradition and of the larger society? Rima Berns McGown's study examining the evolution of Islam among Somalis in Canada and Britain, notes that the indigenous religious traditions of the Sufi Shaykh, which were part and parcel of Somali Islam, have "given way to a sense of Islam as a vital force in understanding how to live in this new world, a force that might require more blatant identification (via, for instance, a beard or the hijab)" (Berns McGown 1999:229).[10] Ironically, while an essentialized Islam, devoid of regional variations or expressions (other than Saudi-Wahabi) may appeal to a wider ethnic cross-section of Muslims, it has simultaneously contributed to a narrowing of Muslim identity to focus almost entirely on the literal, visible and ritualistic aspects of the religion.

Globalization

The pressures and processes of globalization also contribute to the homogenization of Muslims. According to European Muslim scholar, Tariq Ramadan, the process of globalization has "erased traditional points of reference for Muslim communities while reawakening passionate affirmations of identity that often verge on withdrawal and self-exclusion" (Ramadan, 2004: 4-5). While this withdrawal is a mode of self preservation, it also leads Muslims to define themselves in opposition to the West and to establish barriers and boundaries of 'us' and 'them'. By doing so they are 'otherizing' not only "Westerners" but potentially also hereticizing other Muslims who do not espouse a puritan view of Islam.

The 'Us (Muslims) vs. Them (Canadians/westerners)' divide is also very much present, thanks to modern technology. Muslim youth are very aware of Muslims and Muslim movements in places as diverse as Afghanistan, Iraq, Palestine, Sudan, Lebanon, Chechnya, Kashmir, etc. These youth constitute a widespread virtual community, a transnational 'Us', and react in a variety of ways including withdrawal, or becoming more vocal and publicly observant as a backlash and as a form of political protest.[11]

Vertovec, Religion and Diaspora , paper presented at the conference on 'New Landscapes of Religion in the West', School of Geography and the Environment, University of Oxford, September 2000, p27-29

[10] Similarly Camilla's Gibb studied Muslim immigrants in Canada from the Ethiopian city of Harar and notes how the vernacular Islam of syncretic saints and cults has been adapted by the immigrant community thereby resulting in "a homogenization or essentialization of Islamic practices, where culturally specific aspects of Islam that are not shared with other Muslim populations are likely to disappear, since they are not reinforced by Muslims from other groups in this context", (Gibb 1998:260)

[11] If Muslims can be said to suffer from the 'Us vs. Them' syndrome, so it seems are many Canadians. Increasingly, there are examples of hate crimes committed against Muslims (CTV 2006)[42], or those believed to be Muslims. Other indirect manifestations are apparent in the coverage of Muslim issues by the media. For

In short, the dynamics of Diaspora communities and the forces of (anti) globalization also lead to an essentialization of Muslims, otherizing/hereticizing Non-Muslims/Muslims and feed into the Us vs Them syndrome. To the extent that a key dimension of the Muslim identity crisis has to do with what Islam does (or does not) 'mean', the struggle is primarily within Islam: within different visions/interpretations and communities, and ultimately within the Muslim psyche, hence the title of Kepel's book *The War for Muslim Minds.* The Us vs. Them syndrome is thus equally present today *within* Islam, as it is between Muslims and non-Muslims.

THREATENED VALUES: FEAR & CONFUSION, AUTHENTICITY & CERTITUDE

As pointed out earlier, due to the forces of modernity and rapid social change further accelerated by globalization, vast numbers of individuals are questioning existing notions of identity, spirituality and religion. One Muslim woman I interviewed explained, "Muslims are now scared, they are scared of losing their children to the West, of losing their values, of not being Muslims." Aspects of Western societies—which have also been criticized extensively by western public intellectuals—such as the culture of consumerism, excessively permissive attitude towards sex, violence in the media, rising divorce rates etc., are seen as a threat to values that many Muslim immigrants have brought with them. For many, puritan readings of religion reinforce values and customs prevalent in their home country and this provides a sense of continuity and an anchor in a rapidly changing world.

Overall what prevails is an atmosphere of confusion and fear, which is further fuelled by socio-cultural displacement(s) linked to immigration. Immigrants are often forced to deal with new family structures (extended vs. nuclear), gender roles, societal values and economic pressures. Migration challenges their identity—not only as Muslims, but as parents and as individuals. Not surprisingly then, the importance given to the family and traditional family values by those supporting puritan readings, strikes a responsive chord with immigrant Muslims. This apprehension regarding eroding family values, has led to a turning to authorities and institutions outside the family in order to persuade the younger generation.

Thus what may have begun as a journey of cultural displacement (immigration) expressed through issues of language and clothing, is simultaneously filtered

---

instance, during the summer of 2006 when the "Toronto 17" were arrested, the two most popular terms used to describe them were "home grown terrorists" and "Canadian born Muslims". The term 'home grown terrorists' already convicts them in the eyes of the public before any trial. And the implications of the phrase "Canadian born Muslim", as journalist Robert Fisk points out, are: " there are now two types of Canadian citizen: The Canadian-born variety (Muslims) and Canadians (the rest)" (Fisk 2006). In short, if some Muslims are defining themselves in terms of "Us vs. Them", so is the larger society and thus a self reflexive, mutually reinforcing vicious cycle has been put in motion.

through historical events, global media and the larger society, and can lead to the mosques/religious centers which are perceived as a sanctuaries and citadels of Islams. However instead of being sanctuaries for diverse religious values, more often than not, many of these centers/mosques (may) have been influenced by Saudi-Wahabi puritan Islam.

Authenticity and Certitude

Unlike in Muslim majority countries, in Canada the Muslim immigrant's religious identity is not endorsed, validated nor shared by the larger society. According to one survey, 80% of non-Muslim Canadians believe that Muslims are discriminated against (CCMW 2004). As such, Muslim's feel the pressure to either conform to what they see as different values, lifestyles etc, and/or see themselves as besieged and victimized because of their faith. As observed by Francis Fukuyama:

> "the question of authenticity arises in a way that it never did in the traditional society, since there is now a gap between one's inner identity as a Muslim and one's behaviour vis-à-vis the surrounding society. This explains the constant questioning of Imams on Islamic websites about what is haram (prohibited) or halal (permitted)" (Fukuyama 2007).

Fukuyama goes on to explain that this identity crisis is not so severe for first generation immigrants since they remain more connected to their home country. It becomes more severe with second and third generation immigrants, however, as they grow up more detached and alienated from their parental culture and neither are they a part of nor fully accepted by the mainstream. Moreover, in the current environment where Muslims and non-Muslims alike are struggling with competing definitions of what exactly is Islam and what precisely does it mean to be a Muslim, puritan Muslim discourse, shorn of complexities, offers a certain security and ideological certitude.

A Muslim woman I spoke to observed: 'Muslims are so confused and there are so many differences among us, we send mixed message to the mainstream community…" She sees the naturally occurring, culturally rooted differences among Muslims to be a sign of 'their' confusion about Islam. Her solution was for all to adhere to one Islam. The either-or, basically exclusionary/exclusivist view of Islam put forth by puritans is attractive as it provides many Muslims with clear-cut, easy answers and allows them to block the confusing cacophony of identity discourses and competing interpretations with which they are bombarded with on a daily basis.

As such, both puritans and moderates represent different coping mechanisms vis-à-vis what Armstrong claims is a 'global response to modern culture'. Within this larger context(s), it must be reiterated that Muslims are not the exception. In resonance with their counterparts in other religions, puritan Muslims try to deal with fear and confusion by a selective retrieval of the past which affords them a sense of authenticity and certitude. Viewed in this light, if heresy is seen as opposition to a predominant ideology, then ironically in resisting modernity and its aggressive pluralism, the puritan too is a heretic.

To conclude, Muslim identity construction/politics is a complex multi layered canvas. To understand its dynamics within Canadian Muslims, one needs to take into account larger global geopolitical issues and socio-psychological forces. These include a crisis within the ideas about modernity, the rise of Wahabi Islam and issues of cultural erosion, displacement and replacement. As has been illustrated, the result of this cultural erosion has been a narrowing of the Muslim identity. Other factors which contribute to the essentialization of Muslims/Islams include transnational identity construction, the pressures of globalization and the perceived threat to values. Furthermore, the confusion within Islam and the need for religious authenticity and certitude has also led many to adopt an exclusive vision. I may have not dwelt specifically on the impact of 9/11 and its aftermath on Muslims, since there is an abundance of literature on the issue, its significance in relation to current Muslim identity politics cannot be overlooked.

Although we have been talking about heresy mostly in theoretical terms, there are countries where allegations of heresy can have serious practical repercussions. In Pakistan for instance, members of the Ahmadiya community-- which has been around for 150 years—have been constitutionally declared non-Muslim, and are faced with steady state sponsored persecution. Like all heretics, the Ahmadis do not see themselves as functioning outside the fold of Islam. However, according to the laws of the country they can be imprisoned and fined for 'posing' to be Muslims or referring to their place of worship as a mosque, and many face the death penalty for blasphemy. This is a vivid example of what can happen when a single vision is privileged above all others. One way of fighting back is to encourage a multitude of religious readings and create a situation where heresies become the norm, and no single religious ideology is viewed/empowered to be the only true Islam.

POSTSCRIPT: AN INVITATION TO HERESY

As discussed, some Muslims are attracted to Puritan Islam due to the clear-cut, either-or, easy answers it provides. While the seduction of certainty/simplification is understandable, it can also be viewed as a form of intellectual inertia. Being confronted with options requires us to (re)evaluate and critically think through our choices. Furthermore, it also means that individuals have to do their own research and investigation to determine which competing view(s)/choice(s) is appropriate for them. Given the emphasis Islam places on critical independent inquiry and reasoning, it can be considered the religious duty of all Muslims to encourage the diversity of religious views and thus heresy. Heresies are often the result of a re-evaluation of religious dogma. And as one young interviewee observed this re-evaluation is a "Farz':

> "To think that in order to be the best Muslim we have to literally follow the rules and regulations devised 1400 years ago is reckless. It is also a

form of injustice to ourselves since we also have to do the work. The scholars of the past did their work and they did it according to their context and the best of their abilities. Now we have to do the work for ourselves, it is a Farz."

When it comes to non-Muslims, discriminatory or not, there is overall a 'hands off' attitude regarding the tensions between Muslim moderates and puritans. However, this seeming neutrality is, by default, being impacted by larger forces and in its own ways, strengthens the Orthodoxy.

The issue here is not so much about a confrontation with puritanism which is ultimately a personal choice, but of its assertive (if not aggressive) promotion at the expense of a shrinking religious (and cultural) diversity. In the context of an environmental crisis in which the diversity of plant and animal life is decreasing, not to mention the extinction of tribes, languages etc; few Canadian's and others living in the global North, would claim neutrality at this ultimate diminishment of life. The vast support for the environmental movement does not mean that everyone has to first be a scientist to publicly support conservation and diversity of planetary life.

Similarly, not everyone has to be Muslim or experts about Islam before deciding that moderates/heretics need their support. What is required is greater awareness of the Islamic rainbow as reflected in the cultures of origin in the Muslim immigrant community. In short there needs to be an engaged awareness and support of all Muslims but particularly the moderates/heretics. Even if the moderates were a fractional minority (and they are not), the support should be actively given as an affirmation of cultural/religious diversity.

REFERENCES:

Abou El Fadl, Khaled (2005). *The Great Theft: Wrestling Islam from the Extremists*, HarperSanFrancisco.

Abou El Fadl, Khaled (2001). *Islam and the Theology of Power*, Middle East Report http://www.merip.org/mer/mer221/221_abu_el_fadl.html 2001 Accessed on 7/7/07.

Ahmed, Durre, "Introduction: The Last Frontier" in *Gendering the Spirit: Women, Religion and the Post Colonial Response.* (ed) Ahmed, Durre. Zed Books, 2002

Armstrong, Karen (2001). *Battle For God*, Ballintine Books.

Berger, Peter L. *The Heretical Imperative.* Doubleday, 1979. New York.

Berns McGown, Rima (1999). Muslims in the Diaspora: The Somali Communities of London and Toronto, University of Toronto Press.

Britannica Concise Encyclopedia, http://www.answers.com/topic/wahhabism. Accessed on 15/09/07.

Canadian Council of Muslim Women (2004). Muslim Women in Canada Fact, Sheet http://www.ccmw.com/publications/Fact_Sheets/Fact%20Sheet%202%20e.pdf Accessed on 12/07/07.

Dowd-Gailey, Jonathan (Spring 2004). *Islamism's Campus Club: The Muslim Students' Association,* Middle East Quarterly. http://www.meforum.org/article/603. Accessed on 07/07/07

Ebrahim, Samina (December 2004). *Newsline*, Interview with Dr. Riffat Hassan,

Eco, Umberto (1995). *The Role of the Reader: Explorations in the Semiotics of Texts,* Bloomington, Indiana University Press.

Fisk, Robert (2006). *Has Racism Invaded Canada?*, CounterPunch, Accessed on 13/09/07.

Fukuyama, Francis, (2007). *Identity and Migration*, Prospect Magazine http://www.prospect-magazine.co.uk/articledetails.php?id=8239. Accessed on 16/09/07

Gibb, Camilla (1998). "Religious identification in transnational contexts: Becoming Muslim in Ethiopia and Canada", *Diaspora* 7(2): 247-69.

Hélie-Lucas, Marieme (2006). "Veil-s Challenging Fundamentalisms", http://www.whrnet.org/fundamentalisms/docs/issue-veil-0607.html. Accessed on 09/08/07.

Irfani, Suroosh; (2004), "Pakistan's Sectarian Violence: Between the "Arabist Shift" and Indo-Persian Culture" in *Religious Radicalism And Security In South Asia,* Satu P. Limaye (ed) Mohan Malik (ed) Robert G. Wirsing (ed). Asia Pacific Centre for Security Studies.

Keppel, Giles (2004). The War for Muslim Minds: Islam and the West, Harvard University Press,

Middle East Media Research Institute, (2002). *Saudi Government Paper: 'Billions Spent by Saudi Royal Family to Spread Islam to Every Corner of the Earth',* http://www.memri.org/bin/opener.cgi?Page=archives&ID=SP36002, Accessed on 07/07/07.

Ramadan, Tariq (2004). *Western Muslims and the Future of Islam* Oxford University Press,

Said, Edward (July 2002)."Impossible Histories: Why the Many Islams Cannot be Simplified," *Harper's,* July 2002.

Sperry, Paul (2002). *U.S.-Saudi oil imports fund American mosques,* http://www.worldnetdaily.com/news/article.asp?ARTICLE_ID=27327. Accessed on 2/6/07.

Vertovec, Steven, (2000). "Religion and Diaspora" paper presented at the conference on 'New Landscapes of Religion in the West', School of Geography and the Environment, University of Oxford

141

When The Military Power Is Used To Restore Freedom

El Mehdi Haddou

In this article, I will address a mistranslation of the verse (27:23) that shows Solomon, a prophet of God, as if he was violating the principle of 'No compulsion in religion' by threatening another community because of their religion (27:37).

From Quran: A Reformist Translation:

27:21   "I will punish him severely, or **I will kill him**, else he should have a clear excuse."

27:22   But the hoopoe did not stay away long, then he said, "I have seen what you do not know, and I have come to you from Sheba with news which is certain."

27:23   *"I found them ruled by a woman, and she was given all possession, and she had a great throne."*

27:24   "I found her and her people **prostrating to the sun instead of God!** The devil had made their work appear good to them, so he kept them away from the path, for they are not being guided."

27:31   "Do not be arrogant toward me and **come to me peacefully surrendering**"

27:37   "Return to them. For we shall **come to them with soldiers the like of which they have never seen,** and we will drive them out humiliated, while they are feeble."

All major translators, as far as I know, have chosen an inappropriate word to translate 'TAMLIKUHUM' (see the 5 translations below).

142

Reformist:	"I found them **ruled** by a woman, and she was given all possession, and she had a great throne."
Khalifa:	"I found a woman **ruling them**, who is blessed with everything, and possesses a tremendous palace.
Yusuf Ali:	"I found (there) a woman **ruling over them** and provided with every requisite; and she has a magnificent throne.
Pickthal.	"Lo! I found a woman **ruling over them**, and she hath been given (abundance) of all things, and hers is a mighty throne."
Shakir:	"Surely I found a woman **ruling over them**, and she has been given abundance and she has a mighty throne."

As you can see in these translations, the translators have chosen the expression *rule them* to describe ' *Tamlikuhum*' instead of 'own them' or 'possess them' which constitute the first and literal meaning of ' *Tamlikuhum*'.

The verb 'Tamlikuhum' and its derivative 'Amliku', 'Tamliku', 'Yamlikuna', 'Yamliku', 'Tamlikuna', 'Malaktum' and 'Malakat' are mentioned 44 times in Quran and in all cases their meaning is 'to own' or 'to possess'.

According to these translations and traditional commentaries, the major information that the hoopoe brought is the existence of a Queen and her people who worship the sun (27:24-25). This information made Solomon angry and decided to invade the kingdom of Sheba if its people do not submit to God (see 27:31-37). By doing so the translators created a contradiction between Solomon's reaction and God's system that recognizes

- the freedom in religion (2:256)
- the freedom to reject the truth (2:193; 10:99; 18:29)
- the promotion of peace among people (2:208).

Solomon was one of God's prophets; therefore we can not imagine him violating this fundamental commandment (freedom of worship). Besides, God did not reprimand Solomon for his attitude.

Now let us see what the hoopoe really said to Solomon in 27:23 that made him upset:

"I found a woman, **who owns/possesses them**, and she was given all possession, and she had a great throne."

As you can see, the bird brought two news:

1. There is a country where its people **are owned** by a woman, in other words, they are **slaves** of that woman (27:23).

143

2,   The inhabitants of the country of Sheba **worship the sun** (27:24).

The bird started with the most important information (which is normal because he knew that he had to show a good reason to justify his absence to avoid being killed by Solomon (27:21)) and kept the less important one at the end. Solomon knew that he was not allowed to force Sheba's people to serve God instead of the sun (2:256). He also knew that he had to rule according to God's laws by promoting truth, justice and freedom of expression (4:135; 5:8, 44; 7:29). As a true submitter (Muslim), Solomon was aware of the fact that he had to stand for liberty (6:164) and fight for the rights of those who are oppressed (4:75; 42:42) especially that he is a descendant of the children of Israel that were at one time the slaves of tyrant Pharaoh.

What really made Solomon angry is the state of slavery that affects the people owned by the Queen of Sheba and not their religion.

Solomon's reaction against slavery and oppression should be an example for every leader who has the power, the means and the potential to free slaves and fight for the rights of oppressed people even if they are living in another country.

What Solomon did in the past is what the United States should do in our time. Their resemblance is reflected in their military power but the difference resides in the fact that only Solomon had submitted to God's laws.

If Solomon was living in the 21st century, who would you think will be at the top of his black list? Yes, many of the so-called Muslim countries.

Polygamy According to Islam

Edip Yuksel

To discuss this important subject, the related verses and my comments in the **Quran: a Reformist Translation** (QRT) are presented:

The translations:

> **4:1** O people, be aware of your Lord who has created you from one person and He created from it its mate and sent forth from both many men and women; and be aware of God whom you ask about, and the relatives. God is watcher over you.*

> **4:2** And Give the orphans their money; do not replace the good with the bad, and do not consume their money to your money, for truly it is a great sin.*

> **4:3** And If you fear that you cannot be just to fatherless orphans, then marry those whom you see fit from the women, two, and three, and four. But if you fear you will not be fair then only one, or whom you already have contract with. So that you do not commit injustice and suffer hardship.*

> **4:127** They ask you for divine instruction concerning women. Say, "God instructs you regarding them, as has been recited for you in the book about the rights of orphans whose mothers you want to marry without giving them their legal rights. You shall observe the rights of powerless children, and your duty to treat orphans with equity. Whatever good you do, God has full knowledge of it.*

Commentary on The Verses

On verse 4:1:

Male and female, with little differences, share the same genetic program. The creation of the female from Adam's ribs found in Genesis 2:21-22 does not fit the Quranic description of creation. There is most likely a misunderstanding or a deliberate distortion of an original word. On the Biblical account of the creation of Eve, the commentator Matthew Henry makes a beautiful comment, which

145

might give us insight into the original meaning of the text: "This companion was taken from his side to signify that she was to be dear unto him as his own flesh. Not from his head, lest she should rule over him; nor from his feet, lest he should tyrannize over her; but from his side, to denote that species of equality which is to subsist in the marriage state."

Ironically, many misogynistic Christian scholars interpreted the Biblical account of Eve's creation to belittle and condemn women. For instance, the 19th century Scottish Presbyterian scholar Easton provides the following information on the verse: "Through the subtle temptation of the serpent she violated the commandment of God by taking of the forbidden fruit, which she gave also unto her husband (1Timothy 2:13-15; 2Corinthians 11:3). When she gave birth to her first son, she said, "I have gotten a man from the Lord" (R.V., "I have gotten a man with the help of the Lord," Genesis 4:1). Thus she welcomed Cain, as some think, as if he had been the Promised One the 'Seed of the woman.'" See 2:36; 49:13.

On verse 4:3:

Polygamy is allowed only to provide psychological, social and economic support for widows with orphans (See 4:127). Muhammad's practice of polygamy must have been in accordance with the condition to serve an important social service. Sure, physical attraction of widows might be one of the factors for marriage and there is nothing wrong with that. Those who could afford practicing polygamy, mentally and financially, should try hard to treat them equally, though 4:129 expresses the practical impossibility of attaining that ideal. Additionally, the consent of the first wife is necessary; otherwise, she can always seek divorce. It is clear that polygamy is not an ideal form of marriage and an unusual practice allowed for difficult times, such as a dramatic reduction in the male population during wartime.

The age gap between marrying men and women creates a surplus of women who will never be able to find a monogamous partner. By a strict prohibition on polygamy, millions of young women are deprived from having a legitimate relationship with men. The only hope for millions of young girls is to get married with already divorced men, perhaps with kids, or to have a relationship born out of promiscuous sexual practices. The Western world does not prohibit polygamy since many males have sexual relationships with more than one woman at the same time. The only thing that modern societies do is deprive those women from the protection of law; they are there to be used, disposed of and recycled by men!

The hypocrisy in the modern attitude becomes clear when homosexuality is defended on the pretext of "consenting adults," but the same standards are not afforded to the polygamists. The conditional permission for polygamy is for the psychological and financial protection of children and their widow mothers, in cases of war or natural disaster. Polygamy, according to the Old Testament, started with the seventh generation after Cain and continued as a common practice in the patriarchal age together with having concubines (Genesis 4:19; 6:2; 16:1-4; 22:21-24; 28:8-9; 29:23-30, etc.). However, the Old Testament also disapproves of polygamy (Deuteronomy 17:17). The Old Testament contains numerous exaggerated stories. One is about the number of Solomon's wives. The roundness of the numbers of wives and concubines and their total, the three numbers being perfectly round, indicate an intentional exaggeration. "And he had seven hundred wives, princesses, and three hundred concubines: and his wives turned away his heart" (1 Kings 11:3). It is highly plausible that the word "hundred" was inserted in the text by later scribes to damage the reputation of Solomon for some political agenda. The following verses depict Solomon as an evil person and idolater. The Quran neither accuses Solomon of indulging in a hedonistic sexual life nor of associating partners with God. Ironically, modern Christians are now bashing Solomon for not sticking to monogamy.

To be politically correct, modern Christians do not hesitate to condemn the common practice of polygamy among Jews and their prophets. Contrary to the Quran, which exhorts muslims to help widows with orphans, the misogynistic Rabbinical teachings inserted into the Old Testament put them in the category of harlots, and finds them unworthy of marriage by the privileged class: priests (Leviticus 21:14).

The expression *Ma malakat aymanukum* has been translated by most translations as "whom your right hands posses" or "captives" or "concubines." We translated this and similar expressions found in 4:3,24,25,36; 16:71; 23:6; 24:31,33,58; 30:28; 33:50,52,55; and 70:30, as "those with whom you have contractual rights." These were the wives of the enemy combatants who were persecuted because they acknowledged the message of Islam and sought asylum at the Muslim community (60:10). Since they did not get through a normal divorce process, an exceptional contract allows them to marry muslims as free women. Marrying them could create some social, economic and personal complications for the husband. They have nothing to do with *IBaD* (slaves), as sectarian translations and commentaries state. As we will learn, the Quran categorically rejects slavery and considers it to be the greatest sin (See 3:79; 4:25,92; 5:89; 8:67; 24:32-33; 58:3; 90:13; 2:286; 12:39-42; 79:24).

The practice of slavery was justified and resurrected to a certain extent via the influence of Jewish and Christian scholars, as well as fabricated hadith and sharia laws, decades after Muhammad's departure. It is ironic that Jews who suffered the most from slavery and were saved by God through the leadership of Moses (Exodus 1:13-14), later justified enslaving other people, including selling one's own daughter, and inserted that practice into their holy books (Exodus 21:7-8; 21:21-22; 26-27; Leviticus 25:44-46; Joshua 9:6-27). Though Jesus never condoned slavery, St. Paul, the founder of modern Christianity, once asked the masters to treat their slaves nicely (Colossians 3:22), and asked the slaves to be "submissive to your masters with all fear" (1 Peter 2:18; Ephesians 6:5; 1

Timothy 6:2; Colossians 3:22; Titus 2:9) justifying the Marxist maxim, "Religion is the opium of masses." The use of religion by the privileged class to enslave or exploit people is vividly depicted by Kenyatta: "When the missionaries came to Africa, they had the Bible and we had the land. They said 'let us close our eyes and pray'. When we opened them, we had the Bible, and they had the land." The word *YaMYN* means "right hand" or metaphorically "right," "power" or "control." However, its plural form *aYMaN* is consistently mentioned in the Quran to mean not "right hands" but to mean "oaths" or "promises," implying the mutual nature of the relationship (See 4:33 5:89; 9:12; 16:91- 94; 2:224-225; 30:28; 66:2; 5:53; 6:109). This unique Quranic usage is similar to the semantic difference between the singular and plural forms of the word Ayat (signs) (see 2:106).

The expression in question, thus could be translated as "those whom your oaths/contracts have rights over" or "those whom you hold rights through your contracts," or by reading *aYMaN* (oaths/contracts) as an object rather than a subject, "those who hold/possess your contracts." The marriage declaration is a mutual partnership between two sexes and is formed by participation of family members. A married woman cannot marry another man without getting divorced from her husband. However, if a woman escapes and joins muslims while her husband stayed behind participating in a war against muslims, she may marry a Muslim man without actually getting divorced from her combatant husband; she will legally be considered a divorcee (60:10). Since this contract is different from the normal marriage contract, this special relationship is described in different words. The same is valid for a man whose wife allies with the hostile enemy. See 24:31 and 33:55. Those who work for another person according to employment contracts are also referred to with the same expression. See 16:71; 30:28. Also, see 4:25,36; 23:6; 24:58; 33:50; 33:52; 70:30. The Quran does not demand those who lived together based on a mutual promise (*aYMaN*) during the days of ignorance, without a marriage contract, to get divorced. Similarly, it does not want those who married two sisters before accepting islam to be a way of life (4:23). This tolerance does not encourage living together without marriage. It only does not want to incur further damage to the family structure and does not want to create hurdles for those who wish to live according to the principles of islam.

On verse 4:127:

This verse has been commonly mistranslated to justify marrying young orphan girls rather than marrying their widow mothers. The mistranslation is so obvious, that it is curious how those who had knowledge of Arabic did not notice it. Unfortunately, this mistranslation helped the justification of marrying girls at a very young age. Though the Quran permits polygamy to men (4:3), it strictly discourages its actual practice by requiring certain significant preconditions: men may marry more than one wife only if the later ones are widows with children, and they should treat each wife equally and fairly (See

4:19-20; 127-129.) Unfortunately, verse 4:127 has been traditionally misinterpreted and mistranslated in such a way as to suggest that God permits marriage with juvenile orphans. This is clearly not the case.

The Arabic expression *yatam al-nisa illati* in 4:127 has been routinely mistranslated as "women orphans, whom..." The expression is also sometimes translated as "orphans of women whom..." This later translation, though accurate, makes the crucial reference of the objective pronoun "whom" ambiguous: Does the phrase after "whom" describe orphans or women? As it happens, the Arabic plural pronoun in this verse is the female form, *allaty* (not the male form allazyna), and it can only refer to the women just referenced, not to the orphans.

This is because the Arabic word *yatama* (orphans) is grammatically male in gender! **All the English translations of the Quran that we have seen have mistranslated this passage**. This is remarkable, because the correct translation requires only an elementary knowledge of Arabic grammar. This error is thus much more than a simple grammatical slip; it is, we would argue, willful misrepresentation.[1] The traditional interpretation of this passage offers an apparent justification for marriage with children, which flatly contradicts the Quran. Like so many passages in the Quran, 4:127's meaning was severely distorted in order to gain the favor of rich, dominant males. Over the centuries, male scholars with active libidos have used fabricated hadith to pervert the meaning of this and other Quranic verses relating to marriage and sexuality (See 66:5). For a comparative discussion on verse 4:127, see the Sample Comparisons section in the Introduction.

---

[1]   Unfortunately, like many reformists, I too did not notice the error in the translations until about a decade ago.

149

Eavesdropping on a Arizona Interfaith Youth Meeting

Dilara Hafiz

Eighteen teenagers jot down on colorful Post-It notes their one-word impressions of the eight religions listed on the poster boards in front of them. Some show no reservations as they work their way quickly down the list, while others hesitate to put down their thoughts for fear of appearing intolerant or ignorant. Is this a Bible study class? No, it's just another monthly meeting of the Arizona Interfaith Youth Movement – a safe, inclusive gathering to which youths of all faiths are encouraged to come together in dialogue, games, and of course, food!

"What if I've never heard of this religion?" asks one of the teens? "That's ok – just write down the first thing that comes to your mind," I reply. As the Youth Director, I'm pleased to see the seriousness which has settled over this group – they're sincerely giving this activity their full attention since it's partly a challenge to their general knowledge as well as an opportunity to share the 'truth' of their religious beliefs. The eight religions I randomly chose contain some familiar to all, but I've also thrown in some lesser known beliefs as well: Catholicism, Islam, Atheism, Sikhism, Christian Science, Buddhism, Judaism, and Church of Scientology. The teens stick up their impressions on the poster boards, grab a water bottle or a cookie, and then return to their seats. I survey the range of words listed by each religion and ask for a volunteer to come up and read aloud the results…somewhat surprised by the religion which has elicited the most negative comments from this diverse group…

According to the Pew Forum's 2008 U.S. Religious Landscape Survey, 83% of Americans identify themselves as belonging to an organized religion, however, "people not affiliated with any particular religion stand out for their relative youth compared with other religious traditions. Among the unaffiliated, 31% are under age 30 and 71% are under age 50. More than one-quarter of American adults (28%) have left the faith in which they were raised in favor of another religion - or no religion at all. If change in affiliation from one type of Protestantism to another is included, 44% of adults have either switched religious affiliation, moved from being unaffiliated with any religion to being affiliated with a particular faith, or dropped any connection to a specific religious tradition altogether." What accounts for this conflict within those of faith – one of the one hand, they identify themselves as being religious even if it

150

means they've left the religion of their childhood, while on the other hand, as Americans age, they seem to leave organized religion behind them?

Is this search for spiritual fulfillment a trend which begins in their youth? As a Sunday School teacher at the Scottdale Mosque for the past seven years – I've observed the diversity in faith from the Kindergarteners all the way up to the seniors in high school. Depending upon their home environment, these kids either skip cheerfully into Sunday School or drag themselves reluctantly into their seats – testing the limits of the dress code which stresses modesty by tugging their T-shirts down to cover their bare midriffs or yanking the required head-scarf into place. How much of their lessons will these teens remember when faced with the overwhelming secularism of their public school environment in which the age-old tensions of peer pressure and cliques rule the day? Religion remains a personal issue – rightly so – but is there a safe space for teens who are interested in exploring their faith beliefs? A brief glance at the teen non-fiction aisle in any Borders or Barnes & Noble reveals the abundance of faith-based books aimed at teens. From Christianity, Judaism, Buddhism – even a Wiccan guidebook – the variety is astounding! So teens are seeking answers through the privacy and safety of books, but is this education encouraging them to leave their parents' beliefs behind as they discover other traditions?

As our inter-faith meeting continues, my son volunteers to read aloud the comments posted on the board under Islam – his own faith group. "Violent, weird clothes, brain-washed…," his voice is subdued as he slowly goes through the impressions. "Tourist? Hey Mom, look, they think Muslims are tourists – that's pretty neat!" I walk over and read the note for myself – turns out he misread the word 'tourist' – the correct reading is 'terrorist'. We briefly review the major tenets of each religion in order to correct misperceptions and reduce stereotypes. Buddhism received the most positive comments by a landslide – even though only one of the kids knew a Buddhist personally. And which religion received the most negative comments? No, not Islam…it was Atheism. Turns out that even if kids switch allegiance from one faith group to another – the thought of not living a life of faith scared them most of all.

Freedom of Thought:
It's Your God-given Right

Irshad Manji

A few years ago, during a trip to Gaza, I conducted an on-camera interview with the political leader of Islamic Jihad, Dr. Mohammed al-Hindi. With his finely trimmed beard and gracious manners, he symbolized the modern — and moderate — Muslim man.

But his interpretation of the Qur'an suggested something else. "Where," I asked, "does it say that you can kill yourself for a higher cause? As far as I know, the Qur'an tells us that suicide is wrong."

Through his translator, the physician assured me that the verses endorsing suicide operations could be found "everywhere" in Islam's holy book. I challenged Dr. al-Hindi to show me just one passage.

After several minutes of reviewing the Qur'an, then calling for help on his mobile phone, then looking through companion booklets, he told me he was too busy and must go.

"Are you sure you're not pulling a fast one on me?" I asked. He smiled, clearly understanding popular American phrases. ("Pulling a fast one" means lying.) "I want to know that you're telling me the truth," I repeated.

Dr. al-Hindi summoned two assistants to the office and made another phone call. His translator shifted uncomfortably, hanging his head as my camera swung past him to film the assistants. With their backs to me, they flipped feverishly through the Qur'an. Minutes later, they presented a verse glorifying war.

But it had nothing to do with suicide. So I asked Dr. al-Hindi yet again. He responded that Islam permits defensive aggression. "If a thief comes to your door and steals your money, isn't it legitimate to protect yourself?" he said through the translator.

Still unable to draw the link between self-protection and suicide, I proposed this comparison: "If my boss steals my job and I kill myself because something that is mine has been taken away, am I a martyr?"

Horrified, the translator shook his head. "No, no, you can't ask this."

"Why not?" I wondered. "It's important, theologically, to ask these questions."

At that moment, my camera batteries died. This, the translator whispered, was a better outcome than *me* dying – which is what Dr. al-Hindi would have arranged if I stayed in his office much longer. Both the translator and I hurried out of there.

Our encounter reminded me of why it is so important for Muslims to ask questions out loud. We have relied far too long on self-appointed "higher-ups" to do the interpreting for us. We have given them the ability to abuse passages and power. We Muslims have forgotten Islam's own tradition of independent thinking: ijtihad.

This concept of creative reasoning has a history of achievement. In the early centuries of Islam, thanks to the spirit of ijtihad, 135 schools of interpretation flourished. In Muslim Spain, scholars would teach their students to abandon "expert" opinions about the Qur'an if their own conversations with the ambiguous Qur'an produced better evidence for their peaceful ideas. And Cordoba, among the most sophisticated cities in Muslim Spain, housed 70 libraries – more than the number of libraries in most cosmopolitan cities today!

From the eighth to the twelfth centuries, the "gates of ijtihad" — of discussion, debate and dissent — remained wide open. That is also when Islamic civilization led the world in ingenuity. So much of what is assumed to be Judeo-Christian culture has, in fact, been shaped by Muslims: mocha coffee, cough syrup, the guitar, even that ultra-Spanish expression, "Olé," which has its root in the Arabic word, "Allah."

At the twilight of the twelfth century, the gates of ijtihad narrowed. Scholars argue about *how* narrow they became, but there is consensus that the artistic and scientific activity that animated the Golden Age of Islam died as stubbornly as my camera batteries did at the end of the al-Hindi interview.

Allow me to be more precise. The fragile Islamic empire, stretching from the Indus River in the east to the Atlantic Ocean in the west, began to experience a series of internal convulsions. Dissident denominations were cropping up and declaring their own breakaway governments. The Baghdad-based caliph — a combination of statesman and spiritual leader — cracked down and closed ranks to secure the political unity of the empire.

To reinforce unity, within a few generations Baghdad supervised the closing of something more: the gates of independent reasoning. Islam's 135 schools of thought were deliberately reduced to five schools, all of them quite conservative. This move produced rigid readings of the Qur'an as well as a series of fatwas that scholars could no longer overturn or question, but could now merely imitate or risk being executed.

For hundreds of years since then, three equations have driven mainstream Islamic practice. The rituals vary in Islam's major sects, but these three equations apply across the board:

- First, unity equals uniformity. In order to be strong, members of the worldwide ummah must think alike.
- Second, debate equals division. Diversity of interpretation is no longer a tribute to God's majesty; it is threat to the unity that Muslims must exhibit in the face of those intent on dividing us.
- Third, division equals heresy. Soon after the gates of ijtihad narrowed, innovation came to be defined as a religious crime. It was *fitna* — that which divides. Because division is the opposite of uniformity, whatever divides must be prevented. Which means that innovation must be stopped. Which, in turn, means that the spirit of ijtihad must be suppressed.

These three equations are not merely theoretical. They have left their mark on modern Islamic history. For example, in the late nineteenth century, a gallant attempt by Egyptian feminists and intellectuals to revive ijtihad failed because of louder calls for Muslim solidarity (read: unity).

This pattern persists a century later and far from Egypt: My mother's imam in Vancouver, Canada, recently preached that I am a bigger "criminal" than Usama bin Laden because my book, *The Trouble with Islam Today*, has caused more "division" among Muslims than al-Qaeda's terrorism has. Apparently, he didn't see the irony in proclaiming that debate is worse than terrorism. Nor did he see how he damned Muslims by acknowledging that literary expression divides us more than the use of violence does.

If ever we have needed to spread the spirit of ijtihad, it is now. The good news is that the gates of ijtihad were narrowed not for spiritual or theological reasons, but for entirely political ones. This means there is no blasphemy in trying to renew Islam's tradition of independent thinking.

I can report that more and more Muslims are seeking to do exactly that. During the Danish cartoon affair, young Muslims flooded my email inbox with questions like, "Is there a way to reconcile religious belief with free expression?" Yes; the Qur'an tells us that there is "no compulsion in religion." This suggests nobody should be forced to treat Islamic norms as sacred.

Fine, many Muslims will retort, but we are talking about the Prophet Muhammad – Allah's final and therefore perfect messenger. However, Islamic tradition holds that the Prophet was a human being who made mistakes. It is precisely because he was not perfect that we know about the so-called Satanic Verses; a collection of passages that the Prophet reportedly included in the Qur'an. Only later did he realize that those verses glorified heathen idols rather than God. According to Islamic legend, he retracted the idolatrous passages, blaming them on a trick played by Satan.

When Muslims put the Prophet on a pedestal, we are engaging in idolatry of our own. The point of monotheism is to worship one God, not God's emissaries. The need for humility demands that people of faith to mock themselves -- and each other -- every once in a while. We will not hear this from the Muslim establishment anywhere. But the fact that a new generation of Muslims is asking such questions tells me that ijtihad has a fighting chance.

Ijtihad can be invoked to restore not only reason, but also humanity, to Islam. Today, a common question comes from Muslim women in the West who have fallen in love with Christian men. Too often, their parents and imams warn them that Islam forbids women from marrying outside of the faith. "Does it?" these young women ask. Not necessarily. As I have explained on my website, the Qur'an tells us that Christians and Jews are fellow people of the book who have "nothing to fear or regret" as long as they stay true to their scriptures. The Qur'an also says that "earlier scriptures" — the Torah and the Bible — are as divinely inspired as Islam's book.

Still, I am not a theologian. Although I have been given many labels, Mullah Manji is not one of them. Therefore, I have asked a progressive American imam and professor of Islam, Khaleel Mohammad, to express his view. He points out that because of its time and place — seventh century Arabia — the Qur'an assumes that women are owned by their tribes and consequently must take the religion of tribal leaders: men. Thus, marrying a non-Muslim man would oblige a Muslim woman to abandon Islam. However, Prof. Mohammad emphasizes, this is not the case for 21st century Muslim women who are exposed to the pluralism of the West. Put simply, "you live in a different time and place."

Wait. What do we say to those who argue that the Qur'an is true for all times and all places? Having exercised ijtihad, Prof. Mohammad replies to that argument, too. You can read his response by visiting my website, irshadmanji.com, and using the search engine to find his scholarship.

By using these examples, my broader point is that Muslims in the West are perfectly positioned to rediscover the spirit of ijtihad. After all, it is in the West that we already enjoy precious freedoms to think, express, challenge and be challenged on matters of interpretation. What a precious gift.

But even if ijtihad is rejuvenated in the West, it cannot stop there. People throughout the Islamic world need to know of their God-given right to think for themselves. Outside of the West, reviving ijtihad might start with liberating the entrepreneurial talents of Muslim women through micro-business loans. The Qur'an states that women are subject to men's authority only if men spend money to "maintain" women. So if a woman earns her own assets, like the Prophet Muhammad's beloved first wife, Khadija, she can make decisions for herself.

Impossible? Then consider this story. An American photo-journalist told me about meeting a woman in Kabul who took a tiny loan from a non-governmental organization. She started a candle-making business and, with her earnings, became literate. For the first time in her life, this woman read the Qur'an for herself rather than relying on local clerics to select the passages she would see. She learned that the Qur'an gives all women the right to reject marriage. And if women choose marriage, the Qur'an advises them to draft contracts protecting their rights as equal creatures of God.

She recited these passages to her husband, who had been abusing her for years. Since then, he has not laid an unwanted finger on her. Could it be that what the United Nations has identified as key deficits in the Arab Muslim world — the deficits of knowledge, freedom and women's empowerment — might all benefit from reviving ijtihad? The possibility commands our attention.

I believe that the spirit of ijtihad should not simply be brought back. It should be democratized and popularized beyond the academics and imams. Some scholars will object, insisting that to exercise ijtihad one must have skills developed by years of training. Otherwise, they say, we wind up with anybody quoting the Qur'an to justify radical behavior, as is already happening with the rise of the internet and the decline of traditional authority.

Yet other scholars say that such elitism only reinforces a pattern of submissiveness that plagues the contemporary Muslim mind — a plague that stops reformist Muslims from speaking up as conservatives take over. According to Ingrid Mattson, professor of Islam at Hartford Seminary in the United States, "because of our very narrow vision, our legalistic vision, and our authoritarian models of decision-making, we are excluding those people who can offer us a different vision of the future". Mattson, the first female president of the Islamic Society of North America, goes as far as to encourage ijtihad among comics, poets and musicians. If she is sincere, then hers is a refreshing message: Before we can know who is worth listening to, we must let a wide spectrum of Muslims find their voices.

Of course, most people — not just Muslims — could use more independent thinking. I was reminded of this point while leaving the Gaza office of Dr. Mohammed al-Hindi. I asked his translator why Dr. al-Hindi would give me an on-camera interview, knowing that he could not find a single verse to prove his claim that the Qur'an justifies suicide operations. The translator replied, "He assumed you were just another dumb Western journalist." He explained that reporters from the West had never asked this veteran terrorist the most basic of questions: Where is the evidence for what you do in God's name?

Maybe it is time that media joined Muslims in embracing ijtihad. I would be happy to supply both groups with security tips.

The Methodology of the Quranic Islam

Caner Taslaman

The world at large is debating at present how to conceive Islam. The recent developments that have paved the way to modernization and urbanization, the eased pressure exerted by traditional religious authorities on the general public and the rapid globalization process of the means of communication like television and internet have had important effects on the current debates about Islam and its expansion over a wide area of the globe.

It is observed that a Quran-centered concept of Islam is gaining ground and opinions not based on the Quran are henceforth discredited. Most of the viewpoints used to be grounded on hadiths, Sunni and Shiite convictions and other persuasions traditionally adopted as Islamic creeds or practices have been abandoned by a wide mass of people. Considering that this revision of the practiced Islam is made under the authority of the Quran in total disregard of the hadiths and sectarian concerns, we have thought it convenient to style it "Quranic Islam."

Method in Understanding Religion

A religious conception devoid of a method and based on pragmatic approach is certainly unsound. What must be done is to lay down the fundamental principles and proceed on to individual issues, since otherwise religion will be exposed to subjective interpretations and conventional practices. Furthermore, without such method, individual cases will run the risk of being contradictory.

Once we set the ball rolling the first question that crops up in our mind should be 'What is Islam?' which, in turn, leads to the question: "What is the source of Islam?" This is the essence of the matter, since the answer we shall provide for this question will clarify all other related queries. Unless this question is answered, a person seeking answer for the religious issues that puzzle him, will fail to see his way clearly. The traditionalist sectarian Islamist will answer this question: "The sources of Islam are the conclusions reached by the sectarian imams who based their research on the Quran and the Hadiths."

According to this view an individual is not permitted to formulate a judgment basing directly on the Quran or the hadiths. He has to abide by the established view and rules of the sectarian imams who see no inconvenience in creating a

157

frame of reference of their own, outside the Quran and the hadiths basing on canonical jurisprudence (ijtihad) and analogy "qiyas". The followers of the imams abide by

1. the Quranic verses approved by the sectarian imams,
2. the hadiths approved by the sectarian imams,
3. the jurisprudence and analogy of the sectarian imams.

For instance, if the sectarian imam is of the opinion that a given verse of the Quran – like in the case of the stoning to death of the adulteress – has been abrogated, that verse is disregarded henceforth. Or else, the sectarian imam may, basing on one hadith, arrive at a decision that a man's calf may be exposed to the view, while he may not approve it basing on another hadith. While the Sunnis follow the dead imams, the Shiites follow the sayings of a Shiite a living scholar who follows the 12 dead imams. The divine inspiration received by the 12 imams is as a reliable source of religion as the revelation to the prophet. The followers of the sects abide by the Quran and the hadiths if approved by the sectarian imams. We must remember that the number of so-called hadiths is much more numerous than the number of the Quranic verses and that the considered opinion of the sectarian imam is more characteristic with reference to the selection and interpretation of the hadiths. If one takes into account the numerical preponderance of the hadiths and the frequent contradictions of the Quranic verses and the hadiths as well as the inconsistency of the latter among themselves one cannot avoid the emergence of sects as source of religion. Individuals who are confused with contradictory hadiths have no choice other than opting for a particular sect of a certain tradition. Here comes the issue of the role of the hadiths in Islam. If one comes to the conclusion that the hadiths have no authority in Islam, this invented source of practiced religion will dry up and consequently the sectarian views based on this source will lose their validity.

Once the authority of the hadiths collapses, we shall have before us the Quran as a unique lawful authority. People are puzzled with regard to questions not mentioned in the Quran. The sects have ventured to make authoritative statements as to the merits of stepping in the bathroom with the right foot rather than with the left or the manner of eating one's food. A person who cannot come across such details in the Quran may be puzzled not to find them. The Quran states that whatever is not mentioned in the Quran has been left to the discretion of the individual (5:101). The individual will thus face the bare reality that many acts to which the sectarian imams have attributed religious connotation have in actual fact nothing to do with religion. To step in the bathroom with the left foot first, to eat food with the hand, man's not wearing golden ring and the segregation of women have nothing to do with Islam. Such false traditions have originated from misinterpretations of the hadiths and of the invented hadiths. A person who has adopted the Quran as the sole authority will not have to dally with invented ways of behavior not just because they are incompatible with the modern lifestyle but because they are not contained in the Quran.

The method in question is the adoption of fundamental principles on which the individual will base all religious issues according only to the dictates of the Quran. This approach may seem easy to practice; what is difficult though is the abolition of preconceived ideas. Many people whose behavior is based on *a priori* acceptance of certain established ways of behavior are puzzled when they cannot find them in the Quran and reach the conclusion that the Quran is not complete, and, consequently must be complemented by the hadiths and sectarian interpretations. What the individual should do is to try to understand religion with all one's due sincerity and adjust our conception of religion accordingly. We cannot find out truth so long as we adopt as criteria the inculcated contents of our minds. The sincere initiation into the mystery might be the following question we would put to ourselves: "Does the religion propounded by God correspond to my own conception of it?" This will pave the way to a differentiation between the revealed religion of God and the religion invented by sectarians and inculcated in our minds through inherited traditions.

One of the wrongful impressions about the Quranic Islam under which the public is laboring is that the religion is being adjusted to the prevailing tendencies of the modern world and globalization. The outstanding feature of the Quranic Islam is the emphasis it makes on the exclusive authority of the Quran and its refusal of the authority of the sectarian imams, heads of religious orders etc. Otherwise, if a religion were to be made up to fit the requirements of modernization and globalization, the values of judgment of modernity and globalization would be taken for a basis on which God's authority (expressed in the Quran) would be appraised. The Sunni and Shiite approaches blended God's authority with Arabic and Persian traditions thus mixing up the divine with the human. In differentiating between what is divine and what is human one must be careful not to interpolate new human elements to what has been revealed. The process of modernization and globalization gathered momentum thanks to western civilization dominated by positivism. A religion that would fit in the requirements of modernization and globalization would be a hybrid combination of the revealed religion with the values of western civilization. For instance, freedom in sexual relations in the west has paved the way to a display of tolerance for perversities and homosexuality, now gaining ground the world over. If we strive to fit Islam in this view of life we cannot avoid committing the error of mixing it with practices outside the religion.

The implacable enemy of religion is the "dominant value judgments". We must remember the war waged against the Prophet was for sticking to the old values with a view to preserving the established order. The values transmitted over from their ancestors provided them the power they needed to protect their idols. The war waged now against the Quranic Islam is for the preservation of such "dominant value judgments" and the historical sovereignty of the Sunni and Shiite concepts are presented as evidence. They rely on the power of dominant values rather than the power of the methods that the said sects have adopted in conceiving Islam. If religion is made up to fit in with the values of modernization and globalization, the old dominant values are superceded by new dominant values. While the former dominant values rely on historicity, the values of modernization and globalization rely on the values of the welfare society, and of the civilization that has brought about the modernization and globalization.

Proponents of the transmitted value judgments mix up reality with what they have inherited from their ancestors. Modernization and globalization mix up the latest developments with truth and assuming that what has been achieved last is the ultimate truth, they deprecate the former state, while the "new" is considered a "relative truth" within the historical framework. The Quran, on the other hand, derives its power from revelation of God and bases its reality on the ontology it establishes. According to this ontology God is the Creator of everything, the omniscient and omnipotent Being. Given its infallible origin in God, it is the only reliable authority invulnerable. The idolaters that had raised arms against the Prophet, those who took sectarian imams for religious references next to God and those who have tried to combine Islam with the value judgments of modernization and globalization and attempted to make a new religion have mixed up religious authority with what is human, denying thus the fact that God has the exclusivity of religion.

What we are trying to get at here is the denial of extra-divine authorities while establishing the authority of God. In our daily life discretionary judgments of extra-divine authorities and the values that have received general acceptance which do not conflict with religious principles may, of course, be acknowledged." For instance there is no inconvenience in wearing a headgear in the fashion of idolaters, the segregation of men and women like in the Sunni sect or wearing jeans, a consequence of globalization. What is dangerous is attribution of religious character to them.

In certain parts of the world traditions are mixed up with religion, while in others the values consequent to globalization and modernization are blended into a whole. The Arabs in Saudi Arabia are more susceptible to the first danger while the Muslims in United States are exposed to the danger that the second alternative presents. Although this cannot be hypothesized, a generalization may be permitted.

All these considerations point to one uncontestable truth: the adoption without reservation of the method of Quranic Islam. The slightest reservation may end up with concoction of an invented religion; one part 1% of the Quran and one part 99% of other elements or vice versa. What is not indicated in the Quran either as duties or prohibitions shall be removed outside religious considerations; however, actions not coming within the purview of religion can be accepted if they do not clash with the provisions of the Quran. For instance one may choose to opt for segregation of women on condition that he does not attribute it a religious character. Moreover, Muslims may well carry on their customs and traditions so long they do not assign to them a religious connotation. Celebrations on the occasion of the termination of the fasting month Ramadan or the feast of sacrifice may be carried on without however attaching them a religious significance. One must take into consideration the fact that the civilization of Islam amassed a great number of customs, traditions and cultural elements in various domains in its 1400 years of history. The Quranic Islam does not deny this fact; what it stands against is the attribution of religious connotation to them. Traditions in which history, arts and culture find a home are surely commendable; this heritage can be preserved. Yet, adulteration of religion with traditions would be a disaster. Categorical separation of these two different domains is absolutely necessary.

One of the greatest calumny heaped on the Quranic Islam is the alleged denial of the Prophet or parsimony in showing him due respect. The Quran has praised him and people heard the Quran for the first time from his mouth. Therefore, the Quranic Islam concept is deeply attached to him. A Muslim who does not love him is unthinkable. Quranic Islam asserts that Muhammad communicated what was revealed to him as the only source of religion and that he mentioned no other source nor made any other bequest. Quranic Islam maintains that the Prophet had not dictated any hadith as source of religion as his banning of such an attempt evidences. It holds that the hadiths have come about as a result of slanders and aspersions, misinterpretations and mixing up of his ways (like winding a turban or eating dates) with religious injunctions. It affirms that denial of hadiths as religious dictates will safeguard the Prophet's memory. In brief, the Quranic Islam lends no authority to the hadiths, in conformity with the will of the Prophet, not against him.

The Quranic Islam removes outside the religious framework a good many cultural traits and traditions, thus facilitating the adaptation of the Muslim population to the global rules of conduct. A Muslim may thus wear a kimono, if he/she so chooses or jeans, he/she may eat mussels, shrimps or study in mixed educational establishments. Divesting man's behavior of religious connotations does not make him less religious. A Muslim well knows that God is omniscient; he frequently remembers Him and never forgets him. What was foreign to religion having been removed, man feels better oriented to the essence of religion. A Muslim even though in domains remaining outside the confines of religion, observes religious principles like justice, honesty, and reliability. Quranic Islam is not a movement whose aim is to make religion easy. However, as the Quran has left many actions to the discretion of man and considering that the sects have interpolated unnecessary elements into Islam, Quranic Islam has certainly simplified many things. The aim has not been a simplification of the revealed religion but the application of the method did facilitate certain things. If people attempt at Islamizing the globalized values in total disregard of the Quran, correction of the outcome may render Islam more difficult. The Quranic Islam movement is, in a sense anti-reformist in that it stands against reforms made in the revealed religion by the Umayyads and the Abbasids. Therefore it should be interpreted as a return to the essence. This conception explains methodically the fact that the existing problems in the world of Islam do not stem from Islam but from the Muslims themselves and shows concretely the difference between Islam as such and the conception of Islam by the Muslims.

The lack of a method will end up by attribution of religious character to traditions, communal acceptances and desires and globalized values. This is making religion out of human elements. To adopt the Quran as the unique source of religion denying authority to all other sources, to make religion the exclusive revelation of God is absolutely necessary for a religion where the sole sovereign is God.

Introduction to Peacemaking

Ayman Abdullah

One would think that peacemaking doesn't need an introduction. Under ideal circumstances people who read the title would anticipate most, if not all, of what will come next just from the title. Unfortunately, the evident lack of peace amongst humankind may require at least a brief introduction.

Those who will read the title and anticipate what I am talking about will recognize that this is about understanding the meaning of the word "islam". The conclusion is in the title. This article will explain how this conclusion was reached and will explore some astonishing implications.

Revisiting the Name

> **22:78.** And strive for the god his true striving. He has brought you and has made no hardship on you in the obligation, the creed of your father Ibrahim. He (the god) named you the peacemakers ("al-muslimeen") before and in this, so that the messenger will be a witness against you and you will be witnesses against the people. Thus, persist in the learning connection and bring betterment and hold to the god. He is your protector, a most excellent protector and most excellent supporter.

Proper names are not translated. Hence, names such as Ibrahim/Abraham, Ismail/Ishmael Isac/Isaac and Maryam/Mary are similar in Hebrew, English and Arabic with some phonetic variations and cross-language mispronunciation. For example, Ibrahim is a proper name and hence in the great reading it is not translated into Arabic from what it meant in Canaanite, Old Akkadian or whatever ancient language Abraham spoke.

On the other hand, let's think about the word "al-muslimeen" in 22:78 for a minute. Were Abraham's followers named what would have been at their time a gibberish word from a future language that wasn't even invented yet? Of course not!

Proposing that "al-muslimeen" in 22:78 is a proper name is no different than proposing that 1400 years ago the followers of the prophet were actually called "The Submitters" long before Modern English was invented. Saying "The Submitters" to Arabs 1400 years ago or "Al Muslimeen" to Ibrahim's followers a few thousand years earlier would have sounded just as gibberish as saying "Qasdhwdkfvwdhcv" to people reading this article. It will still be gibberish to the readers even if thousands of years from now some yet to be invented language will have "qasdhwdkfvwdhcv" as a meaningful word. So definitely "al-muslimeen" is a common noun and thus should be translated.

The next question becomes what should the common noun "al-muslimeen" be translated as?

The word "al-muslimeen", when translated, is most commonly translated as "the submitters". In fact, a new sect named The Submitters has sprung and in their case the word reverted to becoming a proper name. But is "the submitters" the right translation for "al-muslimeen"? Rightly so, a thoughtful person would immediately point out that the terms "submitter/submission" sound incomplete. In other words, the natural question that arises when one says "submitter/submission" is submitter/submission to what?

Since, "'al-muslimeen" is a common noun and there is no further explanation for the "to what?" given in 22:78, one would expect that if a better translation is to be found, it must be a self-contained word that doesn't require further explanation.

As usual, the next step for the study is to examine all the passages where the Arabic root "slm" and its derivatives occur to see the common thread that runs across most of the occurrences. The meaning of "peace" seems to be prevalent. For example, 47:35, 8:61, 4:90-91, 4:92, 4:94, 5:16, 6:54, 6:127, 7:46, 8:61, 10:10, 10:25, 11:48, 11:69, 13:24, 14:23, 15:46, 15:52, 16:28, 16:32, 16:87, 19:15, 19:33, 19:47, 19:62, 20:47, 21:69, 25:63, 25:75, 27:59, 28:55, 36:58, 37:79, 37:109, 37:120, 37:130, 37:181, 39:73, 43:89, 50:34, 51:25, 56:26, 56:91, 59:23, 97:5.

It can be noticed right away that the same exact form "silm" is used in passages such as 2:208, 8:61, 16:87 and 47:35. However, all translators translated the same exact form in two completely different ways in those passages. In some instances it was translated as "submission" and in others it was translated as "peace". For example, let's consider 2:208 and 47:35.

002.208

> **Yusufali:**   O ye who believe! Enter into Islam whole-heartedly; and follow not the footsteps of the evil one; for he is to you an avowed enemy.

Pickthal:	O ye who believe! Come, all of you, into <u>submission (unto Him)</u>; and follow not the footsteps of the devil. Lo! he is an open enemy for you.
Shakir:	O you who believe! enter into <u>submission</u> one and all and do not follow the footsteps of Shaitan; surely he is your open enemy.
Khalifa:	O you who believe, you shall embrace <u>total submission</u>; do not follow the steps of Satan, for he is your most ardent enemy.

047.035

Yusufali:	Be not weary and faint-hearted, crying for peace, when ye should be uppermost: for Allah is with you, and will never put you in loss for your (good) deeds.
Pickthal:	So do not falter and cry out for peace when ye (will be) the uppermost, and Allah is with you, and He will not grudge (the reward of) your actions.
Shakir:	And be not slack so as to cry for peace and you have the upper hand, and Allah is with you, and He will not bring your deeds to naught.
Khalifa:	Therefore, you shall not waver and surrender in pursuit of peace, for you are guaranteed victory, and GOD is with you. He will never waste your efforts.

Unlike "submission" which wouldn't fit in 47:35 or 8:61, "peace" fits well in all those passages. Hence, passages such as 2:208 and 16:87 make good sense when substituting "peace/peacefulness" in the translations. For example, here is 2:208:

002.208

Yusufali:	O ye who believe! Enter into peace whole-heartedly; and follow not the footsteps of the evil one; for he is to you an avowed enemy.
Pickthal:	O ye who believe! Come, all of you, into peace; and follow not the footsteps of the devil. Lo! he is an open enemy for you.
Shakir:	O you who believe! enter into peace one and all and do not follow the footsteps of Shaitan; surely he is your open enemy.
Khalifa:	O you who believe, you shall embrace peace; do not follow the steps of Satan, for he is your most ardent enemy.

The words "salam" and "islam" have a relation that is a fairly common one in Arabic. It is found in the forms "Fa'AL" and "If'AL". Some examples of those same forms include NajaH - InjaH: Success - making successful, Halal - IHlal: Allowed - making allowed, SalaH - IslaH: Good -making good, Ta'am - It'am: Food – feeding, 'amar - I'mar: Prosperity - making prosper and many more. Thus, similarly, "salam" means peace and "islam" means peacemaking.

If "slm" means peace, "islam" means peacemaking, and "muslim" means peacemaker then what are the implications? Why is the concept of peace so important?

The Prevalence of Peace

In order to understand how the concept of peacefulness is prevalent throughout the great reading, even when not mentioned, let's take an example.

> 6:165.   And He is the one who made you leaders of the earth and raised in grades some of you over others, to test you in what He gave you, indeed your Lord is swift in punishment and indeed He is forgiving and merciful.

> 35:39.   He is the one who made you leaders of the earth, so whoever is ungrateful, on him is his ungratefulness. The ungratefulness of the unappreciative doesn't increase anything at their Lord except abhorrence and the ungratefulness of the unappreciative doesn't increase them anything except loss.

> 2:30.   And when your Lord said to the controllers: "I am making in the earth a leader". They said: "Do you make in it one who corrupts in it and sheds the bloods, while we exalt with your praise and sanctify for You?" He said: "I know what you don't know."

With the understanding that "islam" means peacemaking, we can now see that since the very beginning, it was always about peacemaking. We can see that in 2:30, the general lack of peace on the part of humans as foreseen by the controllers was the cause of their objection to making humans leaders of the earth.

With this understanding, let's reexamine 22:78. The clear signs were in it all along:

> 22:78.   And strive for the god his true striving. He has brought you and has made no hardship on you in the obligation, the creed of your father Ibrahim. He (the god) named you the peacemakers before and in this, so that the messenger will be a witness against you and you will be witnesses against humankind. Thus, persist in the learning connection and bring

betterment and hold to the god. He is your protector, a most excellent protector and most excellent supporter.

We are told that the reason for naming us "the peacemakers" is two fold:

1. The messenger will be a witness against us.
2. We will be a witness against humankind.

The definition of a witness can be summed up as one who testifies the truth in the case of a dispute. We know from the great reading that the messenger and the message are practically synonymous. What is the issue in dispute and how is the message a witness against us?

The issue in disputation is mentioned right at the beginning of the passage. By saying "true striving for the god", it is implicit in that statement that there is false striving for the god.

The message of the passage is us being named "the peacemakers" by the god. This message will be a witness against us in the dispute of what constitutes true striving ("jihad") for the god as opposed to false striving ("jihad") for the god. Thus, we cannot corrupt and cause destruction in the earth and shed blood as the controllers foresaw in 2:30 and claim that we are doing it because we are striving for the god. By describing us as the peacemakers in the god's message, it will be a witness against us. Similarly by being the peacemakers, we will be witnesses against those who do not strive for the god the true striving and instead corrupt in the earth and shed the bloods while claiming to strive for the god.

Another interesting passage that can now be better understood is 37:103.

037.103

Yusufali:	So when they had both submitted their wills (to Allah), and he had laid him prostrate on his forehead (for sacrifice),
Pickthal:	Then, when they had both surrendered (to Allah), and he had flung him down upon his face,
Shakir:	So when they both submitted and he threw him down upon his forehead,
Khalifa:	They both submitted, and he put his forehead down (to sacrifice him).

Notice that Yusufali and Pickthal had to insert "to Allah" to have the passage make sense because "submitted" by itself is incomplete. An important word in the passage is the Arabic verb "tal". Here are what Classical Arabic dictionaries say about this word:

167

"Tal": something in his hand: Place it on the hand or push/pull it to one's self. For example, if I say ""tal" the object to me", this would mean I pushed/pulled the object to me. So "tal" to my forehead: Place it against my forehead or pushed/pulled it to my forehead.

Now let's retranslate the passage with the new understanding about the meaning of "aslam":

> 37:103. So when they became peaceful and he (Ibrahim) pulled him (his son) to his (Ibrahim's) forehead.

Is having a knife and getting ready to slaughter someone and throwing him down "becoming peaceful"? Does the above passage give the image of someone with a knife who is pushing another person and is about to slaughter him? Of course not and a knife is not even mentioned!

Now with this improved translation, we can see that the passage actually gives the image of Ibrahim and his son becoming peaceful and Ibrahim lovingly hugging his son. This is an example of the application of 22:78. Ibrahim strives for the god the true striving by doing the peaceful thing even after believing that the dream was an order from the god.

Many evils in the world and many wars and destruction have taken place in the name of striving for the god. This goes against our most basic purpose to serve the god by being good leaders of the earth and not corrupting in it and shedding blood. With a single word, the god's message stands as an irrefutable witness against those who cause wars and destruction while claiming to strive for the god.

This is why in the great reading fighting is only prescribed in self-defense. Fighting is never prescribed to spread religion or conquer others. Our true "deen"/obligation to the god is "islam"/peacemaking. This is what those who had faith are told in passages such as 2:193 and 8:39.

> 2:193. And fight them until there is no more persecution and the obligation is to the god (i.e. peace is established), so if they desist, there should be no aggression except against the aggressors.

There are many implications to understanding "islam" as peacemaking. Now many things fall into place. Now we can see why a behavior as trivial as calling each other bad names is strongly condemned in the great reading and made almost as important as having faith. It is because such behavior doesn't promote peace between people.

049.011

> **Yusufali**: O ye who believe! Let not some men among you laugh at others: It may be that the (latter) are better than the (former): Nor let some women laugh at others: It may

	be that the (latter are better than the (former): Nor defame nor be sarcastic to each other, nor call each other by (offensive) nicknames: Ill-seeming is a name connoting wickedness, (to be used of one) after he has believed: And those who do not desist are (indeed) doing wrong.
Pickthal:	O ye who believe! Let not a folk deride a folk who may be better than they (are), not let women (deride) women who may be better than they are; neither defame one another, nor insult one another by nicknames. Bad is the name of lewdness after faith. And whoso turneth not in repentance, such are evil-doers.
Shakir:	O you who believe! let not (one) people laugh at (another) people perchance they may be better than they, nor let women (laugh) at (other) women, perchance they may be better than they; and do not find fault with your own people nor call one another by nicknames; evil is a bad name after faith, and whoever does not turn, these it is that are the unjust.
Khalifa:	O you who believe, no people shall ridicule other people, for they may be better than they. Nor shall any women ridicule other women, for they may be better than they. Nor shall you mock one another, or make fun of your names. Evil indeed is the reversion to wickedness after attaining faith. Anyone who does not repent after this, these are the transgressors.

It is all about peace as clear from 2:132 and 3:102.

> 2.132.   And this was the legacy that Abraham left to his sons, and so did Jacob; "Oh my sons! The god has chosen the obligation for you, so do not die except while you are peacemakers."

As 2:132 indicates, the primacy of the concept of peacemaking is not a new invention that was not already very well known to the people of the book since the time of Abraham. As a matter of a fact, the noun "submission" is never mentioned in the Bible while the concepts of peace, peacemaking, and peacemaker are mentioned no less than 450 times in the Bible.

Conclusion

In the international media we increasingly hear many untranslated Arabic words. Examples include words such as Islam, Muslims, Islamist, Jihad, Al-Qaeda, etc... By taking such words as proper names or meaningless labels, those who spread corruption in the earth have been able to attach whatever meanings they

169

want to those words. Both Arabic and non-Arabic speakers have been deceived by such tactics.

For example, when the word Jihad is mentioned, the first image that is evoked in the minds of the majority of Arabic and non-Arabic speakers is that of a religious holy war. This meaning has taken hold despite the fact that all Arabic dictionaries say that the word "jihad" simply means "striving". Of course, "striving" is a positive word that doesn't carry violent connotations in the minds of the audience. Being Arabic speakers has not helped people avoid this trap because the proper name blocks the true meaning of a word even in Arabic.

As we have seen, by transforming a word into a proper name, a new meaning has been attached to a neutral or positive word. This phenomenon has worked both ways and thus we also see Arabic words with a negative meaning being used as proper names whose inventors have intended as positive.

For example, ironically the opposite of those who strive ("al-mujahidun") in the great reading is the idle ("al-qaedun") according to passages such as 4:95. Those who lied to the god and his messenger are said to have been idle ("qaed") in 9:90. Generally the word "qaed" in the great reading has the meaning of "stop/idle/hinder". Thus, the "qawaed" are what stops a building from falling (2:127, 16:26) and "qawaed" are also women who stopped desiring marriage (24:60). We also hear about the descendents of Israel who disobeyed Moses as being idle ("qaedun") in 5:24. Even the devil himself is described as hindering ("qaed") humans from the straight path of the god (7:16). In Arabic, the feminine form has the same meaning as the masculine form but depending on the context may add a sense of collective classification. So in the context of striving, "al-qaeda" actually is the opposite of the true striving and it means "the idle".

Whoever chose the name Al-Qaeda for an outfit that we often hear about on the news as a symbol of "extreme Islamic Jihad", must be completely clueless about the great reading, the connotation of the word in it, and the fact that in the context of striving it actually means the opposite of striving ("jihad"). Indeed, they scheme and scheme but the god is the best schemer. The god's message continues to be a witness against those who claim to strive for the god in order to commit corruption in the earth.

How do we strive for the god his true striving? The answer is given in 22:78:

> 22:78.   And strive for the god his true striving. He has brought you and has made no hardship on you in the obligation, the creed of your father Ibrahim. He (the god) named you the peaceful ("al-muslimeen") before and in this, so that the messenger will be a witness against you and you will be witnesses against humankind. Thus, persist in the learning connection and bring betterment and hold to the god. He is your protector, a most excellent protector and most excellent supporter.

We strive for the god his true striving by continuing to learn and teach others about his message, bringing betterment as opposed to corruption in the earth, and holding on to him.

This is not really a conclusion but is a humble step forward in a long journey. It is a step for restoring the true meaning of the striving for the god. We can start by teaching people about the real meaning that was blocked by the proper names. When such barriers are removed, the world will be a better place. Suddenly, "extreme peaceful striving" doesn't sound so bad.

Unless the god wills otherwise, this study will continue in a forthcoming book entitled Introduction to Peacemaking. The book tries to answer the question of why would an organization who is supposedly the embodiment of extreme Islamic Jihad be given a name that has the diametrically opposite meaning of striving (jihad). It also tries to explain how billions of people, including so-called experts, were duped by such foolishness. It is hoped that the answers found in the course of this research would help correct other widely held and age-old misunderstandings and perhaps, in a small way, change our world for the more peaceful.

IMPORTANT DISCLAIMER:

     2:2.   This is the book no doubt in it, a guidance for the forethoughtful.

This article reflects my personal interpretation of the passages of the great reading as of March 28, 2008. I will try to improve my understanding of the great reading and the universe, except if the god wills and perhaps my lord guides me to what is nearer in rationality. Please verify all information within for yourself as commanded in 17:36, and remember that simply "none" is the forethoughtful answer to 45:6. If the god willed, the outcome of this article will be beneficial.

The Humanistic Approach vs. the Religious Approach
How the Focus Matters

Arnold Yasin Mol

What is the purpose of revelation? What is the main focus and how does this affect society? The answers to these questions I believe lay at the core of the current problems within the Muslim world and they give a direct solution to the long road of Islamic reform. The majority of the Muslims, in fact people of any religion, believe revelations were send to mankind to erase idolatry, instruct how to perform worship, how to redeem themselves, gain personal salvation and the list goes on. The main reason is mostly a religious one. Worship and beliefs mostly come first and then the second purpose comes along, the structure of society, the human rights and freedoms of mankind. The current Muslim theology has put the religious goals above the humanistic goals. No sect within Islam denies justice or the need for structure in society as these are clearly to be found within the Quran and Sunnah. But is worship really more important then humanitarian action? In the beginning, Christianity has separated these two, and taught that the law and deeds did not matter as much, it was faith that determined your destiny.[1] Within Islam also, faith and worship gained a more dominant position then the humanistic side of the religion, a person is more judged on his worship instead on his positive participation within the respective society.

The position of these two separate goals affects deeply the mindset of the Muslim people in their daily affairs, the pursuit of knowledge and the structure of their society. The time, the energy, put within upgrading their level of worship and the upgrading of their social level differs immensely. Muslims have endured oppression by their own rulers, by landowners, slavery, tribalism, colonialism, dictatorship, continious poverty and countless wars, but as long as their worship is sustained, they feel their duty as Muslims has been fulfilled. The dominance of worship in the Muslim mind is summarized in the famous five pillars of Islam; prayer, alms-tax, shahada, pilgrimage and fasting during Ramadan. When these are fulfilled, you can be deemed a succesful Muslim according to tradition.

But what has the Quran to say about the dominant mindset, what does it give as its main goal? Does God demand or need acknowledgment? The demand for acknowledgement of power was also present among human rulers as kings and

---

[1] The Bible, Saint Paul in Romans 3:28

dictators which may hint towards the source of the human view on power. Mankind learns definitions and relations through experience. The majority of absolute rulers demanded and displayed their power and rule through festivals, rituals, but also by brute force.

If these absolute rulers represented the mortal human version of absolute power, God must demand much more of mankind, He must be the ultimate version of an absolute ruler. But how does the Quran describe God? In a small chapter called *Ikhlaas* it says:

> 112:1-4 Say, "He is God, the One! God is *Samad*: Absolutely Independent, Absolute, Eternal, Unique, Self-sufficient Sustainer, Perfect, the Uncaused Cause of all that exists. He begets not, nor is He begotten. And there is absolutely none like Him."[2]

> 14:8 And Moses said: "If you deny the Truth, you and all those who live in the earth, know that Allah is indeed *Al-Ghani*, Self-sufficient, Owner of Praise."

> 3:97 .... One who denies verily, Allah, *Al-Ghani*, the Rich is Self-Sufficient, want-free of any peoples.

The Quran constantly stresses the independence of God. He is complete and self-sufficient. Nothing we will do will add or take away any power God has. Human rulers want complete obedience to their rule and will persecute traitors, those that uphold other people as their rulers, as of course this would take away their power. God does not care if you praise Him, or believe in other gods. A human ruler is dependent on his subjects to have power, God is not, so we cannot mix up the human form of power with that of God. Although this is acknowledged by almost all sects within Islam, an important factor has been overlooked by many of them. If God is needless, why would He demand worship, or at least, make it so important within His message? The answer traditional Islam gives, which is similar to many religions, the reward of worship is attained in the hereafter, as worship is showing our gratitude to our Creator for making us. But does the Quran also see this so, and what is there to be thankful for if the majority on earth only experiences hardship? Islam doesn't profess a belief in an original sin as in Christianity[3], but life on earth is seen as a test and

---

[2]   Page 321-322 under the root Samada. Dictionary of the Holy Quran by Abdul Mannar Omar, 2006 4th edition. And page 91-92. Islam: A Challenge to Religion by G.A. Parwez, 1996 3rd edition saying: "The second verse refers to the Divine attribute of Samadiyyah or self-dependence. The term connotes independence, self-reliance and self-sufficiency. "Samad" is the being which depends only on its own and on nothing else, a being which is eternally enduring and absolutely free."

[3]   39:7 says: No laden one will bear the burden of another. And thus rejects the concept of original sin.

by many as a place which much be detested.[4] The philosopher Marx claimed that the poor where being deluded and controlled by saying they cannot change their low status in this life, that they must endure it and hope for their reward in the hereafter.

So the next question would be: does the Quran say to the people, endure your misery, accept it and wait for the hereafter, your worship is more important than your human rights?

13:17   While what is of benefit to mankind, abides on Earth.

42:38-43   They respond to their Lord by establishing *Salaat,* and conduct their affairs by mutual consultation, and they keep open for the welfare of others what We have given them. And whenever gross injustice is inflicted upon them, they defend themselves and stand up for their rights. But requiting evil may become an evil in itself! So, whoever pardons and makes peace, his reward rests with God. Surely, He does not love the violators of human rights. And those who stand up for their rights and defend themselves, when they have been wronged, for such, there is no blame. The blame is on those who oppress people and cause disorder on earth resorting to aggression, unprovoked. They are the ones for whom there is an awful doom. Certainly, whoever is patient and forgives, that is from the strength of character.

Throughout the Quranic text, justice and rights of people are seen as important, which again is acknowledged by most sects within Islam. But what comes first in the Quran; religious goals or humanitarian goals?

According to the Quran, there are several reasons the belief in God as one is important. It gives examples that believing in deities is wasting man's energy and time, that it doesn't solve their problems, that it is a wrong perception of reality and especially, that people will follow goals which gives them nothing in the end.

22:73-74   "O Mankind! Here is an example for you to listen and ponder! Behold, those beings you invoke instead of Allah, cannot create as much as a fly, even if they were to join all their forces to do so. And if a fly robs them of anything, they cannot get it back from it. Weak indeed is the seeker and weak indeed the sought." They esteem not Allah as He must be esteemed. In fact, Allah is the One, Mighty, All Powerful.

---

[4]   While the Quran clearly sees life on earth as something beautiful if we make it so. 16:97 says: Whoever - male or female - does works that help others and is a believer, we shall certainly cause them to live a good life, and We shall grant them the rewards considering the best of their actions. (see also, 10:59, 16:6, 7:32, 34:12)

According to the Quran, believing in one God is the simple truth, it is a direct observation of reality. To see God as one, is the first step to distance one's Self from *Kufr*. The Arabic word *kufr* has multiple meanings as *"To close the eyes to reality, To bury the truth for one's Self"*.[5]

This observation of reality is beautifully expressed in the story of Abraham:

> 6:75-79   We gave Abraham insight, the ability to reflect, into the Mighty Dominion of the Universe so that he might attain firm conviction. One night when it grew dark upon him he saw a planet (Venus). Abraham exclaimed to them, "This is my Lord!" But when it went down, he said, "I love not the things that go down." Then when the moon was rising, he exclaimed, "This is my Lord." But when it went down, he said ; "Unless my Lord guides me, I surely will go astray." Then he saw the sun rising in splendor, and he said, "This is my Lord! This is greater!" But, as the sun went down, Abraham exclaimed, "O My people! I am free from all that you associate with God." "I have focused firmly on Him Who initiated the heavens and the earth; as an upright man I turn away from all that is false. I will never be an idol worshiper in any form."

Abraham saw that believing in idols is not based on reality, but on self-imposed belief. It is not based on evidence.

We can see clear order in the Universe. Everything works through fixed laws and not through chaos. This is clear evidence of a single Control. If there were more deciders on the Universe's purpose and governance, the Universe would be in chaos as every controller would have imposed their own will unto their part. Order means there is only one Will that governs the Universe. Allah clarifies this also with the verse:

> 21:22   If there were other gods besides God, there would have been chaos in both, the heavens and the earth. Glorified is Allah, the Lord of Supreme Control, above all that they contrive.

So believing in one God, one Creator is a confirmation of reality. This is why we also say:

> 3:18   Allah Himself witnesses that there is no god but He and so do the Malikah, the laws of the universe, and men and

---

5   Page 489-491 under the root Kafara. Dictionary of the Holy Quran by Abdul Mannar Omar, 2006 4th edition. The word means to be ungrateful, to cover something. Inside the Quran the term got the definition of denying the truth, to be ungrateful for life, to bury the truth for yourself and society, to cover thr rights of others.

women of Science who research in the right direction. There is no god but He, the Almighty, the Wise.

This is why the Quran teaches us monotheism, not because God wants or needs acknowledgement, but to prevent mankind wasting their time on self-made beliefs that contradict with reality and thus waste the precious gift of life on nonsense. After we have confirmed this reality, the Quran then urges us to research nature and it's workings so we can use it to our advantage.

> 3:190-192 Indeed, in the creation of the heavens and earth, and in the alternation of night and day, there are signs for men and women who will to understand. Standing, sitting, and reclining, they reflect upon the wonders of creation in the skies and earth, saying, "Our Developer! You have not created all this without purpose. glory to You! Save us, then, from (being negligent in attaining knowledge and thus from) the doom of the fire (as we burn our potentials to waste)." "Our Developer! Any individuals and nations whom You admit into the fire, You have brought them low (for failing to harness the forces in Nature)." There are no helpers for those who displace knowledge with conjecture and thus wrong themselves. [Zaalimeem =those that replace truth for falsehood]

When we understand nature, we can harness it and use it for the development of mankind.

> 45:13 And He has made subservient to you, from Himself, all that is in the heavens and all that is on earth. Therein, are signs for people who reflect..

> 13:17 When they use fire to refine metals for their jewelry or equipment, foam is produced like it. In this way, God is citing for you the example of the truth and falsehood. For, as far as the foam is concerned, it passes away as scum upon the riverbanks - While what is of benefit to mankind, abides on earth. This is how God uses analogies for you to understand.

In the above verse a very important and many times ignored sentence is given: *"While what is of benefit to mankind, abides on earth."* It reveals the focus of the Quran, to make people benefit each other for the betterment of mankind. Throughout the Quran it is made clear people are judged on their conduct towards other people, not on their amount of worship.

> 18:7 We have adorned what is on earth so that We may let them test themselves as to who is best in conduct, and lives a balanced life. [Ahsanu 'amala includes 'best in conduct' and 'balanced life']

18:30   As for those who attain belief and do the works that help others, certainly, We never fail to reward such benefactors of humanity. (As-Salihati are the works that reform and improve society. Ahsana amala refers to conduct that is good to others and is balanced.)

18:46   Wealth and children are the joys of the life of this world. But good deeds that fulfill the needs of others, their fruit endures forever. Such actions are of far greater merit in the Sight of your Lord, and the best foundation of hope.

19:76   God increases in guidance, those who seek it and wish to live upright. The lasting good deeds that fulfill the needs of others, are eternally rewarded by your Lord, and are best for eventual returns and better for resort.

49:13   O Mankind! We have created you male and female, and have made you nations and tribes so that you might (affectionately) come to know one another. Surely, the most honored among you, in the sight of God, is the one who is best in conduct. God is Knower, Aware.

There is a belief to be found between the followers of most religions, which is if their worship is not correct or good, God's punishment will befall them. But according to the Quran, the laws of cause and effect present in the universe do not react to the beliefs of a people, nor their worship or rituals, but on their righteous behavior towards other people.

11:116-117 But, Alas! Among the generations before your time, only a few were virtuous enough to discourage disorder in the land. We saved those few, whereas those who continued to violate human rights only pursued material riches. And they were guilty of stealing the fruit of others' labor (and they were requited). Your Developer never destroys a community for wrong beliefs alone[6] as long as its people are *Muslihoon*: reformers, setting right their own, and one another's condition.[7]

---

[6]   Page 351. Dictionary of the Holy Quran by Abdul Mannar Omar,. Zulm comes from Zalama and means to displace something from its rightful place. Raghib says this can be between man and God where it refers to shirk, between people where the human rights are violated and between a person's own self, where he wrongs himself.

[7]   Page 438-439 Volume 4, Arabic-English Lexicon by Edward William Lane, based on Taj-Ul-Roos, 2003 2nd reprint. Muslihoon comes from Salaha. It gives under Salaha: "To make whole sound, set things right, amendment, reformation, reformer, one who is upright, righteous, a person of integrity, peacemaker, suitable."

The famous *Imam Razi* mentions in his commentary on this verse:

> *"God's chastisement does not afflict any people merely on -account of their holding beliefs amounting to shirk and kufr, but afflicts them only if they persistently commit evil in their mutual dealings, and deliberately hurt (other human beings] and act tyranically [towards them]. Hence, those who are learned in Islamic Law (al-fuqahd') hold that men's obligations towards God rest on the principle of [His] forgiveness and liberality, whereas the rights of man are of a stringent nature and must always be strictly observed"* [8]

As the commentary shows, this verse completely destroys the concept of religious duties being the dominant focus as the law of God judges deeds not beliefs. What is an important note, is that beliefs create deeds. So without the correct vision on reality, eventually a people will fall into wrong behavior. This is why God sends Revelation to guide mankind towards the correct understanding of the universe.

A Muslim's main duty is to be a *Muslihoon*, a reformer of society who benefits all of mankind in all of their acts and duties. The Quran continuously puts faith and creating peace, *iman*, next to *salaha*, to contribute to society. This is the true concept of *ibādat*, servitude and obedience to God. Normally is *ibādat* purely understood as worship, but the above explains we serve God through serving mankind. This is also a famous *hadith* attributed to the Prophet Muhammed where he was asked how we must serve God, his answer was: *"You want to serve God? Then serve mankind."*

Open the famous collections of *Hadith*, history reports on Prophet Muhammed, the *Tafseers*, explanations of the Quran, or go to any Muslim bookstore or website, and the majority of the writings are focused on worship and rituals. How to perform them, and how you will be punished if you do not perform them correctly or on time. The religious focus dominates the humanitarian focus in Muslim writings, be it on Quranic interpretation or how Muslims must spend their lives.

Also when somebody has done wrong, it is believed this act can be restored by worship, so God will forgive you. But the Quran says:

> 21:47 We will set up the scales of justice on the Era of Resurrection, and no person will be wronged in the least. Though the good or evil be of the weight of a mustard seed, We will bring it forth. We are Sufficient for reckoning and none can take account as We do.

---

[8] Page 374, The Message by Muhammed Asad, 2003. Commentary 149 on verse 11:117. Quoting Abu 'l-Fadl Muhammed Fakhr ad-Din ar-Razi(d. 606 H.) in his At-Tafsir al-Kabir.

So every deed will not be neglected, nor forgiven in the form of Salvation. The Quran uses a different system, one of compensation. In 11:114 it says:

> 11:114 *Al-Hassanat*, good deeds towards other humans removes the ill effects of *Al-Sayyi*, the bad that was done to others.

The famous Quran commentator *Ibn Katheer* quotes *Hadith* which he claims explains that the good deed mentioned in this verse is praying, which will erase the sins.[9] But the word *Al-Hasanat* means to benefit a person.[10] Which in itself explains that *Hasanat* can only be done between humans or God giving Hasanat to humans, but the Hasanat cannot be directed towards God since He is above laughter and in need of any goodness. Same accounts for *Al-Sayyi*, which is to make someone sad and sorrowful by spreading corruption and be vicious, something that is done between humans alone.[11]

You can only compensate for your wrong deeds by doing good to others. A concept explained also in the other verses mentioned earlier. This system of compensation is made easy as every good deed is seen as ten times more compared to a bad deed.[12]

---

[9] Isma'il Ibn Katheer in his Tafsir al- Quran on verse 11:114, Cairo. English translation.

[10] Page 206-208 Volume 2, Arabic-English Lexicon by Edward William Lane: . "Make good, seem good/beautiful/comely/pleasing, be excellent, make or render a thing good or goodly, to beautify/embellish/adorn a thing, strive or compete in goodness, to do good or act well, act or behave with goodness or in a pleasing manner towards a person, confer a benefit or benefits upon a person, act graciously with a person".

[11] Page 181-183 Volume 4, Arabic-English Lexicon by Edward William Lane. "To treat badly, do evil to disgrace, be evil/wicked/vicious, ill, anything that makes a person sad and sorrowful, bad action, mischief and corruption"

[12] 6:160. He who does a good deed will receive ten times its worth; and he who does evil will be requited to an equal degree; and no one will be wronged. See also 27:89-90. The word Ghafara has also been presented in a very wrong way. In the Quran, Ghafara means to protect against dirt or harm as 99:7-8 and 21:47 rejects the concept of salvation or forgiveness. Page 405-406 under the root Ghafara. Dictionary of the Holy Quran by Abdul Mannar Omar, 2006 4th edition.It says: "To give protect, to cover over, shield, suppress the defect, set the affairs right. Ghafar al-Mata'a means He put the goods in the bag and covered and protected them. Mighafar is a shield and helmet. Ghafr means covering with that which protects a thing from dirt. Ghafour, name of God: The Protector." God is also called Al-Afaa, Afaa means to remit previous deeds, it also means the surplus of something (2:219) Page 379-380 under the root Afa. Dictionary of the Holy Quran by Abdul Mannar Omar, 2006 4th edition.It is used 7 times for God who remitted those that upheld their present life above the better one. He is Al-Afaa because people are given time to remit their wrongdoing and because He gives more (surplus) for every good deed (6:160). The effects of their deeds on their own Self will be judged according to these factors:

The whole focus of the Quran is thus clearly a humanitarian one whereby even the judgment laid upon mankind in the next life is based on their conduct towards one another.

> 23:61-62 It is those who race with one another to improve the quality of life for humanity, and it is those who are worthy of winning good things. We do not burden any human being with more than he or she is able to bear. And with Us is a Record that speaks the truth (about what you can and cannot do). And so, none shall be wronged.

> 41:46 Whoever does good to others, does good to his own 'self', and whoever causes imbalance in the lives of others, hurts his own 'self'. Your Lord is never unjust to His servants.

Within the global Muslim society answers are sought to find the keys to success, to find a way out of the misery the *Ummah* has been in for the last couple of centuries. I believe one of the key factors that will create this long sought-after success is that the *Ummah* must change its main focus from worship into humanitarian action. The governments of the Muslim countries must be chosen on their beneficence towards all the people within the society and the education in the countries must teach people how to benefit society with their profession and behavior. Now precious energy is given mainly on worship while the Quran urges us to spend it on each other so we can create an earthly paradise. This was the success of the first generations of Muslims.

Today Muslims judge each action they do on its religious merit. Actions are done to earn blessings from God, and by this every action is turned into worship. Societies will not change by this, as worship does not require education nor the

---

- The person's is judged on intention (2:225, 5:89).
- Has no knowledge of the law or the Divine Law or doesn't understand it correctly (6:131).
- Is minor or insane and not capable of understanding (17:36).
- Is forced to do a thing (16:106).
- No action would go un-recompensated (3:25).
- Everyone will get the consequence of his own deeds. (7:147, 52:16, 37:39).
- Absolute and full justice will be done, and no one will be dealt with unjustly, as the selection is made by laws and not by emotions (16:111, 40:17, 39:70).

The above mentioned factors that will determine the recompense of the person's deeds, and these are also used in almost all courts of law in the world. In the Quran, forgiveness stands for giving room to compensate for wrong deeds done. The Quran: An Encyclopedia says: "Forgiveness involves a change of heart that may advocate that the wrongdoer receives punishment or be considered accountable for redressing the wrong." Under Forgiveness, page 213-216 by Bahar Davary. The Quran: An Encyclopedia edited by Oliver Leaman, 2008 Paperback.

presence of the basic human needs and development, but being beneficence does require education and the means to develop as a people and nation.

> 13:11 Each person has, *Malikah*, Divine laws surrounding him. They record his actions according to the command of God. Most certainly, God does not change the condition of a nation until they first change themselves. And when God intends a nation to suffer punishment (as a consequence of their misdeeds), there is none who can repel it. For, they have no defender besides Him.[13]

The Muslims must change their governments by changing their own focus, strive for betterment of society as a whole and demand the human rights given to them in the Quran.

> 16:97 Whoever - male or female - does works that help others and is *Muminun*, a protector of others[14], We shall certainly cause them to live a good life, and We shall grant them the rewards considering the best of their actions.

> 42:38 They respond to their Lord by establishing *Salaat,* and conduct their affairs by mutual consultation (*Shura*), and they keep open for the welfare of others what We have given them.[15]

> 20:118-119 "Indeed, you are living the life of Paradise (on this very Earth) where you are guaranteed never to go hungry, nor go unsheltered." "Neither do you go thirsty, nor are you exposed to the burning sun." [Well-provided with food, clothing, shelter, the basic needs for all]

> 6:132 The ranks of all individuals and nations are determined solely by their deeds, and your Lord is not unaware of what they do. [Calling yourselves 'believers' will not help. 2:8]

---

[13] QXP commentary: 8:53, 82:10-14. Hifz: Protect, Preserve, Save, Record, Guard. Ma bi anfusihim: What is in themselves, What is in their own 'self', What is in their hearts, Their psyche, Their way of thinking, Their intentions, Their will to change, Their innate 'self'.

[14] From Amina, To feel and make safe. To be secure and make others safe. Giving security, rendering safe Page 33-34. Dictionary of the Holy Quran by Abdul Mannar Omar. A Concise Dictionary of Koranic Arabic by A.A. Ambros, 2004. On page 29 where he discusses how the religious understanding of Amina as 'To believe" was a later creation coming from the Aramiac and/or Ethiopic. See for example verses 3:97, 9:6, 106:4 where the root Amina is used in to make people safe and secure from harm.

[15] QXP commentary: Establishing Salaat = Establishing the System where following of the Divine Commands is facilitated. Nafaq = Open-ended tunnel = No hoarding. Salaat means To follow closely, to remain attached.

2:177   But righteousness is that: [..] And that he gives of his cherished wealth to:- Family and relatives, Orphans, Widows, *Al-Masakin*, which are those left helpless in the society, whose hard-earned income fails to meet their basic needs, whose running businesses have stalled, ones who have lost their jobs. Whose life has stalled for any reason, The disabled. And *Ibn al-Sabil*, The needy wayfarer, son of the street. the homeless, the one who travels to you for assistance. And *Al-Sa'ilin*,Those who ask for help, and *al-Riqab*, Those whose necks are burdened with any kind of bondage, oppression, crushing debts and extreme hardship of labor. […]…

51:19   And in their wealth was the Divinely ordained right of those who ask and those who are deprived.

9:111   God has bought from the *Mu'minina*, those entrusted with the safety of others, their persons and their goods, for (in return) theirs is Jannah, the state of constant evolution. They shall fight in the cause of God, and shall slay and be slain. It is a promise that is binding on Him in the Torah and the Gospel, and the Quran. Who can fulfill a promise better than God? Rejoice then in the bargain you have made, for that is the Supreme Triumph.

21:10   O mankind! Now We have revealed to you a Book that is all about you and it will give you eminence. Will you not, then, use reason?

3:103-105 You must hold fast, all of you together, to the Bond of God and be not divided into sects. (The Bond or Rope of God is the Quran which is an Unbreakable Support 2:256.) Remember God's favor upon you when you were enemies and, almost overnight, He brought mutual affection in your hearts. Thus, you became brothers and sisters by His grace. And recall that you were on the brink of the pit of fire, and He saved you from it. (Various tribes used to attack one another, and personal enmity plagued them.) This is how effectively God has made His messages clear for you to journey on the lighted road. Let there be a community among you that invites to all that is good, advocating virtue and deterring vice. They are the truly successful. Do not be like those who became divided and disputed after all evidence of the truth had come to them. For, they have incurred a tremendous suffering.[16]

---

[16]   QXP commentary: 6:165, 30:31-32, Huda: Guidance, Walk the right path, Travel on a lighted road. Verses 2:143, 3:110 and 22:78 assign this duty to the entire

The Quranic human rights:

a. Equal human dignity by birth (17:70, 95:4)
b. Gender equity (4:32, 33:35)
c. Superiority by character only (49:13, 46:19)
d. Rule of law, not of individuals (3:79)
e. Full compensation of work (53:39, 53:41, 39:70, 37:39)
f. Provision of basic needs (20:118-119)
g. Security of faith, life, mind, honor, and property (6:109, 6:152, 2:269, 17:36, 24:2, 22:40, 6:152, 5:90, 2:195, 5:32, 17:32, 17:35, 17:29, 83:1)
h. Choice of spouse (4:3, 4:19)
i. Freedom of religion (22:40, 6:109, 2:256)
j. Freedom of expression (2:42, 3:71)
k. Redress of grievances (4:148)
l. Privacy (33:53, 24:27)
m. Care of the handicapped (4:36, 70:24)
n. Presumption of innocence (49:6)
o. Sanctity of name and lineage (49:11, 33:4)
p. Right to residence (4:100, 2:85, 6:41)
q. Aesthetic choice (18:31, 76:13-15)
r. Protection of chastity (17:32, 24:2)
s. Race, color, gender, lineage, wealth are no criteria of superiority.
t. Degrees of people according to their deeds (2:212, 3:163, 6:132)
u. Man must explore the workings of nature to progress and this must be part of Muslim education system (17:36, 3:191, 45:3, 16:12-18)
v. Economy is free of interest (2:275-80, 3:130, 30:39)
w. Social welfare system is there to provide the weak, sick and the poor (2:177, 51:19, 76:8-9, 89:17-18)
x. No clergy ruling the people, can only work on an advisory level (7:30&66, 2:49, 27:87-89, 34:34-35, 43:23, 5:63, 9:31&34, 6:112-113, 3:7)
y. Every person having the right for running water, sewage system and housing (7:43, 39:20)
z. Fight against oppression and liberate the oppressed (4:75, 2:190-3)[17]

This is the difference and importance of approach. Believing in one God is a confirmation of reality and the first step into uniting mankind and the Muslims. But it is the humanitarian approach to life which will truly uplift the Muslim

---

Muslim community. Ma'roof: Virtue, Kindness, All that is good, Declared Ma'roof by the Quran. Munkar: Vice, Evil: All that is wrong, Declared Munkar by the Quran. 2:143, 3:109, 23:1, 61:2-3.

[17] Islam as I understand by Dr.Shabbir Ahmad, 2007 7th edition. A-V given by Dr.Shabbir Ahmad. U-Z added by the author.

societies. It is clear the Quran is focussed on us, not on worship. He has given us the Quran so we can become the best people on Earth. To make Paradise on Earth which will be continued in the Hereafter.

Then we can claim:

> 3:110 (Since you have been empowered by the Quran), you are indeed the best suited Community that has been raised up for the good of mankind. You shall enjoin the Right, by example and close the doors to Wrong, by example, since you have conviction in Allah (and accept His Final Word as the Criterion of Right and Wrong 3:4. The Quran educates you on the Permanent Moral Value System and distinguishes clearly what the otherwise vague terms of 'right' and 'wrong', and 'good' and 'evil' would mean). Now if the People of the Scripture had attained this kind of belief, it would have been for their own good. Some of them do embrace belief, while most of them continue to drift away.

"The original impetus of Islam, so tremendous in its beginnings, sufficed for a while to carry the Muslim commonwealth to great cultural heights-to that splendid vision of scientific, literary and artistic achievement which historians describe as the Golden Age of Islam; but within a few more centuries this impetus also died down for want of spiritual nourishment, and Muslim civilization became more and more stagnant and devoid of creating power. I had no illusions as to the present state of affairs in the Muslim world. The 4 years I have spent in those countries had shown me that while Islam was still alive, perceptible in the world-view of its adherents and their silent admission of its ethical premises, they themselves were like people paralysed, unable to translate their beliefs into fruitful action. But what concerned me more than the failure of present-day Muslims to implement the scheme of Islam were the potentialities of that scheme itself. It was sufficient for me to know that for a short time, quite at the beginning of Islamic history, a successful attempt had been made to translate that scheme into practice; and what had seemed possible at one time might perhaps become really possible at another. What did it matter, I told myself, that the Muslims had gone astray from the original teachings and subsided into indolence and ignorance.

What did it matter that they did not live up to the ideal placed before them by the Arabian Prophet 13 centuries ago-if the ideal itself still lay open to all who were willing to listen to its message?" [18]

DRC 2008

---

[18] Page 304-305 Road to Mecca by Muhammed Asad

Bibliography:

Quran translated and commented from the Arabic by the author *Dr.Shabbir Ahmad* -QXP Quran
  Translation, 2007 4th edition, Galaxy. ISBN 187-9402696 **Important Note:** Many of the
  presented Quran verses are an interaction between my understanding and Dr. Shabbir's
  understanding. Thus many times I will present QXP with a slight adaption where I have
  translated words as *Jahannam, Jannah* or *Rabb* differently within the verses. QXP and my
  presentations of the Quran are very different then most translations as we try to convey the
  root meaning of the Arabic words in a neutral way, preferring scientific and sociological
  meanings. Also many explanations are given within the verses in brackets or in the footnotes
  of the Arabic meanings.
Islam as I understand, 2007 7th edition. Galaxy
www.ourbeacon.com
Arne A. Ambros A Concise Dictionary of Koranic Arabic, 2004. Reichardt Verlag Wiesbaden. ISBN
  3-89500-400-6
G.A. Parwez Islam: A Challenge to Religion, 1996 3rd edition
*Al-Raghib al-Asfahani Al-Mufridaat Fi Ghareebil Quran, Edited by Haitham Tu'aimi. Dar Ihia al-
  Turath al-Arabi-Libanon. ISBN 9953-420-07-6*
Abdul Mannar Omar Dictionary of the Holy Quran, 2006 4th edition. Arabic-English. ISBN
  09632067-9-6. This comprehensive dictionary is a summary of authoritive dictionaries on the
  Arabic language as: *Bahr al-Muhit, Tafsir Kashshaf, Lisan al-Arab, Mughni al-Labib, Qamus
  al-Muhit, Al-Mufridaat Fi Ghareebil Quran, Taj al-urus, al-Muhit fi al-Lughat* and many
  more.
Edward William Lane Arabic-English Lexicon, based on *Taj-Ul-Roos* by *Murtdza Husaini* (D 1205
  CE), 2003 2nd reprint. Asian Educational Services. ISBN 81-206-0107-6
Muhammad Asad
  The Message, Quran Translation, 2003 ISBN 1-904510-00-0
  Road to Mecca, 2005 2nd edition, The Book Foundation, ISBN 1-887752-37-4
The Bible
Arnold Yasin Mol
  The Quranic Rules of Interpretation, 2008 DRC
  Quranic Cosmology: A short introduction by Arnold Yasin Mol, 2008 DRC
Isma'il Ibn Katheer Tafsīr al- Quran, Cairo. English translation
The Quran: An Encyclopedia edited by Oliver Leaman, 2008 Paperback. Routledge, ISBN 978-0-
  415-77529-8

Islam and Democracy:
Why There is No Democratic
Government in the Muslim Countries?

Ali Behzadnia

Let us first clear some of the misunderstandings about Islam before addressing the topic.

Islam finds its root from two sources, "Taslim" i.e. submission or surrender and "Salam" meaning peace. As a complete and integrated ideology, Islam covers both the relationship of man and his creator and the relationship of human beings with themselves or human relationship with the universe.

The relationship of mankind with his creator is total or absolute submission. This is the essential meaning of Islam and it is not confined to the faith that was revealed through Mohammad. He was the last of the chain of many prophets, who were also called Muslims, none was distinguished from the other and they all delivered the exact same message. (26:67, 68, 103, 104, 121,123, 139, 140)

Those prophets who came after Abraham (Ebrahim) including Muhammad were addressed to follow the creed of their forefather. (22:78)

The Qura'n uses the same term "Muslim" for many prophets, those whose names are mentioned like Adam, Noah, Salih, Lute, Abraham, Ishmael, Isaac, Moses, Jesus, Mohammad and all those that are not mentioned in the book. (2: 133-139)

The Qura'n addresses the believers, the Jews, Christians, Zoroastrians and all others who believe in God and do good deed, that they will be rewarded and should have no fear and no grievance. (2:62) Islam is the religion for entire universe. All creatures, visible and invisible (Jinn) are willingly and unwillingly are submitted to His will. (62:1; 64:1; 87:1) Man was exempted, when he was gifted with free will and wisdom. He/she had the choice to accept or reject even the religion itself. This is how the foundation of our freedom, individual and social responsibility, critical thinking, human rights and democracy was established. He further left the monitor within us (self-consciousness) to guard our behavior and gave us Knowledge so we can use it wisely to find our way. Then to every nation, at different periods he sent His messengers as the reminders and models, like lighthouses to illuminate our way. (6:104-106; 88:22)

But God did not want us to be passively obedient. As is mentioned in the Quran, in symbolic story of Adam and Eve, which is the same in other scriptures, the

186

first reaction of the couple was to rebel, but later to find their mistake after receiving the knowledge and choosing to repent. (2:28-35)

So it is not a surprise to see that Qura'n says "Religion the eyes of God is Islam". (3:19, 83, 85)

The universe is created as Muslim. Human embryo is shaped by Him and delivered at term by as a Muslim, which is the faith of every infant, and child who then have to choose their faith at maturity. (3:6) Religion is not in the genes, not inherited, not intimated and not familial. In selecting one's faith, the Quran teaches us not to follow the belief of our parents if you do not see them on right path and they do not use their wisdom. (29:8, 31:14-15)

Religion is sensed, learned and experienced. Not two people, even the identical twins, will have the same concept of God, purpose of life and the world vision. In fact, in every individual, at different stages of life these concepts will change. Belief is a dynamic phenomenon that is constantly variable. How often we see that an observation, experience or incident has changed some ones belief and the entire life.

We are created not to believe the same. After all, people's belief is in their mind and there heart. Wherein we have no access to see or measure the religion or the degree of their religiosity. We can only see people's action, not even knowing their intention. Our judgment as to their deed is also limited to our perception, interpretation and many other factors. (53:30; 10:108)

The Quran tells the believers not to tease or humiliate those who do not believe and not to be arrogant if you think you are among the believers. (4:171; 5:77). Qura'n advises the prophet not to feel sad if the people reject the message and speed on their wrong path. (3:176; 5:41) God says if He wanted, would have sent a sign to bend the neck of unbelievers and make them all believe the same. (26:4)

None of the prophets used force, imprisonment or punishment for those who rejected the faith. Noah could not save his son. Lute could not change his wife, Abraham only felt sorry for his father. Moses came to save his people form the oppression and slavery of Egyptian Pharos but the same people rejected him, leaving him in the desert and asking him to go and see his God. Jesus came to spread love and mercy but his companions and ran away, the day the saw him being taken to the cross. Mohamed's own family tortured him and so too the families of many companions on them. The Jews and Christians were among the first people to join him in Medina, when the Muslim were few and new immigrants. None of the prophets was holy and neither one of their companions. They were like ordinary people. They were mostly illiterate and poor people. They called people to worship their creator and they were not to be worshiped.

As for the second part of meaning of Islam, it defines the relationship among human beings, not only the Muslims. This is the first interaction and greeting of two people Muslim or non-Muslim. It means peace and justice that entails tolerance and mercy. The Muslims are not to fight with each other. Permission is given to them to engage the non-Muslims only if they are threatened by latter. (22:39)

The source and goal of religion, i.e. all faiths, is love and mercy. It is to establish peace and security within each person and with the society and nature. The call to fight in the name of or for the sake of religion, it is a total falsehood. The reasons behind the bloodshed of the past or present Crusaders, is all fake and not the faith.

Democracy is a political term meaning, a government by the people or the rule of majority. The meaning is some time expanded to cover having free media, freedom of speech, equal opportunity etc.

Islam does not specify or recommend any special form of government. Most of the prophets had no leadership role but some have been in position of kings especially among the children of Jacob. Moses had a general leadership with his brother Aaron, but did not have a government.

Jesus prophecy was quite short and acted mostly as a spiritual leader. Mohammad had a very special form of state when he was in Medina. In a multi Tribal community, he was involved in most functions of his small community. He assigned people to different tasks at different times. He had eyes on individual member of his community. He consulted his people on major issues especially when they were to engage in the battles. When he died, he left no established organization, did not assign any one for leadership. Obviously his prophecy was not replaceable, but his companions selected, the oldest and long-term companion of him, as his successor. He lasted for a short period and three successor Caliphs were all assassinated and for a short period after the fourth caliph the format changed to kingdom and then again to caliphate. With all the expansion and heroism that was the political agenda of different caliphates, with little exception they were mostly corrupted. Even though Islamic territory had expanded to a vast area .The entire Middle East, most part of Africa, part of the east and even west Europe, Russia, Asia and Far East were the Islamic territory. Today the biggest Muslim country is Indonesia. The remnant of empire was defeated in Turkey and countries were divided into small pieces. This fractionalisation was not limited to the geographical territory but they highlighted minor differences among Islamic sects to further damage their unity. Muslims on the other hand, being depressed and humiliated, lost their contact with the Quran, the source of their strength and unity and ended up in today's chaos. We have all kinds of governments in the Muslim lands. Some still in tribal format, mostly are a hidden dictatorship, under false names of Democratic, with the possible exception of Malaysia that is close to democracy. And yet a newly invented system of government, by Khomeini, called "Velayate Faqeeh" was established in Iran, wherein a bunch of Mullahs with the Pharoah's mentality, claim to be the representatives of God, having an ideology that is totally alien to Islam of the Quran. They have done the worst to Islam and Muslims in the last thirty years. Unfortunately those who are not able tolerate democratic movement in this part of the world mostly support them.

Iranian people had three revolutions in less than hundred years. First was the "Parliamentarian Movement" or "Mashrooteh Revolution" that was defeated by the British and their allies, when they brought Reza Pahlavi to power, through a coup d'etat. Next was the "Nationalization of Oil" by the late Dr. Mossadeq that was over thrown by US backed coup d'etat in 1953. The last king, Mohammad Reza, was brought back to power. And lastly the Democratic Revolution in 1979 that forced the Shah out of the country and put an end to near 2500 years of kingdom and dictatorship in Iran.

Unfortunately the revolution was highjacked by the Mullahs. Most of the intellectuals found themselves being deceived by Khomeini's false promises. Once again her allies and US could not see the Democratic movement in the area. So in a two-stage coup d'etat, they first forced the transitional government of Bazargan[1] to resign, by the dirty trick of hostage taking and then by secret negotiations with the Mullahs to expel Banisadr, the first democratically elected president after the revolution, now in exile in France.[2] Those negotiators were now in power. Their ruling has forced more than a million of the most educated professionals and business managers to leave the country and hundreds of thousands of Iranian to lost their lives or became disabled from eight years nonsense fighting of two Muslim neighbors.

Islam wishes liberty and justice for all and not for a specific nation or parts of the planet. While we may be required to apply for citizenship, when migrating from one country to the other, but we all hold the citizenship of the same planet, no matter which part of it we were born. Therefore we should exercise our rights for voting not only for the local government but also in major decision-makings for the world affair. This idea was the principle of having Assembly of the United Nations. However by considering the right of Veto for a few big nations and inefficacy of its resolutions, when it comes to the big powers or those small ones with special interest, it is becoming a useless organisation.

The idea of separation of church and the state that is considered in Christianity does not apply to Islam, whereas there is no state in Christianity, there is no church in Islam. A Muslim can be part of the government in a majority Muslim country or non-Muslim country. Non-Muslims have the same right. There is not such thing as "Islamic Government". The Quran and scriptures are the books of

---

[1] Bazargan was a Professor of Engineering, Muslim Scholar, founder of Iranian Liberation Movement and head of the first Transitional Government of Iran after the Iranian Revolution. He asked people to vote for Democratic Republic of Iran, but Khomeini said "Islamic Republic with no addition"!

[2] *My Turn to Speak: Iran, the Revolution and Secret Deals With the U.S.*by Banisadr former President of Iran. McMillan Publishing Co. USA, 1991.

guidance for those who believe in them. People may benefit by considering some of their religious principles in writing their local constitutions, but they should not replace each other. Here are some facts about the position of leadership in Islam,

The concept of "Shura" or consultation was being exercised in the early Islamic Society, even among the tribal communities. Every one has only one vote and no other power or privilege. Furthermore, while the vote of majority is counted, for certain major issues a unanimous agreement is encouraged.

In Islam the ruler is elected for certain period and is the employee of the nation.

The positions are held by those most qualified and are conditional. People have the right to give mandate and the right to withdraw it at any time.

The ruler is not hostage to the special interest groups, the elite or nobility.

Community volunteer work is highly encouraged for every Muslim. Some have considered this as a duty or religious obligation.

Now that we have explained Islam and agreed that there is not much of a democratic regime in so-called Islamic countries, and we also gave some of the reasons for it, we should ask those who phrase the question of lack of democracy in Islam, to further humiliate the Muslims, do they see a true democracy in other parts of the planet? How much the practice of current western democracy meets the criteria of true democracy? May we ask where the Christian or Jewish countries are? Is there a true democracy in those nations? In our most civilized, most educated, wealthiest and most diverse nation on earth, the United States, wherein people seems to be having more freedom than many parts of the world, do we really have a democratic regime? What percentage of those eligible will vote for different election, including the presidency? If our repeated statistics shows this being much less than one third of qualified voters, have we asked why? Are we concerned that the elected candidate is not representing the majority? Was this not the basic principle of Democracy? Have we asked why the candidates have to spend millions of Dollars for their campaigns to get the people vote? Who pays for all these expenses and what for? Is it not the duty of each citizen to deeply search and study about their candidates, in their everyday life, rather than rely on the media, pressure groups and lobbyists, who during the short period before the elections, advertise for those candidate of their interest? Where is the democracy, wherein millions of citizens and their delegates vote but the candidate for the highest rank of responsibility and world leadership, is selected by the court order! Is the selected candidate the most qualified for the position, in the country that is blessed to have hundred of thousands of the most brilliant minds and experts in many fields? Have we thought of having special classes or schools for training proper officers for the leadership position? Finally may we ask how much this democracy has brought stability, peace and security for our citizens? Why are we living in such high level of debt and anxiety, depression and fear of terror? And how long this is going last?

I am concerned as a citizen. Please do not get angry and do not tell me "Love it or leave it". Be patient, think of a third alternative "stay and change it". I came here more than forty years ago, escaping from the dictatorship where I was born. I came with my Doctorate in Medicine as a physician, researcher, educator and a healer. My children were all born here. This is my home and my country as much as may be yours. "My home is where my grandchildren are going to play and not where my grand mother was born." I love my neighbors, my patients and my new home. I want to see them in peace and happiness. I respect them as human and expect to be treated like. "Salam" Peace be upon you.

Are Muslims or Islam a Threat to Our Security?

Ali Behzadnia

It is almost seven years since the destruction of the twin towers in downtown New York.

There is still much ambiguity as to how and why this happened. Who was the actual planner of this unforgettable crime? Because those who were accused to be involved in this operation, happened to be Muslims from Saudi Arabia, ironically a staunch ally of the United States, suddenly all Muslims were accused to be "Terrorist" and Islam was viewed as a "Doctrine of Terror".

Since that tragic event, there has been a co-ordinated effort in the media, among special interest groups, many politicians and unfortunately some teachers and preachers—relentlessly stereotyping Islam and Muslims the results of which have perpetuated hate crimes, unfair targeting and profiling of American Muslim citizens in general and especially those who are activists.

Some preachers have gone so far as to claim that Muslims do not believe in God since they worship "Allah". Many websites, newspapers and magazines, in addition to radio and broadcast media, have been humiliating Muslims and publishing books and cartoons blaspheming Islam and its messenger Mohammad (PBUH). They are misrepresenting the crime of a group of terrorists and creating a negative association with an entire world population of Muslims. These few criminals are not representative of the over nine million Muslims in the United States, the peaceful citizens whose contributions to our nation's education, science, technology, medicine and business are innumerable.

Furthermore, we cannot ignore the fact that 1.8 Billion people on this planet are Muslim and the population is increasing at a rate of 2.9% annually. This has been further supported by the Vatican, which recently announced that Muslims outnumber Catholics in the world for the first time in history.

In spite of all the carpet bombings, mass murders, and genocides that have been taking place, in the last two decades in Muslim lands including: Bosnia, Chechnya, Pakistan, Palestine, Iran, Iraq, Afghanistan, Lebanon, Kashmir, India, Somalia and many parts of Africa, to name a few; Islam continues to have the highest growth rate. What is most amazing is the number of people who have advanced their belief (converted) among our youth, by self-studying the Quran

192

and showing interest to learn about Muslims. Many not only have turned to Islam, but also have become scholars, speakers and writers of Islam.

There appears to be no world war, but most of the Muslim world has been burning in fire, especially the Middle East. The home of the greatest prophets and the cradle of human civilization has turned into boiling blood baths simply because oil runs beneath their earth. God knows the exact number of casualties, but we know that at least hundreds of thousands of innocent men, women and children are killed and those that survive are either adversely afflicted or perish from poverty and illness. What was once considered beautiful, fertile land is now home to mass burials and graveyards? All of this inhumanity and injustice is done to rob the oil and yet oil today is at its highest price in history!

It is the average working citizen, not just here but in the global village that has to pay the price. Taxes and extra taxes are to be paid for every ticket you buy, every room you occupy, every mile you drive, every phone you call and every item of basic necessity you purchase. This is what is happening now and God knows what will happen to the generations to come. What would happen to the gun manufacturers and our economy if those scattered wars in the third world were to be eradicated by the effort of some peace loving people?

Our country is the richest in the world, yet the average American citizen in spite of working hard, often working multiple jobs, is more in debt than the people who live in less wealthy countries. Many people in Africa do not have enough to eat, but they are not in debt either. We destroy the surpluses of our products to save the Dollar and yet we are economically in recession and mentally in Depression. "The materialistic ideologies are not compatible with the life of human beings, whose needs are beyond material."

Communism promised peace and social justice by crushing the rights of individuals for the social benefit. It killed hundreds of thousands of its opponents or drowned them in the icy lakes of Siberia, but it did not last more than decades. When it collapsed we were there to help to absorb the shock of such destruction. We could never imagine seeing the leader of the Soviet Empire, kneeling at the feet of the capitalist asking for help to provide basic needs for his nation!

Conversely, capitalism has ignored and crushed the society for the benefit of individuals. The Dollar-oriented capital giant needs to expand in order to survive. If it does not change direction, it will ultimately collapse. Now imagine who would be able to absorb the shock of such a disaster.

For many years we scared our people with the fear of Communism and the Russian threat, to justify the development of the most advanced, expensive and sophisticated army and arms manufacturers. In spite of being blessed by having two great oceans on our right and left and the friendliest nation to our North, we have been spending and continue to spend most of our nation's income for our defense budget.

Now that Russian bubble has burst and the level of poverty, the deceptive dictatorship is no more behind the Iron curtain and the Cold War is over, who is going to absorb the product of our gun factories? If we decided today to change our war economy to the economy of peace, what would happen and how much time and sacrifice would be needed?

Are we actually willing to do it? Do we think about a change? Have we not learned after all these wars, that bloodshed only causes more blood to be shed? Never has war brought peace and security for any nation. So we either have to destroy the product of our gun factories in the oceans, as we do with our produce or continue for securing the capital benefit of a few, sucking the blood of average citizens and forcing them to tolerate multi-billion dollar war machines and gunship to go abroad and shed the blood of innocent people with whom we have no relationship and for whom we have no animosity!

So in the absence of real giants we have to find pseudo-giants. Our old "friends" become our biggest enemies. The number one wanted man on the list of world's criminals—Osama Bin Laden is a Saudi hero. He and his father modernized Saudi Arabia in such a short period. The US had a very close relationship with his family and did significant business in the process of the remodeling. The US encouraged him and his team to go to Afghanistan and gave him whatever he asked for to fight the Russians who had partially invaded the Northern Afghanistan and was trying to proceed south, to get access to the open sea, through Pakistan (A long-time dream of the Russians). After he defeated the Russians, wanted to return home but it was dangerous if such hero would have returned to his country, after what had taken place in Iran. We invaded Afghanistan and killed most of his people but ended up facing the Taliban who was another old "friend" that was now angry with us and whom we are still there fighting.

Another old "friend" was Saddam Hussein. We supported him with all the arms he wanted, including chemical and biological weapons, plus almost a billion a day of Saudi oil income, to fight the Iranians for eight years. A war that had erupted for the sole reason of preventing Khomeini's army from potentially expanding into Iraq and the Middle East. No one was victorious in this war. There were significant human casualties for both sides. Eventually as Saddam grew in power he stood in the way of our interests. So we encouraged him to invade Kuwait. He did not realize that he was digging his own grave, when he was looting and evacuating the country making it ready for the US Army to establish its bases to eventually invade Iraq. The Army could not enter from the North because of the heavy mountains and the Turks and Kurds being very patriotic Muslims. They would not allow US invasion. The Saudi's were not happy having US soldiers on their ground. The Sheikh of Kuwait was brought to the US, was treated as a guest and then returned back to his position, now to support us when we get there.

Today Saddam is gone and Iraq is destroyed. But the oil wells are intact. We cannot stay there, but we do not know how to get out. Most other countries have already left.

Our focus is now on Iran. We helped the Mullahs get rid of Bazargan,[1] and Banisadr,[2] who were establishing a democratic system in Iran. We have supported this existing cruel dictatorship for almost thirty years, and now they are going to have an atomic bomb and its President has declared many times that he wants to wipe Israel from the map! Which is equivalent to the end of the world as far as the US is concerned! Keep in mind, when there is no big giant, the fear must sound gigantic. What greater fear is there than the end of the world?

You see the problem is not Islam or Muslims. In fact, there are many Millions of Muslims in other parts of the world, but there is no war. The population of West Pakistan is almost twice that of Iran, they have more hard liners Muslims and atomic energy and an atomic bomb. Yet, why are we not afraid that they will destroy the world?

I assure those who are concerned, that the real threat is not from a few radicals who were once our 'friends'—who have been either killed or are finding refuge in caves, oceans and continents away from us. History teaches us that no empire has collapsed because of poverty or lack of warriors. They were destroyed when the people's morals decayed. Study the fall of the Roman and Persian Empires or

---

[1] Mehi Bazargan was a Professor of Engineering, Muslim Scholar, founder of Iranian Liberation Movement and head of the first Transitional Government of Iran after the Iranian Revolution. He asked people to vote for Democratic Republic of Iran, but Khomeini said "Islamic Republic with no addition"! It is important to know that there was no single Mulla among the people that he selected for the transient government. Many were graduates from world's famous universities; some were long-term U.S. residents. His first deputy, and once the foreign minister was a U.S. citizen (E. Yazdi). Still this cabinet was not acceptable to us and it was forced to resign by the trick of taking hostages. Stage one of the codetta of the US against Iranian Revolution.

[2] Aboul-Hassan Banisadr was also an Islamic scholar, writer, thinker, economist, a long term resident in Paris, Who received Khomeini, when Saddam expelled him from Iraq. He was a key counselor of Khomeini, for preparing the Statements and interviews with the foreign media, while he was in Paris. He came to Iran with him. Became the Foreign Minister for a short period. Over eleven Million of Iranian voted for him, in a most democratic election in Iranian history, Khomeini was not one of them. Soon after he took the office, the Iran-Iraq war started, he was assigned as the Commander In Chief of the army. Even though he never had served arm forces, but his loving attitude inspired the forces to defend their country in spite of all the accusations and humiliation by the Mullahs. He was finally impeached by the Mullah dominated Parliament and forced to return back to exile in France. The second stage of the US codetta against Iranian Revolution. *My Turn to Speak: Iran, the Revolution and Secret Deals with the U.S.* by Banisadr former President of Iran. McMillan Publishing Co. USA, 1991.

the most recent collapse of the Soviet Union and Communism to realize this fact.

The threat comes from within. When there is a major social gap, hidden racism and slavery, social injustice, poverty, consumerism, economic insecurity, a sick economy in which people may lose all they have overnight, it results in a negative wave of broken families, alcohol, drugs, homicides, suicides, all other social maladies and a life full of fear in debt and depression, shamelessness and chaos.

Also a careful review of history shows that Muslims, Jews, Christians and people of other beliefs, with few exceptions, have lived for many centuries together in peace with patience and tolerance. The source of all religions is peace and love. Our diversity is part of our being and is beautiful. We are all transients and guests on this planet. It is time for everyone to reflect on what we believe and how this affects our behavior and our interactions with others no matter what they believe in. Religion is not inherited, it is learned to help us to be self-conscious and live humanely and preserve our self-dignity.

Far from all the stereotyping that is taking place, I highly recommend to those who are concerned, to self-search in the Quran and find out why in Islam there is room for every one.[3] Room for the believers and those who claim to be unbelievers, without any prejudice you will find out that Islam is a treat and not a threat.

---

[3] See, the Quran: 1:1-7; 2:133-139; 3:1; 26:67, 68, 103, 104,121,123; 22:78, 2:62. Also see, 49:13. This verse in engraved in a wooden Arc at the entrance of United Nation (A Gift by the Moroccan).

Hadīth as Scripture:
Discussions on the Authority of
Prophetic Traditions in Islam

Aisha Y. Musa

This work examines the development of Muslim attitudes toward the Hadīth as a scriptural source of religious guidance and law the classical period by examing the debates recorded in the works of Muḥammad ibn Idrás al-Shāfiī (d. 204 AH), Ibn Qutayba (d. 276 AH) and al-Khaṭīb al-Baghdādī (d. 456 AH). In addition to these three authors, supporting evidence found in a variety of other early works including those dedicated to the issue of problematic Hadīth, commentaries on the Quran, prophetic biography/war chronicles biographical dictionaries, histories, and the Hadīth collections themselves. An analysis of information found in these sources identifies the central ideas and arguments related to the authority of the Hadīth. Key figures and arguments over the authority of the Hadīth in the modern period are also examined and compared with their historical counterparts. Such a comparison of the historical debates and their modern parallels offers valuable insights into the debates at both the popular and scholarly levels.

Part I deals with the early controversies over the authority of the Hadīth, focusing primarily on the works of al-Shāfiī, Ibn Qutayba, and al-Khaṭīb al-Baghdādī. These three figures address objections to the Hadīth more directly and in greater detail than other early sources. Moreover, they shed light on the evolution of the debates over the Hadīth from the second through the fifth centuries A.H. In addition to these three authors, supporting evidence found in a variety of other early works including those dedicated to the issue of problematic Hadīth, commentaries on the Quran, prophetic biography/war chronicles, biographical dictionaries, histories, and the Hadīth collections themselves is also examined.

Part II deals with recent and contemporary challenges to the authority of the Hadīth, focusing on the most prominent figures, including Rashad Khalifa, Edip Yuksel, Kassim Ahmed, and Ahman Subhy Mansour, together with the key arguments that have dominated the debates during the last several decades.

Part III of this work is a translation of al-Shāfiī's Kitāb Jimā al-ilm, which is both the earliest known and also one of the most important works on the authority of the Hadīth. The arguments articulated by al-Shāfiī in the Jimā have remained a cornerstone in mainstream Muslim defense of the authority and necessity of the Hadīth in Islam.

Jews in the Quran: an Introduction

Aisha Y. Musa,

Today, it often seems as if the relations between Muslims and Jews are dominated by bigotry, intolerance, and even downright hostility. Some claim that Muslim hostility toward Jews is taught in the Quran itself. How does the Quran portray the Jews? Is it inherently hostile toward them? Are they described, as some have claimed, as apes and swine"? The simple answer to the latter question is no, the Quran never says the Jews are "apes and swine". We will take a closer look at this claim later in this essay. Before that, however, let us take a broader look at the overall image of Jews in the Quran. The present essay focuses entirely on the Quran and is meant as an introduction. Beyond the Quran, Muslim opinion is also shaped by the Prophetic traditions (Hadith) and centuries of commentaries and interpretations. Future essays will examine other such sources and aspects of the question.

There are approximately 60 verses in the Quran that speak directly about or to the Jews. Two thirds of these use the phrase "Children of Israel" (bani Isra'il), others use the terms "Jews" (yahud) or "those who are Jewish" (alladhina hadu). In addition to verses specifically about or addressing the Jews, the Quran also speaks of the people of the Book (ahl al-kitab) and "those who have been given the Book" (alladhina utu al-kitab). These verses are generally understood to refer to both the Christians and the Jews, those who received the scriptures which preceded the Quran. The Quran also mentions the Torah more than a dozen times. It also mentions the Pslams of David. In addition to the variety of verses that speak to or about the Jews, chapter 17 of the Quran is entitled "The Children of Israel."

In order to better understand the Quran's portrayal of the Jews it is important to understand the Quran's portrayal of religion itself. Right religion, according to the Quran, is submission to God (lit. islam in Arabic). Those who submit to God are, by literal definition, muslim. Thus, islam, in its generic, literal meaning is the religion of all the prophets and messengers from Noah to Abraham to Moses, Jesus, and Muhammad, according to the Quran (10:71-72, 84; 2:128-131; 5:110-111). Thus, there is a distinction between the Quranic use of the term muslim as a generic term, which refers to someone who submits to God, and the proper noun Muslim, which refers to a follower of the religion founded by Muhammad in the seventh century. Does one need to be a Muslim to be a muslim? Must a Jew who recognizes Muhammad as a messenger and the Quran as scripture convert to Islam? The perhaps surprising answer, from a Quranic perspective, the answer is, no.

All of the prophets before Muhammad were, according to the Quran, muslim, as were those who believed them and followed them. The children of Israel enjoy a special status: "O children of Israel, remember my favor which I bestowed upon you, and that I favored you above all creation." (Quran 2:47, 2:122).*

The Quran discusses God's favors and covenant with the Children of Israel in detail:

> 20:80   O children of Israel, indeed we delivered you from your enemy and made a covenant with you on the right side of the mountain, and we sent down for you manna and quails.*

> 45:16   Indeed we gave the children of Israel the Book, and wisdom, and the prophecy, and we provided them with good things and favored them above all creation.*

> 2:83   We made a covenant with the children of Israel: "Serve none except God. Be good to parents, relatives, orphans, and the poor. Speak kindly to people. Establish prayer and give alms." Afterward, you turned away, except a few of you, and you were averse.*

Their special status and covenant with God gives the children of Israel a great responsibility: the responsibility to uphold the covenant and abide by the law and guidance God has given them. So, what of the Quran's criticism of Jews? An indication of the problem appears at the end of verse 2:83, above: Afterward, you turned away, except a few of you, and you were averse. Just as it provides details of God's favors and covenant with the children of Israel, the Quran also discusses violations of that covenant.

> 2:92   Moses came to you with clear proofs, yet you took the calf [for worship] in his absence, and you turned wicked.*

> 2:84-85 We made a covenant with you, that you not shed each others' blood, nor evict each other from your homes. You agreed and bore witness. Yet it is you who are killing each other and evicting a group among you from their homes, supporting each other against them unlawfully and aggressively; and if they should come to you as captives you would ransom them-- while evicting them was unlawful for you. Do you then believe in a part of the Book and disbelieve in the other?*

> 2:65   You have known those among you who violated the Sabbath, so we said to them: "Be despicable ape."

It is in a similar context that the Quran uses the term "apes and swine," in Quran 5:60, though in that verse, it is not said in reference to Jews. Here is 5:60 in its entirety:

> 5:60   Say: "Shall I inform you of something worse in the sight of God: those whom God has cursed and with whom he is angry, and he has made some of them apes and swine and servants of evil. These are in a worse position and more astray from the even path." *

While some people may claim that the above refers specifically to the Jews, reading the verse in its context shows this is not necessarily accurate. This is clear from verses 5:57-58.

> 5:57-58 O you who believe, do not befriend those who make a mockery of your religion from among those who were given the Book before you or the disbelievers. Reverence God, if you are truly believers. When you call to prayer they make a mockery and a game of it. This is because they are a people who do not understand. *

As these verses show, the discussion is about those who make a mockery of religion, whether they are those who received previous scripture or those who are disbelievers. Of course, Jews are among those who received previous scripture, which is the basis of the claim that verse 5:60 refers to Jews. However, there is no Quranic basis for claiming that it refers exclusively or even primarily to Jews. The emphasis in the discussion is not the religion of, or lack thereof, of those with whom God was so angry that he cursed them and some of them apes, swine, and servants of evil. The emphasis is on the actions that may lead to such retribution from God--making a mockery of the religion of those who believe in God and in a scripture the mockers do not accept. Some of those mockers are among those who received previous scriptures:

> 5:59   Say, "O people of the scripture, do you resent us because we believe in God, and in what was sent down to us, and in what was sent down before us, and because most of you are not righteous?"*

But does this mean all of those who received the previous scripture? Other verses of the Quran make it clear that it is not.

> 3:113-115 They are not all alike; among the people of the Book there is an upstanding community. They recite God's revelations through the night, and they fall prostrate. They believe in God and the last day. They advocate good and forbid evil, and they hasten to do good works. These are among the righteous. Whatever good they do will not be denied. God knows those who are reverent.*

> 5:69   Surely those who believe, those who are Jews, the Sabians, and the Christians, whoever believes in God and the last day and does good, has nothing to fear nor will they grieve.*

The above verses clearly extend the promise of God to all who believe and do good, whether they are believers in the Quran or not. Those who are criticized in the Quran are those who fail to uphold their covenant with God. Nothing in the Quran calls on the Jews to abandon the Torah in favor of the Quran. Quite the opposite. The Quran repeated declares that it comes to confirm the previous scripture, not to supplant it. Indeed, the Quran criticizes the Jews of Medina for coming to Muhammad for judgment when they had the Torah:

> 5:43   How do they make you a judge while they have the Torah in which is God's law? Then they turn back after that--these are not believers.*

The following verse further emphasizes the importance of the Torah, and the fact that those who follow it are submitting to God.

> 5:44   We sent down the Torah, in which there is guidance and light, by which the prophets who submitted judged the Jews, as did the rabbis and the priests, according to what they were required to observe of God's Book, and thereunto were they witnesses. So do not fear people, but fear me, and do not sell my signs for minor gain. Whoever does not judge by what God has sent down are disbelievers.*

Considering all of these verses, whether they are speaking to or about the children of Israel, or the Jews, or people of the Book, it is clear that Quranic criticism and condemnation is aimed not at the Jews as a people, but only at those among them who fail to reverence God and uphold their covenant with Him. Moreover, the Quran calls on Jews to adhere to what God has sent down in the Torah. So, if a Jew recognizes Muhammad as a messenger and the Quran as God's Book, should follow the Torah. To do otherwise would be to disobey the Quran. The Quran also offers a clear remedy for religious bigotry and intolerance:

> 5:48   We have sent down the Book to you in truth, verifying what is before it of the Book and a standard of comparison for it; therefore judge between them by what God has sent down, and do not follow their low desires, turning away the truth that has come to you; for each of you we have ordained a law and a way of doing things. If God wished, He would have made you a single community, but he tests you according to what he has given you, so compete with each other in doing good. Your return is to God, and then He will let you know about that in which you differed.*

Let us consider these words from the Quran with care and open our minds and our hearts to the possibility of accepting that God has given our communities different traditions and practices by which we serve Him, so that we can begin to compete with each other in doing good for His sake and our own.

* To see this document with the Arabic text please to go to Aisha Musa's site: www.askmusa.org

I Refuse to Be a Hostage

Aisha Jumaan

In recent years, the world has learned that it is easy to manipulate Muslims emotions; it is rather simple, cheap, and requires only a few people; all a person needs to do is insult Islam or what Muslims consider sacred. This was illustrated by the Danish Cartoons that resulted in violent demonstrations by many Muslims around the globe. Since then others who do not believe in coexistent or a domination of one group over another to coexist have found a treasure box to prove their pre conceived notion that there is no place for Islam in our world today unless it fits their definition of what Islam should be.

Of course like many things in our lives, many factors are interrelated in this phenomenon.

Free speech: some people feel that it is a matter of free speech. I, and most people, believe in the essential role free speech plays in our own lives; however, under the guise of free speech, some people spread hate. Recently, Geert Wilders released a movie which he named "fitna" against the Quran, the Muslim's Holy book.

In a world that has become more diverse, where many people of different faiths races and ethnic groups live together, respect for the other and not just tolerance is an essential social responsibility for peaceful coexistence. Mr. Wilder ignores these basic principles and continuously insults Islam and Muslims. Wilders is not motivated by free speech, but rather by prejudice and hate. He has advocated banning the Quran in the Netherlands; a position that contradicts his claim for free speech. It is one thing to bring issues up for debate; it is another to incite hate towards over one billion people.

Free speech does not mean that we accept expressions of hate without challenging them, especially when they cause emotional turmoil to the targeted communities and incite prejudice and hate towards them. It is a civil duty of citizens of the world to counter such expressions of hate and expose them for what they are. It is especially crucial for people not belonging to the targeted communities to dissociate themselves from such expressions and assure the attacked communities that they don't support such hateful messages by speaking up against them.

Muslims' reactions: it is unfortunate that many Muslims react to such hateful expressions by holding violent demonstrations which is exactly what people like Wilders want to happen because it feeds into the stereotypes of violent Muslims that are repeatedly shown on media outlets around the world. Furthermore, threats of death to those who spread hate is not acceptable by the vast majority of Muslims around the world who should make their strong opposition known to such behavior because it contradicts Quranic teachings as is illustrated by the following verses.

> 4:140 And, indeed, He has enjoined upon you in this divine writ that whenever you hear people deny the truth of God's messages and mock at them, you shall avoid their company until they begin to talk of other things - or else, verily, you will become like them. Behold, together with those who deny the truth God will gather in hell the hypocrites,

> 6:68 Whenever thou meet such as indulge in [blasphemous] talk about Our messages, turn thy back upon them until they begin to talk of other things and if Satan should ever cause thee to forget [thyself], remain not, after recollection, in the company of such evildoing folk.

As a Muslim, I refuse to be held hostage to people like Wilders and their hate messages, who orchestrate their expressions to illicit strong emotional responses. That does not mean however, that we should be passive. There are multiple ways to express our opposition and concerns to such messages including peaceful demonstrations, making information available about who we are and what our faith is (as we see ourselves, and not as others define us, or how minority extremists define our faith). We can write articles to journals and news media expressing our views, and we can also engage in interfaith activities in our communities to help dispel myths about us as Muslims, but also bring us closer to people of faith.

People generally fear what they don't know and that is the chord that people like Wilders play on; we can break that by becoming active participants with other members of our large communities. Finally, citizens of the world who are concerned about justice, peace and equality should be concerned because although these messages may start targeting one community, unless stopped can easily expand to include more different communities.

Freedom of choice

In the recently held Muslim Heretic conference on March 2008 in Atlanta USA. I learned a valuable lesson. What will happen if the Muslim world adopted the message that some of the conference organizers presented?

The most attractive part of the conference was the promise that each individual has the right to practice his/her faith without being judged or preached to. As the conservatives Muslims try to define how I should be as a Muslim, I found myself in the conference being preached to by the "progressive Muslims" the same way. Since, I have rejected the conservative call in defining how I should be as a Muslim; I also reject the "progressive" call as well. I also found it distressing that some seem to fall into the same trap of engaging in criticizing people and making generalized statements about others. It was distressing because many of those in the group have experienced first hand the pain of individual attacks and generalizations.

Faith is an individual choice and as long as we don't hurt others or even ourselves, what faith we chose or how we practice it should not be a subject of judgment by others. For me, my faith is a relationship that I have with God and I perform it in a way that makes me comfortable and brings me closer to God. No one has the right to tell me how that relationship should be since no one can tell what is in m heart, except God. One of the most horrifying things to me is the casual way people use in making judgment about others and defining who is good and who is not.

As I heard some of the speakers tell me what I should accept or reject, I thought about my sisters, all wearing the hair cover and wondered what their status would be if we lived in a world where the mandate of the progressive Muslims were to be the norm? Would they be forced to take off their hair cover? Would other Muslims have to convene a conference using the same name.

I was lucky to have been raised in a house where practice of faith was a choice, none of my parents asked any of their 6 children to perform any of the religious practices, we all chose for ourselves whether to pray, fast or read the Quran and as we got older, we all came to our individual faith at different points in our lives and in different ways. What my parents insisted on teaching us were respect for others regardless of their faith or status in society, speak the truth even if it was to be used against them and stand up for the weak and for what we believed to be just, and take care of the poor and the needy and orphans and women were at the top of the list.

These values have served me well for almost ½ century, I feel comfortable with people of all faiths, nationalities and ethnic origins. Some of the most valuable lessons I have learned about myself and my faith have come from Christian ministers, Muslims from all school of thoughts and even from people who don't believe in God. Having said that, I am, in no way free of prejudice; however, I am aware of my prejudices and I put myself in situations to challenge those feelings in the hope that I will learn to shed them away, and to some extent, I have succeeded, yet I still have a long way to go.

Understanding "Spending in God's Way" (*Zakat* or *Sadaqa*) under the Quranic Light

Abdur Rab

The Significance of Spending in God's Way

One of the central tenets of Islam relates to spending in God's way—*zakat* (or *zakah*)[1] or *sadaqa*. Some of the reasons why those in society who can afford to engage in such spending should spend are as follows:

- Such spending is part and parcel of the very worship of God;
- It is through such spending that we bring about greater egalitarianism in society;
- Such spending is self-purifying, and it brings real contentment and happiness for the giver; and
- Such spending also makes economic sense.

Whether one calls it *zakat* or *sadaqa*, spending on the poor and one's disadvantaged fellow beings or for God's cause is part and parcel of the very worship of God—for expressing our gratitude to God for His manifold blessings we enjoy (6:141), and for our livelihood that really originates from Him (2:57, 126, 172, 212; 3:27, 37; 4:130; etc.).

There is also a deep philosophical reason for humanitarian spending on the part of the rich people in society. They are just custodians of their wealth and income[2]; they need to spend that wealth and income for godly purposes—to serve only God (12:40). There is no merit in the amassing of wealth, as it has no value as a measure of virtuousness of a human being before God (34:37). Those who are stingy in humanitarian spending and amass or hoard wealth would eventually find that wealth too burdensome for them—such wealth would be tied to their necks like a collar on the Day of Resurrection (3:180). The Quran

---

[1] The word zakat is generally understood as a kind of obligatory poor-due at a certain fixed fraction of one's wealth. The word has also another meaning – purification. The use of the word zakat in the same verse after "spending for the poor" suggests that the word zakat in this verse should be taken to mean purification, rather than poor-due. In that case the meaning of the later part of the verse "akimus-salat o-atuz- zakat" should be like "establish prayer and attain purification".

[2] Current earnings make up income, and wealth is accumulated earnings and/or inherited assets

directs us to be fully alive to the need for ensuring distributive justice in society. It strongly urged the Prophet Muhammad (peace be upon him), who was an orphan and a needy person, not to be oblivious of the needs of the orphans and the needy (93:6-10). The Quran envisions for us an egalitarian society. A society is neither egalitarian nor healthy for its all-round development when some people swim in wealth while others are ill-fed, ill-clad and ill-housed, and when they cannot provide for their health and education even at a basic level. Spending on the helpless and disadvantaged groups in society helps overall moral and spiritual uplifting of all humankind, which is the only way we elevate all men and women and help develop their latent potentials and bring about all round progress in society.

****

*This article is a summarized, consolidated and revised version of the discussion on the same subject in some parts of the author's recently published book *Exploring Islam in a New Light: An Understanding from the Quranic Perspective*. An earlier version under the title "The Significance of Spending in God's Way" can be seen on the website: http://free-minds.org

Zakat means "purification". Spending in a benevolent or God's way is a way of purifying oneself (92:17-21), and often a way of atoning for mistakes or misdeeds or for inability to perform other desirable religious acts. The Quran is emphatic in proclaiming that we cannot attain piety until we spend of that which we love (3:92). The rationale for spending for others is also to be found in the consideration that a human being can hardly live alone in happiness without sharing his or her earnings and possessions with others. God-loving people spend for the poor, the orphans, and the captives out of love for, and pleasure of, God—which is essentially their own pleasure, and they seek or expect no reward or thanks in return (76:8-9; 92:20-21).

> **3:92** Ye will not attain piety until ye spend of what ye love. And whatever ye spend, God is well aware of it.

> **92:17-21** As for the righteous, he will be spared it (the blazing Fire), one who giveth from his riches for self-purification. He seeketh nothing in return, but seeketh (only) the pleasure of his Lord, the Most High. It is he who verily will find contentment.

> **9:103** Take (O Muhammad) contributions (*sadaqa*) from their riches to purify them, and make them grow (in spirituality), and pray for them. Verily thy prayer is reassurance for them.

Spending thus works essentially like prayer, or can broadly be conceived as part of prayer itself. Indeed, as God warns us in the Quran, neglecting needed help and support to needy people renders one's prayer null and void (107:1-7). Spending in God's way is thus an essential component of righteousness (2: 177).

The Quran emphasizes spending in God's way as a greatly virtuous act:

90:12   Ah, what will convey unto thee (O Muhammad) what the
Ascent is!

90:13   (It is) to set a slave free,

90:14   And to feed the hungry,

90:15   An orphan near of kin,

90:16   Or a poor person in misery,

90:17   Then he has become one of those who believe, and enjoin one
another patience and kindness.

90:18   Those are the people on the right path. (90:12-18)

2:261   The example of those who spend their wealth in God's way is like a grain that groweth seven ears, with a hundred grains in every ear. God giveth increase manifold to whomever He pleaseth.

It is only the wrong-headed people who dispute the case for spending for others:

36:47   When they are told: Spend of what God hath provided you, those who disbelieve say to those who believe: "Shall we feed those whom God could feed, if He so willed?" Ye are clearly misguided.

From even a purely economic point of view, a high concentration of income and wealth in fewer hands is counter-productive. Such a concentration adversely affects the development of human resources, and holds down effective demand and holds back economic expansion. High inequality of income and wealth destroys social cohesion, peace and harmony, and breeds bitter feelings on the part of the poor and deprived people, and creates scope for social crimes, immorality and frustration. The have-nots at some time may feel so frustrated that they may even feel prompted to rise against the haves to pull them down.

The Scope of Spending in God's Way: the Wider Meaning

"Spending in God's way" means much more than is conventionally being understood. A careful reading of the Quran does reveal that such spending should be from both income and wealth, that the amount we should spend should be a considerably higher proportion of our income and wealth than is currently being practiced, and that the purposes for which we should spend are much more varied than are usually thought.

The Quran urges us to spend out of our wealth and income or production (2:254; 6:141). Besides, we should use part of our income for our and our families' current consumption, and save and invest part of our income for future consumption, but we should not keep it idle or hoard it. Hoarding is bad for an economy. It deprives others; it curbs effective demand in the economy and holds back economic expansion, and if the hoarding is done in goods, it creates artificial scarcities and high prices of the hoarded goods. The Quran strongly condemns hoarding (3: 180).

Though, everything prescribed in the Quran is *fard* or obligatory for us, God specifically mentions *sadaqa* as *fard* for us, and He mentions where such spending should go:

> **9:60** The alms (*sadaqa*) are for the poor, the needy, and those who administer them, and those whose hearts are to be reconciled (to truth), and to free the slaves and the debtors, and for the cause of God, and (for) the wayfarers; an obligatory duty (*fard*) imposed by God. God is Knower, Most Wise.

Such spending is for those who beg or are needy, and for those who are deprived or poor (70:25), and also for parents, near relatives, orphans, wayfarers, and for those who ask (2:177), and for other causes of God, including that for freeing of captives or slaves and for necessary reconciliation or rehabilitation of new converts to religion (2:177, 215; 8:41; 9:60; 24:22). Spending is also for those who are in need of help, but being involved in the cause of God, are unable to move about in the land, and who do not beg importunately (2:273). Likewise, we need also to spend for other noble causes such as for relieving the burden of those who are heavily laden with debt (9:60), and for miscellaneous other noble purposes, which can be termed as causes of God. As for the spending for the new converts, the Quran speaks well of the God-loving believers during the Prophet's time, who were so generous to those who came to them for refuge that they gave preference to the refugees over themselves in helping them, even though they were poor (59:9).

God advises those of us who are affluent that we should not make such promises as not to help our relatives, poor people, and those who leave their homes for the cause of God; and we are urged to forgive them and ignore their faults (24:22). He loves those who spend not only when they are in affluence or ease, but also when they are in hardship (3:134). He admonishes us to give others what is good, and not what we regard as bad and do not want to receive for ourselves (2:267). God characterizes freeing of war captives or slaves or marrying them as equal partners as very important righteous deeds. Spending for such purposes is likewise a great virtue in the sight of God (2:177; 9:60).

Although unlike in the case of *sadaqa*, the Quran nowhere mentions where the *zakat* should go, and by how much in relation to income or wealth, both *sadaqa* and *zakat* appear to mean the same thing in principle, and also in practice. The current practice of *zakat* at a low proportion (2.5 percent) of one's wealth (which includes the value of most of one's assets with some exceptions such as the family house) appears inadequate in light of the Quran, especially for high-income people, as well as from the point of view of the demands of society for a multiplicity of beneficial works (for God's cause) on top of provisions for the poor.

Concerning what to spend in God's way and how much, the Quran explicitly states:

2:267   O ye who believe! Spend of the good things which ye have earned, and of what We bring forth from the earth for you, and seek not the bad to spend thereof when ye would not take it for yourselves unless ye close your eyes.

2:219   They ask thee concerning what they should spend. Say: That which is in excess (of your needs). Thus God maketh clear (His) revelations, that you may think.

25:67   And they, when they spend (in charity), are neither extravagant nor niggardly; they keep a just (balance) between these (two limits).

In these verses, the Quran asks us to spend out of what we earn and produce (i.e., from our income and production), out of what we like for ourselves, and from that which is in excess of our needs. Our needs can be understood as those for our own consumption, including needs that accommodate provisions for savings and investments for our needed future consumption. "Need" is a subjective term, and hence can be interpreted variously. The same is true of the term "niggardliness"—in one of the above verses the Quran exhorts us not to be niggardly in spending as well. When deciding about how much to spend in God's way, individuals concerned need to make their decisions according to what they feel or think about their own needs and what they consider as niggardly. Thus the amount of spending in God's way should be in excess of our needs, and a reasonable balance between extravagance and niggardliness.

Two other verses of the Quran also shed more light on how much one should spend out of windfall income or wealth like the spoils of war and other gains:

8:1   They ask thee (O Muhammad) about the spoils of war. Say: The spoils of war are for God and the Messenger. So be careful of (your duty to) God, and settle matters of your difference, and obey God and His Messenger if ye do believe.

8:41   And know: Of anything ye gain, a fifth is for God and His Messenger, relatives, orphans, the needy, and the wayfarer, if ye do believe in God and in what We have revealed to Our servant.

The first of these verses relates to gains such as the war booties. Such gains wholly belong to "God and the Messenger", which means that such gains should be distributed entirely for God's cause—for meeting the needs of the poor and needy people and other welfare needs. The handling and distribution of these gains should be done and administered by the state or by state-sponsored appropriate public or private sector organizations (modern-day NGOs, for example). There may be other gains of the nature of what economists call "windfall gains", the handling and distribution of which warrant similar treatment. Some examples of such gains are instant treasure troves found by some people, and real estates, bank deposits and other assets left by deceased people who have no near relatives with any legitimate claim to such assets. Lottery earnings also fall in the category of windfall gains, which deserve to be heavily taxed by the state for welfare needs. Note, however, that the Quran strongly discourages us to indulge in games of chance (2:219; 5:90–91). Hence, in Muslim countries lotteries and gambling should not be allowed in the first place. However, if any citizens in these countries receive profits from lotteries overseas, such profits deserve to be highly taxed by the Muslim state.

The second verse (8:41) calls for spending or distribution of a fifth of other gains or income we earn for God's cause, and for near relatives, orphans, needy, wayfarers, etc. That implies that there should be a twenty percent tax on normal or regular gains or income for both state and other welfare activities. These verses warrant drawing the following summarized implications concerning how much we should spend in God's way:

- First, we should spend in excess of our needs, and choose an appropriate balance between extravagance and niggardliness;
- Second, the excess over needs implies a more than proportionate ability to spend in relation to income and wealth of a person suggesting a need for progressive taxation for welfare needs;
- Third. windfall gains such as war booties and other gains of the essentially same nature should be spent entirely in God's cause, and their distribution should be left at the discretion of the public authority, i.e. the state; and
- Fourth, we should spend in God's way one fifth of our normal gains— income or wealth, which are gains other than windfall gains of the nature of war booties. This entitles the state to tax people's normal income or wealth at the rate of 20 percent for meeting the welfare needs of the state.[3]

These directions of the Quran highlight that the proportion of our income, wealth or gains to be spent in God's way should normally be a considerably higher fraction than the 2½ percent (of wealth), which is generally believed as the *zakat* amount. Note that such spending should go not only to the destitute and needy, it should be used also for a multiplicity of noble causes, which we

---

[3] I am grateful to Layth Al-Shaiban. who manages the Internet website http://free-minds.org and is also a co-author of *Quran: A Reformist Translation*, for a comment on an earlier interpretation of mine, which has helped to rephrase the interpretation into the present one.

can lump together as God's cause. A substantial chunk of such causes is best handled at the governmental level, while others may be left for private individuals. During our Prophet's time, considerable resources in the forms of believing men and goods were mobilized for conducting war against the invading infidels.

> **9: 41** Go forth (O ye who believe), equipped with light arms
> and heavy arms, and strive with your wealth and your lives in
> God's cause. That is best for you if ye only knew.

Resources mobilized in the forms of men and goods used for purposes of defense are spending in God's cause. There are many such needs in God's cause that need to be met at the government or public sector level. The government should cater to such needs, and *sadaqa* or appropriate taxation should finance such needs. All those parts of government expenditure, which are meant for social welfare—feeding and rehabilitation of destitute people, provisions for unemployed workers, education, labor training, health and hospital services and similar spending directed especially to amelioration of the conditions of the poor, and those which are meant for making available what economists call "public goods" that are best produced at the public sector level—are indeed instances of spending for God's cause. Public goods are those goods and services, the production of which, if left to the private sector alone, is grossly neglected or inadequately met. Public goods are similar to what Muslim scholars recognize as acts or goods of public interest (*maslaha*), but they are not exactly the same. Some examples of public goods are social peace and security, defense against external aggression, administration of law and justice, promotion of social, cultural and spiritual development, economic policymaking and general public administration for miscellaneous government functions. All such state functions should count within the purview of God's cause. And in an impoverished developing economy, the state has a special role to play in promoting economic development, which indeed is the best answer to alleviation of poverty for the poor. For promoting economic development, considerable investment is needed in physical infrastructure (such as roads, highways, railways, waterways, ports, telecommunications, power and energy, etc.) as well as in human skills and education, technology and research. Promotion of such development is crucial for expanding employment opportunities and raising living standards and, in the long run for dealing with the problem of the poor.

It is clear that spending in God's way covers a lot more things than are currently covered by the *zakat* or *sadaqa* system. It matters little whether one calls it *zakat* or *sadaqa*. But this system is in need of major reform in light of the directions given in the Quran and in light of recent developments in the conception of functions of a modern state. Spending in God's way then of individuals will comprise both the taxes they pay for benevolent works of the government at the government level and whatever they can afford to spend voluntarily at the private sector level on top of the taxes they pay. It should be recognized that what the government can or should do efficiently is inadequate to deal with the total problem of social inequity and to promote overall social welfare; and there is much still left to be done at the individual level. But limiting such benevolent and humanitarian spending to just 2½ percent of one's wealth will be taking a very narrow view of spending in God's way in light of the Quran. Such spending should not be limited just to a proportion of wealth alone as is generally understood in the case of *zakat*. The verses (2:267; 6:141) cited above clearly point to spending from earning and production. Hence earning or production could also be used as a base for such spending. And the proportion should be a flexible one depending on how much one can afford neither being too generous nor too niggardly as directed in verse (25:67) cited above, taking into account what he or she has already paid to the government in the form of taxes for God's cause.

The ultimate aim of the *zakat* or *sadaqa* system should be to eradicate poverty, and help people get work opportunities and become self-reliant, and not to perpetuate a beggars' class in society, which is not only degrading for them but also a nuisance in society. To the extent possible and economically efficient, such spending should be handled at the state level. Many modern developed countries have well-planned public welfare and social security systems embodying unemployment benefits and certain medical benefits and administered at the state level in conjunction with enterprise level retirement, lay-off and medical insurance benefits, and it is not left to the whims of individuals to cater to such welfare needs. Social security systems existing in some of the developed countries essentially exhibit the basic principles of the *sadaqa* system that the Quran propounds. Though there is some debate as to what developed countries are really doing for developing countries (they often take back what they give in different ways[4]), the concessional aid they give and what their sponsored multilateral development financing institutions give to the developing countries is also a kind of *sadaqa* at state level on the part of the rich countries to the poor ones. Such aid should also be counted in the calculation for how much more resources the government should mobilize domestically to cater to the needs of the poor and development and social welfare needs. The need for paying *sadaqa* at the individual level will last as long as the state cannot pay full attention to the problems of helpless people. The state in many developing countries is almost invariably unable to take full care of the poor and the needy. Also considering that public sector welfare systems in developing countries are

---

[4] One important case in point is the system of protection that the developed countries themselves provide to their domestic activities through government tariffs on imports from developing countries and government subsidies to their farmers for production of agricultural products, and in some cases, through subsidies on exports of certain agricultural products. According to recent World Bank estimates, such trade restrictions of both developed and developing countries hurt the poor developing countries more than they receive by way of aid from the rich countries.

found to be almost always plagued by significant corruption as available evidence suggests, there remains considerable room for charities at the individual level. When a believing man or woman can afford to spend and perceives the need for such spending, it becomes incumbent on him or her to do it. That is as good as his/her prayer for his/her own spiritual advancement. And a significant part of such spending should be given to reputable international charitable organizations and international and domestic NGOs (non-governmental organizations), which engage in development and social welfare activities, and which are known to be more efficient and less corrupt than the relevant government departments.

Another point to be noted in this regard is that the scope of such spending should also embrace interest-free or concessional lending, which the Quran calls *qarz-hasana* (beautiful lending) (2:245; 57:11, 18; 64:17; 5:12; 73:20). In modern days, some of this concessional financing function is being performed in developing countries by developed country aid agencies and multilateral development financing institutions. The Quranic message of interest-free loans is applicable only for disadvantaged borrowers, who deserve to be treated with a humanitarian approach. The Quran also encourages the lenders to remit interest on remaining loans, and postpone or write off the original loans in cases where the borrowers are in difficulty to repay them (2:278-280). In cases, which deserve humanitarian considerations, loans should indeed be extended free of interest, and where appropriate, such loans should be given as grants or alms, which is *sadaqa* in the Quranic terminology.

Conclusion

Spending in God's way should be understood in a much broader sense than the generally understood *zakat* system. It involves considerable spending on the part of a modern state for a variety of functions financed through a well-devised taxation system, besides charitable spending at the individual level. The best kind of spending in God's way is helping others stand on their own feet. To help another person in a way, which makes him or her look for help all the time, is inherently ill motivated, and is like that of those who like to be seen by men, and is of no intrinsic virtue to them (2:264). From this point of view, the modern state should take appropriate measures to promote investment and development to increase opportunities for gainful employment of unemployed people, along with crafting a well-devised social welfare and security system. At the individual level, such efforts should include savings, investment and work that would help build infrastructure and industries for employment-generating development, along with their humanitarian spending in deserving cases.

Are Muslims a Part of the American Story?

Mike Ghouse

I am inspired by the article "Between American society and the American story" by Professor Sherman Jackson. (http://www.altmuslim.com/a/a/a/2808/)

The distinction he has made is crystal clear "Thus far, however, Muslims remain outside the American story, which is why, despite their positive contributions to society; they seldom enlist empathy when they are jailed, deported or discriminated against." And he offers the solution, "Hopefully, however, it will not be long before Muslims come to understand this. Once they do, while guilt by association may continue, Muslims will be able to fight back. For in this they will be joined by others."

Indeed, we are not connected enough with the mainstream society for a vast majority of Americans to stand up for us, empathize with us or even understand the truth about us that we are no different than them in our endeavors and aspirations of life. We must however express our gratitude to the millions of Americans who have stood up for us, compelled by their sense of justness and fair play.

Refreshing our identity

As good citizens it is not only our right but it is our duty to be self critical of our society; the American society. I hope that the conservatives among us will get beyond the self righteous criticism and value the freedom that we have to exercise with pride and care.

We must learn to re-examine our attitudes towards others and push the refresh button to understand the essence of Islam. We must do our inner jihad against the temptations to reduce Islam to rituals, we should not only be identified as Muslims by the ritual aspect of our religion, but also be recognized by the spiritual aspect of "being a Muslim".

Being a Muslim is volunteering one's time and effort in the well being of the society, serving the community with blinders. A Muslim is some one who is engaged in mitigating conflicts and nurturing goodwill amongst our neighbors and countrymen, to help create a just and more viable society for all. (indeed, prophet Muhammad set those examples of Aswad, the title of Amin was the first model)

A Muslim respects the otherness of the other (http://quraan-today.blogspot.com/2008/07/sura-kafirun-un-believers.html) and grasps the essence of Islam; Justice and peace. Rituals are not an end in themselves; they are simply markers of being a Muslim. They are the most important aspect of our faith paving the way to achieve humility and spirituality. A Just person is one who cares for what surrounds him or her; life and the environment. Isn't that what the will of God is? Isn't submitting to the will of God means working for a Just society, and bringing equilibrium between living beings and the environment?

To be just one has to shed arrogance, indeed Prophet Muhammad (pbuh) said to his associates after returning home from a victorious war; the biggest Jihad begins now, he said, it is the war with one's own seductions. It is to reign in our temptations to avenge, being revengeful or getting even; it is getting hold of our anger. Anger leads to injustice. He said God's favorite person is the one who forgives others and repents his own short-comings. Islam is about being a just human in treating ourselves, our families and the societies we live in.

A majority of Muslims certainly practice this refreshed identity, but a few loud mouths define Muslims otherwise and sadly they get the most coverage in the media, drowning the good and encouraging the ugly. But vigorous effort to project our real identity has begun and Insha Allah, we will succeed with a realization that what is good for Muslims has got to be good for the mankind and vice versa for it to sustain. We cannot have advantages over the others, such benefits are deleterious and of temporary nature.

Where did we go wrong?

The average Mohammed and Amina have realized that to be a spiritual part of the society, we have to connect, we have to care and be cared for, and we have to be with the society emotionally as they would be with us. To feel a complete sense of feeling "at home" we have to live the essence American life, which is not different from the essence of Islamic life. Please don't jump to conclusions, it does not mean you have to give up an ounce of your identity, it simply means the sense of difference "they" v "us" has to vanish from our thoughts and "us" to be ingrained in our language and actions.

The traditional religious leadership and the leadership that runs Muslim organizations is yet to grasp this, in the name of identity, they dig in their heels. That has been the hallmark of all closed minded religious leaders to keep the flock tethered.

To be religious is to bring about a balance within oneself and with others who surround us; through humility religion seeks to dissolve the barriers between the peoples. We, and every one in America need to embrace other flocks, we need to look for permanent solutions of co-existence and honor every one's God given space.

We chase our own tails; we spend all our disposable hours at the Mosques or engaging in big talk about love for Islam and attend lectures on how to be a ritual Muslim. Unquestionably, it is a part of what makes one a Muslim, but that is not all that Muslims should be concerned with. Our focus ought to be, to become a part of that American story. Please remember no one is pushing us out or excluding us, it is us, who are not integrating to become a part of the whole and it is our loss, as many of us do not feel that we are a part to this land; that engenders an undesirable insecurity.

Justice alone cannot carry us far

In case of the Holy Land Trial; justice won, but justice alone cannot carry us far. There was no sympathy when Professor Arian was on trial, there was no support when Tariq Ramadan's visa was rejected to visit and teach in the United States. There is a long list is and such incidences happen *ad nauseam*

There are several organizations making the efforts to make that change "to become a part of the American Story" but it is not their priority to grow the feeling of hominess, something that solidly bolts us to the ground. Our priorities must take us from a ritual Muslim to a civic Muslim and be a part of the American story. Where the three hundred million of us feel connected with each other and talk and act as one nation. Those of us who have not grown up yet, being American is our identity as much as being a Muslim is. Our ability to build relationships with people other than our own kind does not negate or reduce our religiosity, but enhance it.

Guts to speak up

The Islamic society of North America (ISNA) is developing a good outreach program, but then there are some, who are shamelessly derailing their effort. Case in Point: the Islamic society of North America (ISNA) engaged an influential Rabbi to become a part of the Muslim-Jewish dialogue, and indeed the Rabbi spoke at their annual convention. Then a few groups of Muslims proclaiming to be legitimate representatives of Muslims (There is no such thing as legitimate representative, none are elected by public at large) wrote to the Rabbi not to be a part of ISNA, as they are the legitimate ones, instead of supporting the efforts of ISNA, they were denigrating them. Both will lose in the situation. Not enough Muslims have picked up the phone and told these other guys to be wise, and start building their own positive relationships rather than negating what others are doing. What does it take? It is the simplest thing that a Muslim can do; to encourage the good efforts of any Muslim or a non-Muslim to build relationships and work for co-existence, peace and prosperity of our nation.

Things to ponder

What are the things Muslims can do to become a part of the American story? What can we do to connect with others on a human level, the level where every one feels like one large family to speak up from their heart when any one of the

300 Million of us is mis-served? Simply put, we have to become part of that family.

We are rightfully concerned with Halal (Kosher) meat and in our subconscious effort to show off that we are Muslims, i.e., ritual Muslims. We prevent ourselves from sharing a meal with others; one of the most connecting activity of a family. People are rightfully afraid to invite us so they do not offend us. It is human to follow the rules, Jews, Hindus and others follow their dietary requirements well, we should not eat what is forbidden, but we should not make a big deal out of it and stay out of homes of friendship and becoming a part of the American story. Let the difference not put a barrier between us.

To develop a sense of oneness with the society, we have to put in conscious efforts till it becomes a part of our psyche and a part of our culture.

For an immigrant to feel home and feel the connection with the community at large, and to bond, we have to find opportunities to serve. Thank God, America is the land of the blessed, it provides tremendous opportunities to the ones who want to feel safe, secure and feel in tune with others and be a contributor and participant in the overall success of each one of the 300 Million of us.

Setting our priorities

Engaging with the society at large must be our priority now. We should quit making excuses that we do not have any time; we must carve out our time from the social activities. We have to invest our time in the long term goodness and to acquire a sense of being at home; we must take our time out from some of the religious activity and lectures that makes us stronger ritual Muslims and invest that time for sustainable goodness. It is our priority. What is good for Muslims has got to be good for America and vice-versa, for that good to be sustainable.

America is our home, we are going to spend our lives here, it is home to our kids and grand kids and their grand kids; and we are going to be buried here, each cemetery plot is our permanent residence till eternity. And we owe it ourselves to make this land safe, secure, peaceful and prosperous for one and all. No one can have peace for themselves, unless others are in peace. It is the responsibility of each one of the 300 Million of us to do our share.

The big small things we can do;

Be a part of some ones birthday celebration or their anniversary, don't be hung up with food or other cultural nuances, just be there for your friend and be a part of his or her happiness. When I go, I don't drink alcohol nor do I eat Pork, but I don't make a big deal or show it off that not drinking or eating makes me a Muslim. I should not draw attention in the party; it is the friends' celebration time. Learn to respect the otherness of others, without you becoming something you are not. Just drink water and eat Salad no will have a problem with it.

The most human thing to do, and by the way it is the most Muslim thing to do is to share the grief when some one passes away and the least thing to do is attend their funeral. You don't have to say one single word to any one, just being there for their family makes you feel good about your humanness. Prophet Muhammad stood up when a funeral passed by him regardless of who they were, the one example often cited is a Jewish funeral procession. Next time, when you hear some one has passed away, whether you know them or not, attend their funeral and see the difference it makes to you and them.

If you are finding it difficult to make friends with people other than your own, consider changing it. Whether it is a wedding, birthday, funeral or any happy or grim occasion, invite people from your work, from where you shop or your neighborhood. Then you have plenty of opportunities year round; Mothers day, Fathers day, Memorial day, Labors day, July 4th and religious holidays of other faiths. Then you are connected and a part of the American Story.

July 4th Celebrations

Go to the 4th of July parties, invite every possible person other than your own kind to your own backyard or create your own party along with a few friends. It does not take a whole lot of money to grill hot dogs (Of course Halal ones for you), hamburgers and water.

Encourage the Muslim leaders and give them your support to do it in the parking lot of the Mosques. Plan it ahead. Let our Imams focus on these things rather than get bogged down with Haram and Halal. Making friends for creating peace and goodwill is unquestionably the Halal thing to do. After all, the name of our religion is peace and we have to act it.

Model Events

Take a look at the models we have created here in Dallas, and look at what it does to ground us. If you are hung with Cultural dances, do something else that connects humans; facts and speeches don't connect people.

I am committed to co-existence and as such, I am willing to spend my time in getting you to set up, provided you have the commitment.

Please go through the following links and grasp their value

Thanksgiving Celebrations:
http://www.foundationforpluralism.com/Articles/ThanksgivingCelebrations-11242008.asp

Unity Day Celebrations:

http://www.foundationforpluralism.com/Articles/UnitydayUSA-2008-PressRelease.asp

II Annual Reflections on Holocaust and Genocides:
http://www.HolocaustandGenocides.org

We owe it ourselves to make this land safe, secure, peaceful and prosperous for one and all. No one can have peace for themselves, unless others are in peace. It is the responsibility of each one of the 300 Million of us to do our share. First, it starts with you and I, we do it because it is the right thing to do and not to keep a score. Let there be purity in our intentions and God will reward every one of us with peace, security and prosperity.

Violence and Peace

(Excerpts from the the *Quran: a Reformist Translation*)

Edip Yuksel

Should Muslims Levy Extra Tax of Non-Muslims?

Verse 9:29 is mistranslated by almost every translator. Shakir translates the Arabic word *jizya* as "tax," Pickthall as "tribute." Yusuf Ali, somehow does not translate the word at all. He leaves the meaning of the word at the mercy of distortions:

Disputed passage: The meaning of the Arabic word *jizya* (reparation/compensation) has been distorted to mean extra tax for non-muslims.

Yusuf Ali	Pickthall	Shakir	Reformed
"Fight those who believe not in Allah nor the Last Day, nor hold that forbidden which hath been forbidden by Allah and His Messenger, nor acknowledge the religion of Truth, (even if they are) of the People of the Book, until they pay the **Jizya** with willing submission, and feel themselves subdued. (9:29).	Fight against such of those who have been given the Scripture as believe not in Allah nor the Last Day, and forbid not that which Allah hath forbidden by His messenger, and follow not the Religion of Truth, until they pay the **tribute** readily, being brought low. (9:29)	Fight those who do not believe in Allah, nor in the latte day, nor do they prohibit what Allah and His Messenger have prohibited, nor follow the religion of truth, out of those who have been given the Book, until they pay the **tax** in acknowledgment of superiority and they are in a state of subjection. (9:29).	"You shall fight (back) against those who do not believe in God, nor in the last day, and they do not prohibit what God and His messenger have prohibited, and do not abide by the system of truth among those who received the scripture, until they pay the **reparation**, in humility." (9:29).

DISCUSSION ON 9:29

You have noticed that we inserted a parenthesis since the context of the verse is about the War of *Hunain*, and fighting is allowed for only self-defense. See: 2:190-193, 256; 4:91; and 60:8-9.

Furthermore, note that we suggest REPERATION instead of Arabic word *jizya*. The meaning of *jizya* has been distorted as tax on non-muslims, which was invented long after Muhammad to further the imperialistic agenda of Kings. The origin of the word that we translated as Compensation is *JaZaYa*, which simply means compensation or in the context of war it means war reparations, not tax. Since the enemies of muslims attacked and aggressed, after the war they are

221

required to compensate for the damage they inflicted on the peaceful community. Various derivatives of this word are used in the Quran frequently, and they are translated as compensation for a particular deed.

Unfortunately, the distortion in the meaning of the verse above and the practice of collecting a special tax from Christians and Jews, contradict the basic principle of the Quran that there should not be compulsion in religion and there should be freedom of belief and expression (2:256; 4:90; 10:99; 18:29; 88:21,22). Since taxation based on religion creates financial duress on people to convert to the privileged religion, it violates this important Quranic principle. Dividing a population that united under a social contract (constitution) into privileged groups based on their religion contradicts many principles of the Quran, including justice, peace, and brotherhood/sisterhood of all humanity.

Some uninformed critics or bigoted enemies of the Quran list verses of the Quran dealing with wars and declare islam to be a religion of violence. Their favorite verses are: 2:191; 3:28; 3:85; 5:10,34; 9:5; 9:28-29; 9:123; 14:17; 22:9; 25: 52; 47:4 and 66:9. In this article, I refuted their argument against 9:29, and I will discuss each of them later.

Some followers of Sunni or Shiite religions, together with their like-minded modern Crusaders, abuse 9:5 or 9:29 by taking them out of their immediate and Quranic context. Sunnis and Shiites follow many stories and instructions falsely attributed to Muhammad that justify terror and aggression. For instance, in a so-called authentic (or authentically fabricated) hadith, after arresting the murderers of his shepherd, the prophet and his companions cut their arms and legs off, gouge their eyes with hot nails and leave them dying from thirst in the dessert, a contradiction to the portrayal of Muhammad's mission in the Quran (21:107; 3:159). In another authentically fabricated hadith, the prophet is claimed to send a gang during night to secretly kill a female poet who criticized him in her poetry, a violation of the teaching of the Quran! (2:256; 4:140; 10:99; 18:29; 88:21-22). Despite these un-Quranic teachings, the aggressive elements among Sunni or Shiite population have almost always been a minority.

BEHEADING?

> **47:4** So, if you encounter those who have rejected, then strike the control center until you overcome them. Then bind them securely. You may either set them free or ransom them, until the war ends. That, and had **God** willed, He alone could have beaten them, but He thus tests you by one another. As for those who get killed in the cause of **God**, He will never let their deeds be put to waste.

047:004 The expression "*darb al riqab*" is traditionally translated as "smite their necks." We preferred to translate it as "strike the control center." The Quran uses the word "*unuq*" for neck (17:13,29; 8:12; 34:33; 38:33; 13:5; 26:4; 36:8; 40:71). The root *RaQaBa* means observe, guard, control, respect, wait for, tie by the neck, warn, fear. "*Riqab*" means slave, prisoner of war. Even if one of the meanings of the word *riqab* were neck, we would still reject the traditional translation, for the obvious reason: The verse continues by instructing muslims regarding the capturing of the enemies and the treatment of prisoners of war. If they were supposed to be beheaded, there would not be need for an instruction regarding captives, which is a very humanitarian instruction. Unfortunately, the Sunni and Shiite terrorists have used the traditional mistranslation, and abused it further by beheading hostages in their fight against their counterpart terrorists, Crusaders and their allied coalition, who torture and kill innocent people even in bigger numbers, yet in a baptized fashion that is somehow depicted non-barbaric by their culture and media. The Quran gives two option regarding the hostages or prisoners of war before the war ends: (1) set them free; or (2) release them to get a fee for their unjustified aggression. Considering the context of the verse and emphasis on capturing the enemy, we could have translated the segment under discussion as, "aim to take captives."

The Old Testament contains many scenes of beheadings and grotesque massacres. For instance, see: 2 Samuel 4:7-12; 2 Kings 10:7, and 2 Chronicles 25:12.

THE MOST FREQUENTLY ABUSED VERSES, 9:3-29

9:1   This is an ultimatum from **God** and His messenger to those who set up partners whom you had entered a treaty.

9:2   Therefore, roam the land for four months and know that you will not escape **God**, and that **God** will humiliate the rejecters.

9:3   A declaration from **God** and His messenger to the people, on this, the peak day of the Pilgrimage: "That **God** and His messenger are free from obligation to those who set up partners." If you repent, then it is better for you, but if you turn away, then know that you will not escape **God**. Promise those who have rejected of a painful retribution;

9:4   Except for those with whom you had a treaty from among those who have set up partners if they did not reduce anything from it nor did they plan to attack you; you shall fulfill their terms until they expire. **God** loves the righteous.

9:5   So when the restricted months have passed, then you may kill those who have set up partners wherever you find them, take them, surround them, and stand against them at every point. If they repent, hold the contact prayer, and contribute towards betterment, then you shall leave them alone. **God** is Forgiving, Compassionate.

Do Not Let Those Who Violate the Peace Treaty Succeed

9:6   If any of those who have set up partners seeks your protection, then you may protect him so that he may hear the words of **God**, then let him reach his sanctuary. This is because they are a people who do not know.

9:7   How can those who have set up partners have a pledge with **God** and with His messenger? Except for those with whom you made a pledge near the Restricted Temple, as long as they are upright with you, then you are upright with them. **God** loves the righteous.

9:8   How is it that when they come upon you they disregard all ties, either those of kinship or of pledge. They seek to please you with their words, but their hearts deny, and most of them are wicked.

9:9   They purchased with **God**'s signs a small price, so they turn others from His path. Evil indeed is what they used to do.

9:10   They neither respect the ties of kinship nor a pledge for any those who acknowledge. These are the transgressors.

9:11   If they repent, and they hold the contact prayer, and they contribute towards betterment, then they are your brothers in the system. We explain the signs for a people who know.

9:12   If they break their oaths after their pledge, and they taunt and attack your system; then you may kill the chiefs of rejection. Their oaths are nothing to them, perhaps they will then cease.

9:13   Would you not fight a people who broke their oaths and intended to expel the messenger, especially while they were the ones who attacked you first? Do you fear them? It is **God** who is more worthy to be feared if you are those who acknowledge.

9:14   Fight them; perhaps **God** will punish them by your hands, humiliate them, grant you victory over them and heal the chests of an acknowledging people,

9:15   To remove the anger from their hearts; **God** pardons whom he pleases. **God** is Knowledgeable, Wise.

9:16   Or did you think that you would be left alone? **God** will come to know those of you who strived and did not take other than **God** and His messenger and those who acknowledge as helpers. **God** is Expert in what you do.

9:17   It was not for those who have set up partners to maintain **God**'s temples while they bear witness over their own rejection. For these, their works have fallen, and in the fire they will abide.

9:18   Rather, the temples of **God** are maintained by the one who acknowledges **God** and the Last day, holds the contact prayer, contributes towards betterment, and he does not fear except **God**. It is these that will be of the guided ones.

9:19   Have you made serving drink to the pilgrims and the maintenance of the Restricted Temple the same as one who acknowledges **God** and the Last day, who strives in the cause of **God**? They are not the same with **God**. **God** does not guide the wicked people.

9:20   Those who acknowledged, emigrated, strived in the cause of **God** with their wealth and their lives are in a greater degree with **God**. These are the winners.

9:21   Their Lord gives them good news of a Mercy from Him, acceptance, and gardens that are for them in which there is permanent bliss.

9:22   They will abide in it eternally. **God** has a great reward.

9:23   O you who acknowledge, do not take your fathers nor brothers as allies if they prefer rejection to acknowledgement. Whoever of you takes them as such, then these are the wicked.

Dedicate Yourself to Establish Peace and Liberty

9:24   Say, "If your fathers, your sons, your brothers, your spouses, your clan, and money which you have gathered, a trade you fear its decline, and homes which you enjoy; if these are dearer to you than **God** and His messenger and striving in His cause, then wait until **God** brings His decision. **God** does not guide the wicked people."

9:25   **God** has granted you victory in many battlefields. On the day of Hunayn, when you were pleased with your great numbers but it did not help you at all, and the land became tight around you for what it held, then you turned to flee.

9:26   Then **God** sent down tranquility upon His messenger and those who acknowledge, and He sent down soldiers which you did not see. He thus punished those who rejected. Such is the recompense of the rejecters.

9:27   Then **God** will accept the repentance of whom He pleases after that. **God** is Forgiving, Compassionate.

9:28   O you who acknowledge, those who have set up partners are impure, so let them not approach the Restricted Temple after this calendar year of theirs. If you fear poverty, then **God** will enrich you from His blessings if He wills. **God** is Knowledgeable, Wise.

9:29   Fight those who do not acknowledge **God** or the Last day, they do not forbid what **God** and His messenger have forbidden, and they do not uphold the system of truth; from among the people who have been given the book; until they pay the reparation, in humility.

NOTES:

009:003-029 The verse 9:5 does not encourage muslims to attack those who associate partners to God, but to attack those who have violated the peace treaty and killed and terrorized people because of their belief and way of life.

According to verses 9:5 and 9:11, the aggressive party has two ways to stop the war: reinstate the treaty for peace (*silm*), which is limited in scope; or accept the system of peace and submission to God (islam), which is comprehensive in scope; it includes observation of *sala* and purification through sharing one's blessings. These two verses refer to the second alternative. When, accepting islam (system of peace and submission) as the second equally acceptable alternative and when the first alternative involves only making a temporary peace, then none can argue for coercion in promoting the Din.

The Quran does not promote war; but encourages us to stand against aggressors on the side of peace and justice. War is permitted only for self-defense (See 2:190,192,193,256; 4:91; 5:32; 8:19; 60:7-9). We are encouraged to work hard to establish peace (47:35; 8:56-61; 2:208). The Quranic precept promoting peace and justice is so fundamental that peace treaty with the enemy is preferred to religious ties (8:72).

Please note that the context of the verse is about the War of *Hunain*, which was provoked by the enemy. The verse 9:29 is mistranslated by almost every translator.

Furthermore, note that we suggest "reparation", which is the legal word for compensation for damages done by the aggressing party during the war, instead of Arabic word *jizya*. The meaning of *jizya* has been distorted as a perpetual tax on non-Muslims, which was invented long after Muhammad to further the imperialistic agenda of Sultans or Kings. The origin of the word that I translated as Compensation is *JaZaYa*, which simply means compensation, not tax. Because of their aggression and initiation of a war against muslims and their allies, after the war, the allied community should require their enemies to compensate for the damage they inflicted on the peaceful community. Various derivatives of this word are used in the Quran frequently, and they are translated as "compensation" for a particular deed.

Unfortunately, the distortion in the meaning of the verse above and the practice of collecting a special tax from Christians and Jews, contradict the basic principle of the Quran that there should not be compulsion in religion and there should be freedom of belief and expression (2:256; 4:90; 4:140; 10:99; 18:29; 88:21,22). Since taxation based on religion creates financial duress on people to convert to the privileged religion, it violates this important Quranic principle. Dividing a population that united under a social contract (constitution) into privileged groups based on their religion contradicts many principles of the Quran, including justice, peace, and brotherhood/sisterhood of all humanity. See 2:256. For a comparative discussion on this verse, see the Sample Comparison section under the title, Why a Reformist Translation, in the Introduction.

Moral rules involving retaliation can be classified under several titles:

- **The Golden Rule**: Do unto others as you would have them do unto you.
- **The Silver Rule**: Do not do unto others what you would not have them do unto you.
- **The Golden-plated Brazen Rule:** Do unto others as they do unto you; and occasionally forgive them.

- **The Brazen Rule**: Do unto others as they do unto you.
- **The Iron Rule**: Do unto others as you like, before they do it unto you.

Empirical studies on groups have shown that the golden-plated brazen rule is the most efficient in reducing the negative behavior in a community abiding by the rule, since the rule has both deterrence and guiding components. The Golden rule, on the other hand, does not correspond to the reality of human nature; it rewards those who wish to take advantage of the other party's niceness. Therefore, though the golden rule is the most popular rule in the lips of people, but it is the least used rule in world affairs. It might have some merits in small groups with intimate relations; but we do not have evidence for that.

The Quran is book of reality, and its instructions involving social issues consider the side effects of freedom. Thus, the Quran recommends us to employ the golden-plated brazen rule. "If the enemy inclines toward peace, do you also incline toward peace." (8:61; 4:90; 41:34). Other verses encouraging forgiveness and patience in the practice of retaliation (2:178; 16:126, etc.), makes the Quranic rule a "Gold plated Brazen Rule," the most efficient rule in promoting goodness and discouraging crimes.

Sunni and Shiite mushriks inherited many vicious laws and instructions of violence through *hadith* books, of which scholars trace their roots to Jewish Rabies and Christian priests who supposedly converted to Islam. Here are some samples of terrifying and bloody instructions found in The Old Testament. We recommend the reader to study them in their context:

> **Leviticus 24:13-16** "The Lord said to Moses: 'Take the blasphemer outside the camp. All those who heard him are to lay their hands on his head, and the entire assembly is to stone him. Say to the Israelites: If anyone curses his God, he will be held responsible; anyone who blasphemes the name of the Lord must be put to death. The entire assembly must stone him. Whether an alien or native-born, when he blasphemes the Name, he must be put to death....Then Moses spoke to the Israelites, and they took the blasphemer outside the camp and stoned him. The Israelites did as the Lord commanded Moses."

> **Numbers 31:18** "Now kill all the boys. And kill every woman who has slept with a man. But save for yourselves every girl who has never slept with a man.".

> **Joshua 6:21** "And they utterly destroyed all that was in the city, both man and woman, young and old, and ox, and sheep, and ass, with the edge of the sword".

1 Samuel 15:3 "Now go and smite Amalek, and utterly destroy all that they have, and spare them not; but slay both man and woman, infant and suckling, ox and sheep, camel and ass".

1 Samuel 17:57 "And as David returned from the slaughter of the Philistine, Abner took him, and brought him before Saul with the head of the Philistine in his hand".

Esther 9:5 "Thus the Jews smote all their enemies with the stroke of the sword, and slaughter, and destruction, and did what they would unto those that hated them"

Jeremiah 12:1-3 "Why do the wicked prosper and the treacherous all live at ease?... But you know me, Lord, you see me; you test my devotion to you. Drag them away like sheep to the shambles; set them apart for the day of slaughter"

Jeremiah 48:10 "A curse on all who are slack in doing the Lord's work! A curse on all who withhold their swords from bloodshed!".

Chapter 20 of Leviticus contains a list of very severe punishments for various sins. For instance, cursing one's own father of mother would prompt death penalty. A man marrying a woman together with her daughter must be burned in the fire. Homosexual men must be put to death. Those who commit bestiality must be put to death together with the animals. And many more death, burning penalties.[1]

---

[1] No wonder, the history of Christianity is filled with massacres, tortures and terror that are perhaps 666 times more violent than the violence committed by Sunni and Shiite radicals combined. Just in the last century alone, the governments of predominantly Christian nations fought hundreds of wars and killed millions of people in atrocious wars, including two World Wars. Of course, there have always been many peaceful Christians and Christian denominations such as Quakers, Uniterians, Universalists, and Jehovah Witnesses, but in general, the Christian Churches have either directly participated or indirectly supported militarism, colonization, imperialistic ambitions, apartheid regimes, invasions, covert operations, torture and terror around the globe. For instance, it was America's Evangelical Christians who overwhelmingly elected and supported the Neocon Bush administration to invade Iraq based on deception and lies, which caused more than a million dead, millions of injured, orphans, and millions of dislocated Iraqis. The same Christians that once dehumanized Jews are now busy dehumanizing Arabs and Muslims and have been the major supporters of Zionist terror and massacres in the Middle East. Just after singing peace and "love your enemy" they voted for wars, for bigger military budget and support for the world's biggest military industrial complex. Here are a few key words from the bloody modern history of Christendom: Holocaust, Nuclear Bombs, Nagasaki, Hiroshima, Abu Gharib, Guantanamo, Shock and Awe. You may also include

DID MUHAMMAD MASSACRE JEWS?

> "There were three Jewish tribes in Medina: Banu Qaynuqa, Banu al-Nadir and Banu Qurayza. They provoked Muslims and the first two tribes were forced to leave the city with their transportable possessions. However, prophet Muhammad did not forgive Banu Qurayza; their necks were struck and their children were made slaves. Estimates of those killed vary from 400 to 900." (Sunni Hadith and Siyar sources)

The Quran refers to the event and never mentions killing or enslaving them, which is in direct contradiction of many verses of the Quran. The Quran, in the Chapter known as Exodus, informs us that a group from "The People of the Book" were forced to leave the territory because of their violation of the constitution and secretly organizing war together with their enemies against muslims (59:1-4). Verse 59:3 clearly states that they were not penalized further in this world.

59:0   In the name of God, the Gracious, the Compassionate

59:1   Glorifying **God** is everything in the heavens and the earth, and He is the Noble, the Wise.

The Mass Exile

59:2   He is the One who drove out those who rejected among the people of the book from their homes at the very first mass exile. You never thought that they would leave, and they thought that their fortresses would protect them from **God**. But then **God** came to them from where they did not expect, and He cast fear into their hearts. They destroyed their homes with their own hands and the hands of those who acknowledge. So take a lesson, O you who possess vision.

59:3   Had **God** not decreed to banish them, He would have punished them in this life. In the Hereafter they will face the retribution of the fire.

59:4   This is because they challenged **God** and His messenger. Whosoever challenges **God**, then **God** is severe in punishment.

59:5   Whether you cut down a tree or left it standing on its root, it was by **God**'s leave. He will surely humiliate the wicked.

059:002-5 The credibility of the story of Muhammad massacring Bani Qurayza Jews has been the subject of controversy since the time it was published by Ibn

---

al-Qaeda and other Sunni and Shiite terrorist organizations that are direct product or indirect product of the imperialistic policy of predominantly Christian nations.

Ishaq. Ibn Ishaq who died in 151 A.H., that is 145 years after the event in question, was severely criticized by his peers for relying on highly exaggerated Jewish stories. He was also harshly criticized for presenting forged poetry attributed to famous poets. Some of his contemporary scholars, such as Malik, called him "a liar." However, his work was later copied by others without critical examination. This is an example of a hearsay used by dubious Jewish reporters for propaganda purposes.

Modern scholars found astonishing similarities between Ibn Ishaq and the account of historian Josephus regarding King Alexander, who ruled in Jerusalem before Herod the Great, hung upon crosses 800 Jewish captives, and slaughtered their wives and children before their eyes. Many other similarities in details of the story of Banu Qurayza and the event reported by Josephus are compelling.

Besides, the lack of reference or justification in the Quran for such a massacre of great magnitude and the verses instructing principles for muslims to abide by takes all credibility out of this story (35:18: 61:4). The Quran gives utmost importance to human life (5:32) and considers racism and anti-Semitism as evil (49:11-13).

IF THEY MOCK GOD'S SIGNS...

> **4:140**   It has been sent down to you in the book, that when you hear **God**'s signs being rejected and ridiculed in, then do not sit with them until they move on to a different subject; if not, then you are like them. **God** will gather the hypocrites and the unappreciative people in hell all together.

NOTES:

004:140 We are not permitted to kill or punish people for their insults and mockery of God's revelation and signs. Any aggressive behavior against those people is against God's law that recognizes freedom of choice, opinion and their expression (2:256; 4:90; 4:140; 10:99; 18:29; 25:63; 88:21,22. Also see: 28:54). In verse 4:140, the Quran recommends us to protest passively those who indulge in mockery of our faith by leaving their presence. Furthermore, it recommends us not to cut our relationship with them; we should turn back in peace and continue our dialogue when they come to their senses and are able to engage in a rational discourse.

Those who react with violence against those who insult the tenets and principles of islam, are not following the very system they claim to defend. The Quran does not recognize the "fighting words" exception recognized by Western jurisprudence. Specific false accusation against a person, however, is not included in expression of opinion, since it is defamation and it can harm a person in many ways. Insult to someone's values or heroes, however, only harms the person who indulges in such an ignorant and arrogant action.

The only unforgivable sin, according the Quran is the sin of associating other partners/idols to God. God allows this biggest sin to be committed in this world. He fulfills his promise to test humans by giving them free choice. He condemns those who deprive others from exercising that freedom of choice. Who then, in the name of the same God, can force others from any expression of their belief or disbelief?

In contrast to how the warmongering Crusaders, Sunnis and Shiites wish to portray, Muhammad was not a man of violence but a man of reason and peace. Numerous verses of the Quran and critical study of history will reveal that the portrait of Muhammad depicted in Sunni or Shiite hearsay books is fictional; a fiction created by the propagandists of rulers of Umayyad and Abbasid dynasties to justify their atrocities and aggression! He and his supporters were threatened and tortured in Mecca for their criticism of their corrupt and unjust theocratic system. They were forced to leave everything behind and immigrate to Yathrib (today's Medina). There they established a peaceful city-state, a federal secular democracy, among its multi-religious diverse citizens. Nevertheless, the Meccan oligarchy did not leave them alone to enjoy peace and freedom; they organized several major war campaigns against the coalition of muslims, Christians, Jews and Pagans united under the leadership of Muhammad. In all the wars, including Uhud, Badr, and Handaq, the monotheist reformers fought for self-defense. They even dug trenches around the city to defend themselves from the aggressive religious coalition led by Mecca's theocratic oligarchy. Muhammad's message that promoted reason, freedom, peace, justice, unity of children of Adam, appreciation of diversity, rights of women and slaves, and social consciousness soon received acceptance by masses in the land. Yet, after ten years in exile, when finally Muhammad and his supporters returned to Mecca as victors, he declared amnesty for all those oppressors and warmongers who inflicted on them great suffering, who maimed and murdered many of their comrades, all because they questioned the teachings and culture they inherited from their parents. However, guided by the teachings of Quran, Muhammad chose forgiveness and peace; he did not punish any of his bloody enemies. After all, he was one of the many messengers of islam, peace and submission to God alone.

The Current Status of Muslims

Shabbir Ahmed

"Surely you will prevail if you are indeed believers."
(Al-Quran 3:139)

1.3 Billion People

Islam is a universal Way of Life (DEEN). Besides Asia and Africa, Europe and North America have substantial populations of Muslims. It is proudly claimed that there are more than one billion Muslims in the world.

However, these more than one billion people are facing a global crisis. The crisis consists of political, economic, social, military, and scientific setbacks. The great Allama Inayatullah Khan Al-Mashriqi in the1940's depicted the state of the East in general, and that of Muslims in particular, in this way:

> "People ask me that having widely traveled the East for years, what have I seen. How shall I tell what I have seen! From this end to that end I saw towns in ruins, broken and shaken bridges, dirt clogged canals, dusty streets, abandoned highways. I saw wrinkled faces, under-nourished bodies, stooping backs, empty brains, insensitive hearts, inverted logic, aberrant reason. I saw oppression, slavery, poverty, pomp and vanity, detestable vices, clusters of disease, burnt forests, cold ovens, barren fields, dirty attire and useless hands and feet. I saw imams (religious leaders) without followings. I saw brothers who were foes unto one another. I saw days without purpose and I saw nights which lead to no dawns."

Let's assess the situation from one more viewpoint. The noted Egyptian scholar Mufti Muhammad Abd'uh (d.1905) visited Paris a hundred years ago. Upon his return to Egypt he startled the world by declaring, *"In Europe I saw no Muslims, I saw Islam. In Egypt I see Muslims, I see no Islam!"* (By the way, he termed the rampant, counterfeit, manmade Islam as THE ESTRANGED RELIGION.)

Dear reader, although there are non-Islamic practices in the West, I can hear the echo of that declaration today. The so-called billion plus Muslims are Muslims without Islam! Their political, economic and social conditions paint a complete picture of misery and chaos wherever they live. Apparently the tree bearing such bad fruit should be blameworthy. Isn't a tree known by the fruit it bears? Let me say at the outset: The tree bearing this bad fruit is what I call THE NUMBER TWO ISLAM. Allama Mashriqi (d.1964) had termed it THE MAULVI'S

WRONG RELIGION. Allama Iqbal (d. 1938) called it AJAMI (alien, Persian, non-Quranic) ISLAM. Sir Syed Ahmed Khan, (d. 1897) had named it the MANMADE RELIGION.

Subjugation to kings, despots, and tyrants, slavery to the Sufi and the Mullah, submission to blind following of weird dogmas, fear, illiteracy, insecurity, lootings & killings, ethnic and sectarian hatred, webs of superstition - what is all this? Rule of slavery, total slavery of mind and body.

Sectarianism

Let's view the situation from another angle. The tree of sectarianism among Muslims has grown to such heights, and *fatwas* (religious edicts) of infidelity have become so popular that there exists not a single Muslim in the world today who would be unanimously accepted as a Muslim by the Ulema (or Mullahs) of any two sects! (According to a Turkish scholar now these sects number 190!) The followers of Islam, which introduced the concept of international brotherhood, are hopelessly divided among themselves.

Muslims by Birth

Many find consolation in, "We are born Muslims", or "Thank God! He created us among Muslims." But the Quran confers no value to Islam by inheritance. It reads:

> **4:136** O You who have chosen to be graced with belief! (and call yourselves Muslims)! Believe in Allah and His Messenger, and the Book He has revealed to His Messenger, and (the fact that He revealed) the Scripture before. [Belief to the point of Conviction can only be attained through reason and not as a birth right 12:108]

> **12:108** Say (O Prophet), "This is my way. Resting my call upon reason, I am calling you all to Allah - I and they who follow me." (We do not invite through blind faith, vague dogmas or by stunning your intellect with miracles). Glory to Allah! And I am not one of those who ascribe divinity in any form besides Him."

The Quran is very particular on using our intellect and reason. It emphasizes on people not to accept even its own verses deaf and blind. (25:73)

Muslims should stop here and think for a moment. Have I ever tried to search for reality? Did I really find the Truth? Or, am I simply imitating the ways of my forefathers? It is only after due contemplation that Islam can be adopted. Unfortunately, today almost all the one billion plus Muslims in the world are Muslims by birth and by blind following, the kind of Islam which the Quran considers of no merit. It has to be a matter of choice based upon reason and understanding. Only then can a Muslim be an effective, enlightened member of the Ummah (Universal Brotherhood).

> *Reason and learning are like body and soul*
> *Without reason soul is empty wind*
> *Without learning body is a senseless frame.*

(Kahlil Gibran, 1883-1931)

Comparison with the Status of Christians

Let us compare the current status of the Muslims with that of the Christians. While there is an increasing bias against Muslims, where are the Christians standing? Objectively speaking, one cannot help but marvel at their scientific, technological and political achievements.

The Bias against Muslims

I know as you do that bias against Muslims has been rising on a global scale. You may wonder why. Palestine, Bosnia, Kashmir, Kosovo, Chechnya have seen the most massive genocides and atrocities since the Holocaust. Anti-Muslim propaganda is on the rise everywhere. Some analysts are calling Iraq a laboratory for further annihilation of Muslims. And the Muslims are getting overjoyed at President Clinton's felicitation on the Eid festival! Meanwhile, Christian missionary work has been stepped up worldwide.

Our response: Mosque upon mosque, religious school upon religious school, is opening. Yet, in these institutions, all is taught but the pristine and glorious Message of the Quran. The magnetic Quran, which contains the Message of global success, has been relegated to mere recitation without understanding. The Quran is being memorized, being sung in competition and being "finished" in so many hours. Muslim scholars and Ulema in great numbers are busy propagating the No.2, counterfeit, ritualistic, cultural, fatalistic, tradition-based Islam. The bearers of the Last Word of God have confined their faith to individual salvation by means of empty, ritualistic worship. Their resulting non-Quranic practices can hardly induce sympathetic or acceptable responses from scientific and rational minds.

> *"The Quran is the only book that can keep up with changing times. Who would like to travel in a bullock cart in the age of horse-less carriage?"*

(Kahlil Gibran, Weekly News, Lebanon, 1921)

Moreover, to my knowledge, there is a great scarcity of books that would simply yet effectively introduce a non-Muslim (or even a young Muslim) to the extraordinary and dynamic practical teachings of Islam. If a non-Muslim is interested in learning about Islam, we either hand-over to him a copy of the Quran (which is not understandable because of wrong translations based upon a thousand year old conjecture-based narratives), or we provide him with a book on Islamic jurisprudence (FIQH). These books of Fiqh talk about menial issues

234

and petty problems such as ways of ablution, size of the beard, type of the head-cover, rituals of worship, etc. These man-made books, unlike the Quran, cannot guide us to establish a workable system in the human society.

Unfortunately, the ignorant opponents and foolish friends of Islam wish to maintain the status quo. Since this kind of Islam proposes no system or way of collective life, it poses no threat to the ruling or dominant class, or to the priesthood. Rather it invigorates both!

We have respect for our Christian brothers and sisters. They are part of God's family. The exalted Messenger Muhammad said:

> *"All humanity is the family of God, so love them all."*

But, Muslims have failed miserably in conveying the highly rational Message of the Last Word of God to humanity. They have done even worse in defining the blissful objective of the Quran i.e. building Paradise in this life and thus achieving it in the Hereafter.

Therefore, even after the western scholars have seen a glimmer of the shining guidance in the Quran, all the above reasons contribute to bar them from looking any further. And noticing the abject political and socio-economic status of Muslims, our Christian brothers and sisters detract from Islam. How would they know that Muslims today are not lagging behind due to Islam but only because of a counterfeit, man-made set of dogmas, beliefs, rituals, customs and traditions, i.e. The Number Two Islam! Who is to blame?

The Status of Christians

Unlike the Muslims, the Christians are performing far better at the political, social, economic, and scientific levels. Their planning and action in these areas is much more organized and rationally based. Why is this?

Ponder that when God commanded the angels ("Forces of Nature" according to Sir Syed Ahmed Khan) to prostrate before Adam, they did. This means that Allah made the forces of nature subservient to mankind. In other words, man has been endowed with the capacity to understand and master the physical laws operative in Nature. This is called the "status of Adam" or "the potential of humanity." The West has attained this coveted status. Muslims, not yet attaining it, are scrambling through life at subhuman levels.

However, let us not ignore the glaring fact that the western civilization is not only imperfect, but according to top western minds, it is heading toward disaster. There is a catastrophic decline of morality. Crime, alcoholism, drug addiction, publicly advertised homosexuality, single parenthood, child abuse, domestic violence, decline of family values, rampant divorce rate, and hard pornography are just a few examples of the evils infesting the materially advanced West. Modernity without spirituality is taking its toll on the western psyche. It appears that, for the Western civilization, the party is over!

It is interesting to note that the Renaissance of the Christian Europe coincided with and heavily depended on the revolutionary thoughts of Martin Luther and John Calvin. When the Europeans moved away from the church they set their course toward becoming scientific and industrial giants. Conversely, Muslims who kindled the European Renaissance slumped into darkness as they departed from the Quran.

The status of the true believers *(MU'MINEEN)*, however, is most glorious i.e. they harness the forces of Nature by mastering physical laws and then use these forces for the benefit of not one nation, race or color, but of all mankind as Allah commands.

> **13:17** The real existence on earth is of the one who benefits mankind.

Thus, the West has attained the status of Adam. The Muslims have lost both statures.

> *"Risen you have not to the human level, how can you find God (and the purpose of life)?"* - Sir Iqbal.

So we come to the question, why I am still a Muslim.

Why I am a Muslim

> *"The Message of Mohammad is not a set of metaphysical phenomena. It is a complete civilization."* (W.A.R. Gibb, Whither Islam)

Basically there are three reasons why I chose Islam to be my way of life and for the same reasons I am Muslim.

1. Islam is not to Blame

As opposed to other dogmas, Islam offers a workable and logical system of life. The Glorious Quran, which embodies the last Word of Allah, guarantees its followers signal victory, success and achievement in this world and in the Hereafter. Then what explains the Muslims' downfall? Is the Message of Islam outdated? I believe that Muslims, and not Islam, are to be blamed for their dismal condition in the last many centuries as we will soon examine.

More than one billion people who call themselves Muslims are so only by name. They have fallen from the high platform of DEEN (The Divinely Prescribed Way of Life) into the swamp of MAZHAB (rituals of worship to achieve individual salvation plus blind following of human 'authorities' and senseless non-Quranic dogmas). Thus, it is their non-Islamic practices that cause their decline and invite condemnation from rest of the world.

> **2:8** And of mankind are those who claim, "We believe in Allah and the Last Day", when they have indeed not attained belief.

Let us hear this truth in the words of the great Sir Syed Ahmed Khan of Aligarh, India:

*" The prevalent form of Islam is not the Deen that was revealed to the
exalted Messenger and that which is preserved in the Quran -----
Muslims have chosen for themselves their ancestors' traditions and
beliefs, their customs and practices, as gods besides God. They have
acknowledged and invented countless prophets (jurists, mystics, sufis,
imams, historians) after Mohammad, the exalted. They have taken
books, written by men as equivalent of the Quran. We do not accept
these false gods, fictitious prophets and fake Qurans. We are the
destroyers of these false gods, fictitious prophets and fake Qurans just
as our father Abraham, the exalted, was the destroyer of his father
Azar's idols."* (Hayat-e-Javaid, Afkar-e-Sir Syed)

Dear reader, if the conviction of Sir Syed has astonished you please reflect on
some verses of the Quran that support him:

3:139   Do not ever, then, lose heart, and grieve not, for you are bound
to prevail if you are indeed believers.

4:141   Allah will not give the rejecters (of the Quran) any way of
success against the true believers.

10:103   It is incumbent upon Us to save the community of true
believers.

21:105   And indeed, after advising mankind, We laid it down in all the
Books of Divine Wisdom that My able servants will inherit the
earth.

24:55   Allah has promised that those nations who will believe in the
Divine Laws and strengthen human resources, He will surely
make them rulers in the earth - Just as He granted rule to the
previous nations (28:6, 33:27). ----.

Now, let us think about the plight of Muslims world-wide. Are they truly
prevailing anywhere? Aren't they subjugated slaves of foreign powers, even in
their own countries? Are they not stagnant in their thought and action? Thus,
either the Muslims are not true believers or the Quran is wrong by declaring that
the believers will prevail.

First, it seems clear that Muslims are not fulfilling God's conditions to prevail in
the earth. Professor A.N. Whitehead rightly points out that *accepting the
customary thought without criticism is a form of idol-worship.* It brings the
development of the human mind to a standstill. Amazingly, the Quran describes
idols as *authan,* things that do not move. These statements support Sir Syed's
assertion that Muslims have become victims of blind following and are,
therefore, stagnant in their thinking and action.

Secondly, there is no doubt about the Quranic Truth that the believers will
always prevail. When Muslims were adhering to the Quran they were the most

237

dynamic force in the world to contend with. History is replete with their accomplishments in all walks of life, be it government, morals, philosophy, science, architecture, military, agriculture, medicine, surgery, physics, chemistry, optics, art, etc. In fact that era provided the most pragmatic test for the Quran with absolutely convincing results for humanity to behold.

According to Robert Briffault; "*The European Renaissance was triggered not from Italy but from the Muslim Spain*".

Conclusion: Sir Syed's claim, that today's Muslims are not true believers, is absolutely correct and confirmed by the Quran. How?

> **25:30** And the Messenger will say, "O my Lord! These are my people, the ones who had disabled this Quran making it of no account."

2. Islam Provides Guidance

While Muslims are to blame for their plight, Islam indeed guarantees salvation and success for all humanity. It explains the role of human beings in the Universe and provides unparalleled guidance. I respectfully submit that nothing but Islam offers to us:

> - A rational, comprehensible relationship between the Creator, the Universe, and the Humans.

> - Guidance to establish a political, social, economic and moral environment where one can grow up to one's full potential. This Guidance, transcending all temporal and spatial boundaries, is for all humankind and promises to solve every single problem of humanity.

These two reasons need further elaboration. Chapter III will further elaborate on Islam As I Understand.

3. Critical Issues With Other Belief Systems

Another reason why I am a Muslim: I find other religions to be extremely dependent on blind faith, supernatural phenomena and irrational mythology. They fail to propose or provide an equitable society free of man-made distinctions. They also fail to offer practical, workable solutions to the problems and crises that humanity is facing. On the other hand, Islam is a challenge to religion. And it is simple. *"If Islam means submission to the Will of God, don't we all live in Islam?"* (Johann Goethe)

While the foundation of Islamic theology is simple, that is, Pristine Monotheism and the Law of Requital (Cause and Effect), other religions offer inexplicably complex doctrines. For example, the Christian doctrines of Trinity, Original Sin, the physical son-ship of Jesus and the Vicarious Sacrifice of 'the Lamb of God' etc are so complex that the Christian Christology has been incessantly revisited by the Church. Top Christian scholars and thinkers feel very uncomfortable with the nature of Jesus Christ as portrayed in the New Testament. This re-visitation is very likely to result in the nature of Jesus being redefined in conformity with that of the Quran. These points will be explained shortly.

See how rational the Quran is!

85:15-16   Lord of the Supreme Throne. Carrying out His Plan according to His Laws.

[In the World of Command He makes Laws as He wills. Then He implements these Laws in the World of Creation - the Universe (7:54). And then He neither changes them, nor makes any exceptions. (17:77, 33:38, 33:62, 35:43, 40:85, 48:23). His Rule is the Rule of Law and not of haphazard tantrums]

So, people do not walk on water, birds can fly, elephants cannot, fire burns, ice cools, water flows downstream, earth revolves around the sun, seeds grow to become plants, living beings taste death, babies are born when male and female gametes unite, seasons alternate in regular fashion, night follows the day and day follows the night etc. There are no such things as the demons or superstitions of any kind.

Islam as I understand

> *The teachings of Islam can fail under no circumstances. With all our systems of culture and civilization, we cannot go beyond Islam and, as a matter of fact, no human mind can go beyond the Quran.*
>
> (Johann Wolfgang von Goethe, the celebrated German poet and thinker, in his letters to J. Eckermann and Sir Henry Elliot))

Dear reader, Islam is DEEN, a perfect way of individual and collective life. All else is *mazhab* or call it religion. The Arabic word *mazhab* does not appear in the Quran. Islam is not a set of irrational themes, empty rituals and rites, myths and omens, pomp and magic, dreams and non-scientific phenomena. Nor, it is just "stories of the bygones". The Quran is the only Book that invariably gives the rational reason behind each and every Command. In fact, Islam is so scientific that the noted Russian thinker, P.D. Ouspensky, stated that *any science that collides with the Quran will turn out to be false.* (Tertium organum)

Relationship of the Creator, the Universe, and the Human Being

1. The Creator:

The Creator is One, all else is creation. He is the Cherisher and Sustainer of the worlds and of all humankind regardless of family, race, sex, color, creed, geography, national origin, religion etc. (1:1, 114:1)

Also, God (Allah) is Omni-present and Omnipotent. He is not confined to the heavens. He does not have a man-like image. He is the Light of the heavens and the earth (24:35). He is High Above the human concepts of needing or having a consort/mistress (6:101) or children (112:1-4). And although Allah is

239

Omnipotent, He uses his Power with Wisdom and Knowledge (2:209). He is the Wise and the Knower, and therefore, never repents on having made a wrong decision.

In the World of Command *(Al-Amr),* He makes Laws as He wills. Then, He implements these Laws in the World of Creation *(Al-Khalq* or the Universe 7:54). These Laws NEVER change (35:43, 48:23). If we reflect, the magnificent gains of science and technology would have come to naught if the proverbial apple of Newton fell on the ground yesterday and flew in the air today.

The entire Universe is operating according to the physical laws designed and implemented by Allah. When we discover some of these laws, we call them Science. Yet, all the creation that exists cannot defy these laws of nature. Senator John Glenn said well that *we can invent a compass but we cannot invent the law for the magnetic needle to point North.* And so, the water will flow down-stream, the apple will fall to the ground, a stone will sink, a boat will float, the day and night will follow each other, the seasons will take their turns, fire will be hot, ice will be cold, the living beings will grow, reproduce and die. Similarly God's Laws in Nature make no distinction between Jews or Gentiles, Hindus or Christians, Muslims or non-Muslims. But, those who submit their free will to His Guidance and try to establish peace, become harmonious with the Divine Plan. He calls those people Muslims. "Islam" embraces both meanings, Submission and Peace.

2. The Universe:

According to the Quran, the Universe is neither Brahma's dream nor Ramji's leela (Rama's play). God is not *Nut Rajan* (the Master Player). The Universe is for real. It is neither an image nor a shadow of the "World of Ideas" as proposed by Plato. It has not been created by chance.

> **44:38-39** For, We have not created the heavens and the earth and all that is between them in idle sport. We have not created them without Purpose. But most of them know not.

The universe is too organized to be the result of an accident.

- Albert Einstein

The Quran further states that all things in the Universe are heading toward their appointed destinations and nothing is stationary. The heavenly bodies are "swimming along in their orbits" (21:33, 36:40). All this is taking place according to the physical laws designed by the Creator. The Universe itself is marching to a designated goal. (51:47)

> *There is a coherent plan in the universe, though I don't know what it's a plan for.*
>
> - British astronomer, author, Sir Fred Hoyle

3. The Human Being:

God has created the Universe in an organized manner and humans are a part of that great organization. However, He has granted free will to the human beings. They are free to choose their own way, and thus, make their own destiny. And, every action of ours must meet with a just recompense in the Hereafter as well.

2:256 There is absolutely no compulsion or coercion in religion. ----.

18:29 And proclaim, "This is the Truth from your Lord. Whoever accepts it let him accept it, and whoever rejects it, let him reject it." ----.

45:22 For, Allah has created the heavens and the earth with Purpose, and that every person shall be repaid what he or she has earned. And none shall be wronged.

Just as all other creations in the Universe are obeying Divine Laws fulfilling their assigned roles human beings must follow the Commands and harmonize themselves with the Divine Plan. To achieve this, humans could use their intellect and science. But the intellect and science are imperfect. Albert Einstein states, *"Science can tell what is, it cannot tell what ought to be. The code of permanent values can only come through Revelation to the chosen personalities* (messengers)." A.S. Eddington maintains, *"The acceptance of God does not mean believing in His existence. Rather, it means accepting God as the Source of guidance."* Thus, in order to help us become harmonious with the Universe, Allah has compassionately shown us the Way. Only we humans can be the losers if we miss the Divine Train which is constantly moving toward an appointed destination.

The Guidance

Now that we have seen a glimpse of the relationship of the Creator with humans, let us take a look at the Eternal Guidance He has provided for us. Al-Quran 2:177 denotes that we must begin with having *IMAN* (Conviction) in Allah, the Life Hereafter, the Angels, the Book and His Messengers. Commonly these are called the Five Articles of Faith.

The Five Articles of Faith (given in 2:177)

1- *Belief in One God: How can we embrace that belief? The Quran invites us to *IMAN* only through reason. A tornado hitting a junk yard will not end up producing a Boeing 747. Even the "Big Bang" must have a Master Mind behind it.

12:108 Say (O Prophet), "This is my way. Resting my call upon reason, I am calling you all to Allah - I and they who follow me." (We do not invite through blind faith, vague dogmas or by stunning your intellect with miracles). Glory to Allah! And

I am not one of those who ascribe divinity in any form besides Him."

Watch this reason applied beautifully. *"The Universe is too organized to be the result of an accident,"* declared Einstein. And Carl Sagan, the renowned American philosopher, exclaimed, *"In order to make an apple-pie from scratch, we would have to reinvent the Universe!"*

2. *Belief in the Hereafter: This entails not only the Afterlife, but Nature's Law of Cause and Effect as well. As you sow so shall you reap! Our thoughts and actions make imprints on our personalities. Thus we start making our hell or paradise right here in this world.

> **20:124** But whoever will turn away from My remembrance, thus ignoring My Commands, his will be a narrow life. (Such individuals and nations will live in economic and moral poverty). And I shall bring such of them blind to the Assembly on the Day of Resurrection.

Accordingly, Sir Iqbal in his beautiful poem;

> *"A Stroll in the Heavens", wrote that when an angel (his tour guide) showed him a dark cold abode for hell, Iqbal looked perplexed! The tour-guide explained:*
>
> *Dwellers of the earth that come here*
>
> *Carry with them own fuel to flare*

Thus, our good thoughts and deeds (actions that are beneficial to the society) culminate in great reward termed "Paradise." Conversely our negative thought and behavior prepare us for the hellfire. It is noteworthy that according to the Quran, the hellfire is such that its flames emanate from, and engulf the hearts.

> **104:6-7** A Fire kindled by Allah (His Law of 'As you sow, so shall you reap') That originates in, and engulfs, the hearts.

Belief in the immortality of human personality (SELF) is, in fact, closely tied to the belief in the Hereafter. Johann Goethe rightly pointed out, *"One who does not believe in the Afterlife is only a cadaver in this world."*

3. *Belief in Angels: This belief holds that the angels are sinless, eternally obedient creation of Allah. Unlike humans, angels do not have free will. The Quran does not expect us to define their exact nature. Sir Syed understood them to be "Forces of Nature" or physical laws of nature in the Universe. The Divine Message was revealed to God's messengers through the Angels. The exalted Prophet, explaining a verse, states that even thunder is one of the angels of God. That statement is completely in agreement with the Quran.

> **13:13** And the thunder and the (other) angels strive to glorify Him by carrying out their duties in awe of Him. And He it is Whose

physical Laws let loose the thunderbolt to strike the earth. And yet they stubbornly argue about Allah's Laws (and fall for superstitions). Though Awesome He is in Power!

4. *The Book: The Message of God revealed to prophets through the angels is called a Book. The Divine Message that was conveyed through a chain of prophets like Noah, Abraham, Isaac, Jacob, Moses and Jesus, took its final form in the Quran. Therefore, the Quran is the Final Commandment, THE BOOK. It is for all times and for all nations.

Moreover, the Quran is the most authentic Scripture in all history. Numerous scholars from all religions agree that the Quran is word for word, letter for letter, the same unchanged, unaltered Message as revealed to and preached by Messenger Muhammad, the exalted.

> *I have studied Islam very closely. I believe from the depths of my heart that the existing Koran is exactly the Book, letter for letter, as written in the lifetime of Mohammad.*

> - Sir Williams Muir, *Life of Mohammad*

> *I am convinced that the Quran is THE WORD OF GOD in its truest and whole meaning.*

> - Rev. Bosworth Smith

Now, watch from another perspective. Dr. Maurice Buccaille, the renowned Christian scholar, historian, and surgeon from France wrote his revolutionary book, *The Bible, the Quran And Science* in the 1970's. He states that *the Quran is replete with scientific narratives such as creation of the Universe, Evolution, the Water Cycle, Geology, Astronomy, History, Embryology, Zoology, Botany, etc.* Dr. Buccaille asserts that *there is not a SINGLE instance in the Quran that is inconsistent with the established scientific knowledge.* On the other hand, according to Buccaille, *"Incongruities are encountered in the Bible at numerous places."*

Furthermore, the Quran challenged all people 1400 years ago to help one another and make one Surah (chapter) like this (2:23 & 10:38). Since the great Arabic writers of that time, the challenge stands to this day with all its majesty.

5. *Messengers: I have avoided using the term "Prophet" here since it conveys the impression of a man making prophecies. The role of a Messenger of Allah is much more comprehensive and sublime. Noah, Abraham, Ishmael, Isaac, Jacob, Joseph, Moses, Jesus, Muhammad (the exalted ones) were all chosen messengers of God. They all were (and still are) the role models for all humanity. They had spotless character and embodied human perfection. They never lapsed in their prime duty of conveying God's Message to mankind.

Contrary to the Bible, the Quran declares that all messengers were men of life upright. They did not commit sins, nor did they violate Divine Values. Therefore, unlike in the Bible:

- Noah never drank alcohol, nor did his daughters made him commit sin with them.
- David did not fall for the beauty of his neighbor's wife.
- Nor did Solomon lean toward worshiping his wives' idols.
- Jacob did not deceive his old father Isaac.
- Nor did he have a wrestling match with God.
- Lot's daughters did not make him drunk nor did they lead him to sin.
- And Abraham did not tell any lies.
- Moses did not kill the Coptic intentionally, nor did he strike him in bias. And Jesus never rebuked his mother. Nor was he rude to his people.

Moment of reflection: If these great messengers faltered in character, who, then, would be the role model of character for us? And how could we expect virtue among their followers and people in general?

Further, God did not repent on creating such human beings. He never gets tired to need a day of rest. No sleep or slumber overcomes Him. He is not an angry, jealous, vengeful God. He favors no peoples or nations. His Laws support those who live by them. (2:255)

Let us reiterate that God sent His guidance to all nations and all peoples through His chosen messengers (10:47). His Message finally was perfected through His last Messenger, Muhammad, the exalted (33:40). The Message has been meticulously preserved in the form of Al-Quran for all places, times and peoples forever (5:3, 34:28, 62:3).

Excerpt taken from Islam as I Understand by Shabbir Ahmed MD. Available at www.ourbeacon.com

Adventures of an Islamic Reformer at Oxford, London, and Istanbul

Edip Yuksel

To publicly discuss my recent book, <u>Manifesto for Islamic Reform</u>, I was invited to give four lectures in November 3-10, 2008. The topics were: A Manifesto for Islamic Reform, and Why Quran Alone through Reason:

MECO, Oxford University, November 3.
MECO, Oxford University, November 4.
The Muslim Institute, London, November 5.
TUYAP Book Fair, Istanbul, November 8.

Prof Taj Hargey, the founder of MECO (Muslim Educational Center of Oxford), picked me up from the airport with an old diesel Volkswagen. I had picked the wrong airport and thus he had to drive more than two hours in a heavy traffic to pick me up. Like all bloody Britons[1], he drove on the wrong side of the road, which made me experience constant anticipation of an imminent bloody traffic accident. Though Taj is a scholar in a prestigious school, he is not a stereotypical one. To my delight, I found him not be a pretentious snob living in ivory towers; he was a humble and a committed activist, a veteran who had tasted victory against the apartheid regime during his years in South Africa. His dedication to the message of rational monotheism or islam appeared to be exemplary. He is both a general and a soldier; a professor and a student; a leader and comrade. Almost single-handedly, with a shoe-string budget, he is putting a good fight against the powerful forces of Sunni and Shiite establishment, and at the same time fighting against the aggression of the British government. Forces of corruption from Saudi, Iran and Pakistan are spending hundreds of millions of pounds to keep the Muslim minority ignorant and backward. The bloody mullahs have interest in keeping the Muslim minority in ghettoes and Taj is struggling to create a British Muslim identity.

Taj told me that his organization lost about fifty percent of its membership for letting Prof. Amina Wadud lead the congregational prayer two weeks before my arrival. Though I find inconsistencies in Amina Wadud's theological position, she is a brave sister who is reminding Sunni and Shiite population the Quranic

---

[1] As one of the principles I have committed myself since my childhood I never use cuss words, but somehow I do not find my habitual aversion against the British cussword "bloody". I am not exactly sure about its complete connotations and subtle innuendoes, but I am going to use it in this article as a British souvenir.

245

verse 49:13, a universal maxim of their holy book, which they have abandoned for the sake of fabricated teachings called *hadith* and *sunna*.

As it seems, a woman leading the prayer was the last straw on *mullah's* back; they unanimously excommunicated Taj and his organization. I was happy to learn that Taj was not naïve about the regressive powers against the reform movement and he was even more determined to fight against misogynistic mullahs. While he was hosting me, he was busy preparing for the upcoming annual music festival. Of course, music too is another divine blessing that mullahs prohibit. Imagine a singing muslim woman in front of men! Music + woman + spotlight! That would be a triple nightmare for them and Taj was going to organize it with an international flavor. Kill those self-righteous hair-splitting mullahs with beauty and music!

Multiple Choice Test or Theological Acid Test

My first lecture at Oxford University was received very well. We had productive discussions. A graduate student argued for historicity, that is, reading and usually limiting the Quran with its historic context. His friend criticized our reliance on science in understanding the Quranic verses. Citing a few abuses of such an approach, she wanted to refute any understanding of Quranic verses according to scientific facts. It took about ten minutes to show her the problems with her allergy against science and the problem with doubting proven mathematical statements. If there is any book on earth that should have complete compatibility with proven scientific facts and mathematics, it would be the books sent by the creator of the universe. I knew that their hidden distrust in Quran was the main factor in their rejection of science and mathematics. It is interesting that they employ impressive academic jargons to make such arguments.

I had prepared a test containing 45 multiple choice questions just the night before my travel. I duplicated them on both sides of a single sheet and I distributed to the audience before the lecture... They were asked to write their name, age, occupation, email address, favorite authors, and their sectarian affiliation. It was a bit awkward to test an audience that consisted of students and professors at one of the world's top universities. The multiple-choice test proved to be a powerful instrument to deliver the message of Islamic Reform under the light of the Quran. The correct answer for each multiple choice question was the E option, and for the Yes or No questions was the B option. So, it would take me a few seconds to evaluate the tests after they were returned to me.

The Sunni or Shiite test-takers found themselves in quagmire of contradiction with their own sectarian teachings. They learned that they were thirty, forty or even more than fifty percent infidels or heretics. Some of those who marked Sunni as their sectarian affiliation contradicted the Sunni teachings on most of the issues. According to their own confessed sects, their lives were worthless; they deserved to be killed! I did not let this mirror or sect-o-meter remain an individual experience; I publicly declared the overall results. Many got all answers correct, including Eric, a monotheist from Unitarian church who already had a copy of the Quran: a Reformist Translation in his possession. Eric knew the original message of islam better than all the mullahs and the so-called "ulama" combined. And Eric was one of those muslims from among the People of the Book described by 2:62 and 74:31.

Let's Have Just One Percent Please, Just One Percent!

A Sunni professor who attended the lecture together with his wife could not handle the questions; he stopped after answering a few. It was amusing how during the discussion session he tried to bargain with me about the teachings of Hadith and Sunna. He realized that he could not defend most of the hadiths and sectarian teachings, so he begged for a compromise: "What about just 1% hadith?" I did not yield. I told him that we did not need to add even a tiny drop of coli bacteria into our food. Even one percent of shirk (partnership with God) is evil, and that one percent would mean that we still rejected God's repeated assertion that His book is detailed, complete, clarified and sufficient for guidance. Furthermore, that one percent hole in the book would be small; yet, it would allow insects, then mice and then get even bigger enough for a litter of pigs, perhaps bearded ones, to intrude. I reminded him that there was no difference between associating one partner or hundred partners to God.

The following night was the continuation of the previous lecture. I focused on the importance of critical thinking and using our God-given 19 rules of inference. I warned them against developing schizophrenic personalities, which almost all religious people do. I started with the following words:

Before putting anything in our mouths we observe the color, smell its odor. If it looks rotten or smells bad we do not touch it. If food passes the eye and nose tests, then our taste buds will be the judge. If a harmful bit fools all those examinations, our stomach come to rescue; it revolts and throws them up. There are many other organs that function as stations for testing, examination, and modification of imported material into our bodies. They ultimately meet our smart and vigilant nano-guards: white cells. Sure, there are many harmful or potentially harmful foods that pass all the way through our digestive system into our blood, such as alcohol and fat. Nevertheless, without using our reasoning faculty much if at all, we have an innate system that protects our body from harmful substances. It would be a mystery then how we can input information and assertions, especially the most bizarre ones, into our brains without subjecting them to the rigorous test of critical thinking. Our brains should never become trashcans of false ideas, holy viruses, unexamined dogmas and superstitions. We should be wise!

How can we protect our minds and brains? Do we have an innate system that protects us from harmful or junky ideas, especially dogmas or jingoisms that could turn us into zombies or self-righteous evil people? Yes we do: our logic is the program that detects and protects us against the most harmful viruses, which usually find their way when we are hypnotized by crowds, salespeople, politicians or clergymen.

The Prominent Imam with an Illiterate Role Model

For the third lecture, Taj took me to London. There I was going to give a lecture at Muslim Institute. I met some of familiar names, authors that I have known decades before, such as Dr. Ziyauddin Sardar and Dr. Ghayasudding Siddiqui. I also met some young reformers such as Farouk Peru, and Yusuf Desai and Nosheen Oezcan of Forward Thinking. I was positively surprised that with the exception of an imam there, who was considered a moderate and open minded one, they did not react in angry temper tantrums to my invitation to follow the Quran alone.

The imam rejected the Manifesto for Islamic Reform wholesale with a passionate opening. He accused me of distorting the facts. To substantiate his opposition, Imam Abduljalil Sajid picked one out of my assertions. He argued that Muhammad must have been illiterate. He did not provide an alternative take against my depiction of such illiteracy to be either an insult to Muhammad's intelligence or his intention. He did not bother to explain how a role model, a divinely selected messenger would not be able to recognize 28 Alphabet letters in 63 years of his life (two years for each letter!), or during the 23 years he received revelation that encouraged its audience to attain knowledge by reading. He did not deal with the problem of the alternative explanation, that is, how a role model could deliberately keep himself illiterate for all his life! Somehow, our imam, like all other religious leaders, had great tolerance for contradictions. His brain was filled with so many; he had perhaps given up from resolving them... A perfect example of intellectually boiled frog syndrome! I had empathy for him, since in my youth I was one of them. I let him vent his frustration.

Imam Abduljalil argued that the word *Iqra* did not mean read, but it meant recite. So, according to him, despite the instruction of verse 96:1, Muhammad could still have been illiterate. It was a late Monday night and we did not have time to engage in a lengthy discussion. For instance, I could remind him his own *hadith* which reported the first encounter of Muhammad and Angel Gabriel. According to that *hadith* report, when he was instructed with the first verse of chapter 96, *Iqra*, to make Muhammad read the visually displayed Quran, the angel squeezed him like a lemon several times when Muhammad claimed *"wa ma ana biqarin"* (I cannot read). Obviously that hadith report did not mean that Muhammad was incapable of repeating a word with two syllabi; it meant that he could not recognize the letters… He was contradiction with the hadith that was the basis for his assertion. I picked another argument.

> -- Let's assume that you are right regarding the meaning of *Iqra*. Then, what is the Arabic word for "read"?

> -- ???

-- Well, there must have been a word for reading in Arabic, since the
Quran talks about books, about pen, about writing...

-- ???

Our imam who started his criticism with a loud denunciation suddenly turned
mute. He could not even come up with a single word. I did not wish to push him
further, since everyone in the room realized that he either did not know what he
was arguing about or he realized that he was wrong. I remembered the most
ridiculous praises in human history, where Muhammad is praised by millions for
his illiteracy with the distorted meaning of the word "*ummy*" uttered together
with another distorted word "*sally*". Thinking about the low illiteracy among the
so-called Muslim population, I did not let the issue go away without a
conclusive ending. I wanted to prove to him and everyone else that Muhammad
was literate.

So, I used one of my successful teaching tools, which I employed first time in
1987 to convince Ali Bulaç, a prominent and prolific Muslim thinker who has
numerous books and a Turkish Quran translation. After following my
instructions, Ali was convinced in less than a minute that Muhammad must have
been literate. Imagine the power of debunking the consensus of all Sunni and
Shiite scholars in less than a minute! Imagine convincing a famous and popular
Sunni author that all his Sunni scholars were wrong about an important issue.
All in less than a minute! Yet, this proof has been implicitly provided in the
Quran with the revelation of its first verses, through the very verses instructing
how to read the Quran. What a marvelous book!

So, I tried that Quranic educational tool. I asked the imam to grab the pen and
write down the beginning of chapter 96: "*Bismillahirrahmanirarrahim. Iqra
bismi rabbika allazi khalaq*" That's it. Surprise: he did not wish to write it.
Perhaps he was scared to continue engaging in a Socratic dialog. Had he written
those few words, I would ask him why he wrote both words the same. Surely, he
would be justified to spell them the same, since both were pronounced the same
and meant the same. Then, I would ask him to look at the spelling of the Quran.
He would notice that the one in *Bismillah* was consisted of three letters, BSM,
but the one in the following verse was spelled with an extra aleph, BISM. So,
even if we assume that Muhammad did not write the revelation of the Quran
with his own hand, even if we believe in the stories of him dictating to scribes,
he must have at least known the letter Aleph. If he knew Aleph, then he was at
least $1/28^{th}$ literate! "I proved that he knew the letter Aleph and now it is your
turn to prove that he did not know the letter B, the second letter in alphabet," I
would nicely ask. If our imam got stuck again, I would perhaps go forward and
ask him about the different spelling of *Mecca* and *Becca* or the curious spelling
of *Bastata* in verse 7:69.

I wanted to end the argument with the imam with an exposition. I knew his
problem and I knew the fastest way to expose it. I told the audience that the

gentleman was arguing about God's system without knowledge and without an enlightening book. I announced that I was going to prove that he did not in fact have respect for the Quran. I started reading from verse 6:145 and then posed him my question: "Do you have any other source or any other witness that adds more dietary prohibitions to the four items listed in this verse?" If he said no, he would contradict numerous hadiths and all sectarian teachings. If he said Yes, he would contradict this verse and would be exposed by the following verses as a "mushrik" (polytheist) for attributing the manmade religious prohibitions to God. He did not rush into saying Yes, as most of the Sunni scholars recklessly do. To my question regarding additional dietary prohibitions, he responded with extreme caution: "May be or may be not!" What? You are an "imam" in your fifties and you have eaten thousands of meals and you still do not know what is prohibited? And you are refuting the Quran alone for a "may be or may be not"? Do you exist? "Maybe or may be not?" Is eating shrimp *haram*? "Maybe or maybe not!" Is eating lobster *haram*? "Maybe or maybe not!" Are you okay? "Maybe or maybe not!"

For some of the audiences, that was the last straw that broke their already stressed respect for the imam. Several people got frustrated with him. One of them loudly yelled at him with animated arms: "If you do not know such a simple thing, then why are you debating with the guest speaker? Let him talk." Hearing his own people reprimanding him, the imam quietly left the room. I felt bad for him, but what he was doing was very wrong. He was trying to keep people in the darkness of ignorance. He was promoting shirk (polytheism) under the guise of monotheism. He was pretending to respect the prophet Muhammad while he was disrespecting the only book he delivered. He was insulting his intelligence by claming that he remained illiterate until his death. Yet, he insisted putting Muhammad's name next to God every time he uttered the monotheistic maxim. I hope that after hearing the message, he will show courage and wisdom to reject the fabricated Hadith and Sunna and uphold the Quran alone.

Detention at the Airport by the Turkish Police

The moment I arrived at the airport in Istanbul, I was immediately arrested by half a dozen young police officers who appeared to be celebrating the catch. After a boring day, they had a Turkish author (again) from the USA. I was informed about three charges against me, all involving political criticism of Turkish government and its policies. Some consisted of distortions of my published articles, exaggerations, or words taken out-of-context. And most did not even belong to me; they belonged to anonymous people who visit my websites and post their political opinions and criticism at the forums.

They took me to a nearby police station. When I entered the room, I noticed a poster filled with flags under the title: Independent Turkish Republics. Yes, in plural! I have no problem with such a sense of Turkish idealism. In fact, years ago, when the Turkish nations declared independence from Russia, I hoped and promoted an aggressive Turkish policy to create a unified block. Unfortunately,

Turkey missed such an opportunity. However, when I heard the phone ring of an officer, I started getting a bit concerned. It was playing the Yeni Çeri march, "Ceddin deden, ceddin baban... hep kahraman Türk milleti..." (Your ancestors your grandparents, your ancestors your fathers... The Turkish nation has always been heroic...) At that point, I knew that I was among an openly racist police department. I have suffered from Turkish racism in many ways. For instance, my young brother Metin Yüksel, a legendary youth leader, was killed by Turkish fascists in 1979. I know first hand the evil of racism.

To my surprise and delight, the Turkish police was very kind and respectful. I am not sure how much of it was because of my American passport, but I think they had a radical change in attitude. They followed the legal procedure to the letter. They informed me about my right to stay silent, my right not to stay more than 24 hour in jail without going to the court. They were music to my ears; I felt as if I was dealing with a nice American police officer. The jail, which I spent the night, was very clean. I laid down on the floor, reading the Newsweek Magazine, a book on Evolution and Intelligent design, and Professor Stewart's Cabinet of Mathematical Curiosities. It was the best night ever I spent in a Turkish jail! Sure, this was a very low traffic police station and they could keep it cleaner than usual. Regardless, I could not believe in such a change, since it was very different from my experience with the Turkish police and jails years ago. During my heydays, in 1977-1987, I was a frequent host of those jails and they were horrible. Some would have raw sewer passing through, rats mingle with detainees, and when I get out, I would always get lice as souvenir. Compared to those Turkish jails, this one was like a five star hotel. I command the Turkish government for this great progress in respecting human dignity and rights.

Kurds, the Oppressed Minority

Well, I had also a bad experience, and should share that too. The chief of the police station treated me like a guest. He took me to his office and ordered food for me where I watched the Turkish TV for about an hour. This made me feel uncomfortable; I was kept unjustly yet I was feeling indebted to my captors. The weekly news program 32nd Day was on. The topic of the discussion was the chronic Kurdish problem. The panel had two Turkish politician or author. There was a good debate about the problem which was the making of the racist Turkish policy. The official racist ideology initially denied the existence of Kurds. Before 1970's, you could not find the word Kurds in the newspapers. The Turkish history text books still consider the Kurdish minority as non existent. Even the great Kurdish leader Salahaddin Ayyubi is described as a Turkish leader. Later, when denial became impossible, the racist Turkish oligarchy described them as Mountain Turks. They did not have a different language, there was no such a language called Kurdish.

Yet, they later shamelessly tried to ban the non-existent language and secured the ban of the language through an article in the Constitution of 1982, which was drafted by the generals who interrupted the young and fragile Turkish democracy, for the third time. The paranoid Turkish racism terrorized those Kurds who were politically active through contra-guerillas, mafia, and Gray Wolf fascists. They kidnapped, tortured and assassinated numerous Kurdish authors and leaders... In a journal article titled "Yes, I am a Kurd," I exposed the racist Turkish policy against Kurds. "My people are denied their identity, their culture, language, naming their own children, using their own land and living in freedom and security." (See: http://www.yuksel.org/e/law/kurd.htm) Kurds were even denied to celebrate their cultural holidays, such as, the Newroz (New Year). Its celebration was banned. When the racist policy politicized Kurds and led to the creation of various Kurdish political movements, including the terrorist PKK organization, the Turkish government was forced to recognize Newroz. Not as a Kurdish holiday, but a newly discovered ancient Turkish holiday! Since like religion, racism is capable of turning smart people into stupid people, they could not even think about the name of the holiday: The name of the officially hijacked Kurdish holiday was made of two Persian or Kurdish words: New (new) Roz (Day). In last decade, Kurds have received many rights, but with a huge cost, after losing the lives of tens of thousands and destruction of thousands of towns in South Eastern Turkey. The desire of Kurdish people for equality and dignity is still an ongoing struggle.

Back to the TV program... While listening to the panelists, the young police officer who had been treating me so nicely suddenly confessed: "If I did not have any expectation from life, I would get a machine gun and kill all of them." The other police officer, who was as young and nice, joined him by declaring his solution for the Kurdish problem: "We should just adopt the ways of our Ottoman ancestors; we should erect hundreds of stakes on the streets and hang hundreds of them on them. Then, you will not hear any Kurdish problem!" Now I knew why their phones were singing Ottoman military marches.

I did not raise objection. It would be futile to discuss with a group of racist police officers while they had me in their possession. Ignorance and arrogance feed each other, and they had plenty of both. Well, later I would be engaging in a Socratic dialogue with a bored nationalist police officer who stood by curiously asking some questions through the bars. Like most racists, he was in denial of his racism. But, all his arguments were biased and Turkish-centered. According to him, there was no problem in forcing Kurdish children to say "My existence should be a sacrificial to the existence of Turkishness" or "One Turk equals to the World," or "How happy is he who says 'I am a Turk'". Our discussion lasted about two hours until he was tired standing on his feet. I think, I was able to penetrate his consciousness, showed him the mirror and placed major doubts in his mind about nationalism, which is one of the worst mental diseases of modern times.

Tried in two Continents in one Day

The Turkish police shuttled me between two courts, one in Asian the other in the European part of Istanbul, rushing to beat the deadline so that I would not stay in jail until the next Monday. I was not handcuffed during this travel; except briefly while I was taken to the car by a new police officer whom later was asked by his superior to unlock the handcuff.

I was also very impressed by the temperament of the judges and their just decision to release me and continue the court. When we arrived in Sultanahmet Adliyesi we rushed to the court's secretary's office. The judge happened to be sitting there. When he heard my name, he ordered the secretary that he knew where was the thick folder was. He pointed at one of the shelves on the wall. Indeed the folder was filled with papers, that is, copies of the hundreds of articles posted by hundreds of people at the forums of 19.org.

The judge initially worried me by telling me that he would continue the ban for my exit. But, he turned to be a very reasonable person. Perhaps he was just bluffing. Not knowing his intention I asked for time for my attorney to come. The judge happily postponed the court to 2 pm afternoon. He read the illegal statements copied from my website's forums. They were primitive and colloquial insult words that I never use. I am puritan and I never use cuss words even in my privacy. They were, according to the complaint prosecutor, insulting Turkishness, insulting Turkish flag, insulting Turkish generals, insulting Turkish National Congress, insulting Turkish judges, insulting Turkish prosecutors, and insulting Turkish police officers. The prosecutor had agreed with the informant citizen that I had violated the article 301 of the Criminal Code and a few others. The charges were based on a complaint letter and supportive documents of a cult member affiliated to Adnan Oktar aka Harun Yahya, whose name was recognized by my attorney who has been defending the victims of this cult leader. (This cult leader has used the repressive Turkish laws to ban 19.org and many other popular sites, such as wordpress.com, youtube.com, and richarddawkins.net. Following his instructions, his followers are spamming the Internet with ugly false accusations against me.)

As later Taj would comfort me during my return to London, "if they did not accuse you of insulting Turkish pizza, Turkish bath, and Turkish coffee, no problem." Well, I had problem with the accusations. First, I would never insult Turkish race, since I am not a racist person. I believe that God allowed the children of Adam to diversify in color, culture and language in order to enrich our lives. I know that the superiority is not by color or ethnic group, but by righteous acts. Besides teaching philosophy at college, I was also teaching Turkish classes at my younger son's K-12 school in Arizona. According to the cultural attaché at the Turkish embassy in Washington, I was the first person in America that started teaching Turkish at a public K-12 school. I display a Turkish flag, its map, the picture of Mustafa Kamal Ataturk, and several beautiful pictures from Istanbul on the walls of the class I teach. Some parents traveled to Turkey just because of their children's exposure to Turkish language and culture. Perhaps, those who accused me of insulting Turkishness would never serve the interest of Turkish people as much as I have done. If I had wanted to retaliate against what the racist Turks had done to me and my family, perhaps I should have joined the ranks of PKK terror organization. I am a Kurd whose mother tongue was banned by the racist Turkish laws, whose brother was killed by Turkish nationalists, and who was imprisoned and tortured for four years for expressing opposing political views, and was forced to serve in Turkish military for 18 months as a "dangerous soldier.".... As a rational monotheist, as a non-sectarian muslim, I could not have acted like my racist enemies. I promote unity and friendship between Kurds and Turks in all my writings on the issue.

I have written numerous articles critical of authoritarian generals who meddle with the Turkish democracy, or have written satires critical of flag-worshiper jingoists, or criticized the unjustified ban on women's headscarf, but they were never crude insults as they were stated. "Those words could not have written by me," I told the judge and the prosecutor on the bench. I was a skilled author and accusing me of authoring those primitive insults were in fact insult to my profession. "If I wished to insult those things," I said, "I could have insulted in style, in a much better language."

Though I find some of the Turkish laws suppressive of freedom of expression, I am very pleased that the legal system and police conduct have dramatically improved to the better. When it became clear that most of the "criminal words" did not belong to me, but belonged to the forum members at www.19.org , I was blamed for not censoring the postings of Turkish or Kurdish people who had expressed insults to Turkish government and national symbols.

The judge was a reasonable person and perhaps had problem with the article 301, which is now under consideration to be discarded. He dictated my statement, and instructed for my release and lifting the ban on my exit from Turkey. He wished to rule on the other two charges too, but they were not under his jurisdiction. We had to rush for the court at Kartal-Pendik region, on the Asian section of the city. We had less than an hour to beat the deadline of 5 pm. Otherwise I had to remain in jail until Monday, the day of my departure from Turkey. I would experience the fastest travel in Istanbul's heavy traffic. The police officers used the siren and zigzagged through the traffic, occasionally using the shoulder, made it to the court just seven minutes before 5 pm.

The middle-aged judge, while browsing my files, looked at me and asked me whether my brother was killed about thirty years ago. I was worried that he could be affiliated with the nationalists. Well, after asking me a few questions, he instructed my release. I am very thankful to the police officers who did their best to make my release possible by the end of the day. I had very little chance to get a release from the three charges.

The following day, I had a great reception at the book fair. This was my third real public appearance since my immigration to the USA, about 19 years ago. For security reasons, I had to limit my activities with TV programs that allowed me to encounter religious scholars through live debates. The lecture room was filled with enthusiastic audience. The reporter from the weekly Tempo magazine later told me about his impression. He was surprised to see a diverse demographics: young and old, men and women, women with headscarves and women wearing modern attire… They were very peaceful and friendly to my arguments.

During the remaining two days in Istanbul, I had an interview for Tempo Magazine's upcoming cover story on Islamic Reform movement, and I met with various groups, including an elite group from another Turkic republic. Contrasting my first night on the floor of the cell, a friend of mine gave me the key of one of his luxury apartments looking at the Bosporus Straight just above Bebek…

I was relieved the moment my airplane departed to London. When I arrived at Atlanta airport, I knew that I was at home. As much as I dislike some of the policies of the US government, especially its imperialistic and Zionist-controlled foreign policy and its promiscuous affairs with big corporations, I consider myself a very lucky person for living in a country with such a Constitution that has allowed me not to worry about expressing my progressive and liberal political and religious views. After my experience during my recent short trip, I became even more appreciative of the Constitution that protects individuals from the tyranny of government. May God reward Jefferson with eternal bliss!

Theometer or Sectometer

(First conducted on the participants of my lectures at Oxford University in November 3-5, 2008)

Edip Yuksel

Name: _____

Email Address: _____

Phone: _____ Age: _____

Occupation: _____

Nationality: _____

Have you read the Manifesto for Islamic Reform? _____

Favorite Books/Authors: _____

Your Sect: (a) Sunni (b) Shiite (c) Salafi (d) Other (d) No sect

Please put a CIRCLE around the letter of your choice:

1. According to the Quran, which one of these is not and cannot be idolized by people?

    a. Prophet Muhammad
    b. Desires or Wishful thinking (Hawa)
    c. Crowds or peers
    d. Ancestors or children
    e. Reasoning (Aql)

2. Which one of these is a true statement?

    a. The Quran is not sufficient to guide us; in addition we need Hadith and Sunna.
    b. The Quran is not sufficient to guide us; we need Hadith, Sunna and follow the teaching of a Sunni sect.
    c. The Quran is not sufficient to guide us; we need Hadith, Sunna and follow the teaching of a Shiite sect.
    d. The Quran is not sufficient to guide us; we need Hadith, Sunna, follow the teaching of a sect and join a religious order.
    e. The Quran is sufficient to guide us when we understand and follow it through the light of reason.

3. Which one of these hadiths narrated by Bukhari, Muslim and other "authentic" hadith books, do you think are fabricated:

    a. Muhammad was illiterate until he died.
    b. Muhammad married Aisha at age 54 while she was only 9 or 13 years-old.
    c. Muhammad dispatched a gang of fighters (sariyya) to kill a woman poet secretly during night in her home, for criticizing him publicly through her poems.
    d. Muhammad slaughtered 400 to 900 Jews belonging to Ben Qurayza for violating the treaty.
    e. All of the above.

4. Which one of these laws or rules does not exist in the Quran?

    a. Stone the married adulterers to death
    b. Do not play guitar
    c. Men should not wear silk and gold
    d. Men are superior to women
    e. All of the above

5. The Quran instructs us to follow the messengers. Following the messenger means:

    a. Follow Hadith and Sunna; Bukhari, Muslim, Ibn Hanbal, etc.
    b. Follow his Ahl-al-Bayt.
    c. Follow hadith, sunna, consensus of sahaba, ijtihad of imams and fatwas of ulama.
    d. Follow Muhammad.
    e. Follow the message he was sent with, which was Quran alone.

6. The Quran is God's word, because:

    a. There are verses of the Quran stating that it is God's word.
    b. The Quran is a literary miracle. None can bring a sura like it surpassing its literary qualities.

c. I do not need to have a reason. Reason is not reliable. I have faith in the Quran.

d. The moral teaching of the Quran is the best for individual and humanity.

e. The Quranic signs (aya) do not have internal contradiction nor does it contradict the signs in nature. Besides, it is numerically coded book with an extraordinary mathematical structure integrated with its composition and Arabic language.

7. Which one of the following is correct for Muhammad:

a. Muhammad was the final messenger and prophet.

b. Muhammad had the highest rank above all humans.

c. Muhammad demonstrated many miracles such as splitting the moon, healing the sick, and crippling a child

d. All of the above´

e. Muhammad was a human messenger like other messengers.

8. In what year he Bukhari started collecting hadith for his hadith collection known as the Sahih Bukhari, the most trusted Sunni hadith collection?

a. During the life of Muhammad in Medina

b. Ten years after Muhammad's death.

c. 130 years after Muhammad's death.

d. 200 years after Muhammad's death

e. 230 years after Muhammad's death.

9. According to Bukhari himself, he collected the 7,275 hadith among the 700,000 hadiths he collected. If each hadith, together with its *isnad* (the chain of reporters) and *sanad* (the text that was attributed to Muhammad) took about half a book page, how many volumes of books with 500 pages would they take to record all those 700,000 hadith allegedly collected by Bukhari?

a. 7 volumes

b. 10 volumes

c. 70 volumes

d. 100 volumes

e. 700 volumes

10. What are the last statements in the Farewell Sermon (Khutba al-Wida) which was reportedly witnessed by more than 100,000

sahaba, making it by far the most authentic hadith among the thousands of hadiths?

a. I leave you Abu Bakr; you should follow him.

b. I leave you my sahaba; you may follow any of them.

c. I leave you the Quran and Sunna; you should follow both.

d. I leave you the Quran and Ahl-al-Bayt (my family); you should follow them.

e. I leave you the Quran, you should follow it.

11. According to some "authentic hadith" found in Bukhari and other hadith books, there was a verse instructing muslims to stone the married adulterers to death: "Al-shayhu wal-shayhatu iza zanaya farjumuhuma nakalan..." According to hadith reports, what happened to those verses?

a. After the Prophet Muhammad's death, Umayyad governor Marwan burned the pages where those verses were written.

b. Angle Gebrail came down and deleted it from the scripture.

c. Ibni Abbas forgot it yet Abu Hurayra never forgot it.

d. There is no reference to such a verse in any authentic hadith books.

e. After the Prophet Muhammad's death, the skin which the verse was written on was protected under Aisha's bed. A hungry goat ate it. Thus, it was abrogated literally yet kept legally.

12. According to both Bukhari and Muslim, when Muhammad was in his death bed, he asked his comrades around to bring him a paper and pen to write something for them so that they would not divert from the right path. According to the same "authentic" Sunni hadith books, Omar bin Khattab stopped a sahaba who was hurrying for a paper and pen and said the following: "The prophet is sick and has fever. He does not know what he is saying. God's book is sufficient for us." According to the hadith, all the prominent comrades (sahaba) agreed with Omar and Muhammad passed away without writing down his advice. What do you think about this hadith?

a. If it is narrated by both Bukhari and Muslim, then it must be true

b. If it is true, then, Omar and all other Sahaba must have betrayed Muhammad and committed blasphemy.
c. If it is true, then, Omar and all prominent Sahaba were followers of the Quran alone.
d. If it is false then all other hadith too should be rejected.
e. C and D must be true

13. Do we need to SAY "sallallahu alayhi wasallam" after Muhammad's name?

a. Yes, every time Muhammad is mentioned we have to praise his name.
b. Yes, but we need to say only once in our lifetime.
c. Yes, the more we say the better.
d. Yes, and those who do not say it after Muhammad's name disrespect him and they will not receive his intercession.
e. No, the Quran does not ask us to say anything after Muhammad's name; muslims were asked (salli ala) to support him, as he was also asked to support them (salli alayhim).

14. What is the correct Testimony (shahada) according to the Quran:

a. I bear witness that there is no god but the God and the Quran is God's word.
b. I bear witness that there is no god but the God and Muhammad is His messenger.
c. I bear witness that there is no god but the God and Muhammad is His messenger and His servant.
d. I bear witness that there is no god but the God and Abraham, Jesus, Moses and Muhammad are His messengers.
e. I bear witness that there is no god but the God.

15. Should Muslims who do not observe daily prayers be beaten in public?

a. Yes.
b. No.

16. Should Muslims who are caught for consuming alcohol for the fourth time be killed?

a. Yes.
b. No.

17. Did the prophet give permission to kill women and children in the war?

a. Yes.
b. No.

18. According to the Quran, are women banned from reading Quran and pray during their menstruation periods?

a. Yes
b. No.

19. In the daily Sala prayers, do you recite "attahiyyatu lillahi wassalawatu .... as salamu alayka ayyuhannabiyyu wa rahmatullahi wa barakatuhu"?

a. Yes
b. No

20. Does the Quran justify taxing Jewish and Christian population under Muslim authority with extra or different taxation called Jizya?

a. Yes
b. No.

21. Does the Quran instruct women to cover their hair?

a. Yes.
b. No.

22. Are woman restricted from leading congregational prayers?

a. Yes.
b. No.

23. Are women mentally and spiritually inferior to men?

a. Yes.
b. No.

24. Does the Quran restrict women from initiating divorce?

a. Yes.
b. No.

25. Is polygamy with previously unmarried women allowed?

a. Yes, up to four women.
b. No, polygamy is allowed only with the widows who have orphans.

26. Do pilgrims need to cast real stones at the devil?

    a. Yes.
    b. No.

27. Is the black stone near Kaba holy?

    a. Yes.
    b. No.

28. May a muslim own slaves?

    a. Yes.
    b. No.

29. Is circumcision a required or encouraged practice in Islam?

    a. Yes.
    b. No.

30. Should converts change their names to Arabic names?

    a. Yes.
    b. No.

31. How much *zaka* charity one should give away?

    a. 2.5%
    b. As much as one can afford, without making themselves needy.

32. Are those who break their fast during Ramadan before the sunset required to fast 60 consecutive days as a punishment for not completing the day?

    a. Yes.
    b. No.

33. Is leadership the right of Quraish tribe?

    a. Yes.
    b. No.

34. Is drawing pictures or making three dimensional statutes a sin?

    a. Yes.
    b. No.

35. Are there more dietary prohibitions besides pork, carcass, running blood, and animal dedicated to idolized names?

    a. Yes.
    b. No.

36. Is displaying Muhammad's name and the names of his closest companions next to God's name in the mosques idol-worship?

    a. Yes.
    b. No.

37. Did Muhammad advise some sick people to drink camel urine?

    a. Yes.
    b. No.

38. Did Muhammad gauge people's eyes with hot nails?

    a. Yes.
    b. No.

39. After following the advice of Moses, did Muhammad, bargain with God about the number of prayers, lowering down from the impossible-to-observe 50 times a day to 5 times a day?

    a. Yes.
    b. No.

40. Does Muhammad have the power of intercession?

    a. Yes.
    b. No.

41. Was Muhammad sinless?

    a. Yes.
    b. No.

42. Did God create the universe for the sake of Muhammad?

    a. Yes.
    b. No.

43. Did Muhammad have sexual power of 30 males?

    a. Yes.
    b. No.

44. Was Muhammad bewitched by a Jew?

    a. Yes.
    b. No.

45. Do some verses of the Quran abrogate other verses?

    a. Yes.
    b. No.

Here is the story and the answer of this test:

Between November 3 and 10 of 2008, I travelled to UK and Turkey to deliver four lectures; first two at Oxford University, the third at Muslim Institute in London and the fourth one in Istanbul Book Fair. I had prepared a test containing 45 multiple choice questions just the night before my travel. I duplicated them on both sides of a single sheet and I distributed to the audience before the lecture... They were asked to write their name, age, occupation, email address, favorite authors, and their sectarian affiliation. It was a bit awkward to test an audience that consisted of students and professors at one of the world's top universities. The multiple-choice test proved to be a powerful instrument to deliver the message of Islamic Reform under the light of the Quran. The correct answer for each multiple choice question was the E option, and for the Yes or No questions was the B option. So, it would take me a few seconds to evaluate the tests after they were returned to me.

The Sunni or Shiite test-takers found themselves in quagmire of contradiction with their own sectarian teachings. They learned that they were thirty, forty or even more than fifty percent infidels or heretics. Some of those who marked Sunni as their sectarian affiliation contradicted the Sunni teachings on most of the issues. According to their own confessed sects, their lives were worthless; they deserved to be killed! I did not let this mirror or sect-o-meter remain an individual experience; I publicly declared the overall results. Many got all answers correct, including Eric, a monotheist from Unitarian church who already had a copy of the Quran: a Reformist Translation in his possession. Eric knew the original message of islam better than all the mullahs and the so-called "ulama" combined.

If you have chosen the wrong option for any of the questions and you are wondering why you have contradicted the Quran, please visit www.islamicreform.org and read the full version of the Manifesto for Islamic Reform. If you prefer to have it in a book form, you may order it by visiting www.brainbowpress.com

CPSIA information can be obtained at www.ICGtesting.com
Printed in the USA
LVOW081248021211

257476LV00003B/50/P

9 780979 671579